Business Biographies and Memoirs: 6 Manuscripts

Jeff Bezos, Elon Musk, Steve Jobs, Bill Gates, Jack Ma, Richard Branson

Business Biographies and Memoirs: 6 Manuscripts

Jeff Bezos, Elon Musk, Steve Jobs, Bill Gates, Jack Ma, Richard Branson

JR MacGregor

Business Biographies and Memoirs: 6 Manuscripts

Jeff Bezos, Elon Musk, Steve Jobs, Bill Gates, Jack Ma, Richard Branson

Published by CAC Publishing LLC.

ISBN 978-1-948489-93-5 paperback

ISBN 978-1-948489-92-8 eBook

Contents

Jeff Bezos: The Force Behind the Brand

Jeff Bezos: The Force Behind the Brand

Insight and Analysis into the Life and Accomplishments of the Richest Man on the Planet

JR MacGregor

Jeff Bezos: The Force Behind the Brand

Insight and Analysis into the Life and Accomplishments of the Richest Man on the Planet

Published by CAC Publishing LLC.

ISBN 978-1-948489-09-6 paperback

ISBN 978-1-948489-10-2 eBook

This book is dedicated to those that dream of changing the world.

Preface

Despite our better angels, we seem to do things without rhyme nor apparent reason. We peer out at our neighbor's new car; we inflict our political views on our family; we judge others by the standards we set arbitrarily for ourselves, and we can't get enough of reality TV. All these factors of the human profile are connected more intricately than we realize.

We do these things because the human species is inextricably connected at a very deep level and the way it manifests is in our curiosity of our fellow man. We are all gifted in our own way but, more often than not, we do not know how to understand our gifts or use them in a way that results in spectacular results.

We don't know how to be our own Elon Musk, or our own Bill Gates, Steve Jobs or Jeff Bezos. All these men (just a short sampling of some of the achievers out there) are extremely successful in what they do, yet there is no duplicate among them. Bezos achieved tremendous success doing something very different to Steve Jobs. Bill Gates contributed something very different – and went about doing it very differently from Elon Musk. But they all contributed significantly and in diverse areas of the life that our species experiences.

We are not looking and, really, we shouldn't be looking to do what they did, but we are looking to understand ourselves in the way they understood themselves and exploited their better angels.

Let me illustrate.

In writing this book about Bezos, I learned so many things about him but, more importantly, I learned something very important about my youngest son who behaves a lot like Bezos did when he was still a kid. As I researched his life, the avalanche of anecdotes that I pieced together in my research – while supposed to paint a picture of Bezos in my head so that I could narrate it for all of you, ended up painting a picture of my youngest son. And that changed my view of him and how I respond to him because it taught me how to understand my youngest better – who has always been a skosh different from typical kids. I don't expect you to do that with your kids, but it could help you explain something about yourself and if you develop that further, who knows where that may lead.

I'll say it here and I will say it again later, biographies are never about the subject and its gossip value. Biographies of great achievers are about ourselves. If you see it in that light, then you are forced to see the good in others so that you can find the power and strength in yourself.

It's a good thing that Bezos is in the news as much as he is and that has created a buzz about him, because the lessons that he can teach us just by dissecting his experience and observing his trajectory will be of huge benefit to large swaths of people – not everyone though. Some of you may get more benefit from Jack Ma; others may get more out of learning about Albert Einstein. My only hope is that my humble attempt at piecing together a small sampling of his interesting life and accomplishments plays a role in touching your life and making it better.

We all have a little voice in our head that can cause success or chaos. If we finetune that voice, it will alert us to things that will catapult us into the realm of our needs and desires. If we trip and start heeding the wrong voice, then we will start to act on our fears and biases. This book is not about choosing which voice you pick but is about a man that has so finely tuned his senses that he knows exactly which voice is telling him what and knows when to listen to it. It is not something that comes from meticulous and articulate definition, but rather comes from mistakes, reflections, more mistakes, learning, and still more mistakes and then, after all the challenges have been surmounted, all the problems solved, and all the mountains climbed, we find achievement on the horizon, and success in the dawn.

Introduction

Let me state up front that you will not see a bad word written about this man in this book. But that is not because this book is written as an adulation to the current wealthiest man on the planet.

Instead, it is written this way because we cannot hope to emulate or learn from a man – any man or woman for that matter – that we are mocking or finding fault with. Biographies are not about the subject of the book. Biographies are about the person reading it, and their quest to find the spark that is within them. Not about paying homage to the subject of the biography.

However, it is easy to get carried away in the evolving narrative of who the person is behind the name. It becomes complex to decipher the man behind the company, and the brain behind the idea. And that is, after all, why we are intrigued by this person – his character, his actions, his reasoning.

He is interesting because of his achievement, and the string of ideas, decisions, and actions he has taken to arrive at where he is at this point in time.

This is also not a book about the rights and wrongs, the vices and virtues, or the ethical or brazen business moves that may or may not impact others. Again, this is about the trek and the soul of a man combined with his chutzpah to make something, see something, perfect something, that is better than anyone else has to that point. There are things you can say about Bill Gates, or about Steve Jobs, Jack Ma, Richard Branson and anyone who has reached a certain level of success that is beyond what most others have dreamed of doing. But judging them will not get you far.

When it comes to Bezos (by the way it's pronounced 'Bay-Zos,' not Bee Zos) there are a lot of you who are going to say that he did this or did that and put this company or that company out of business. I understand your sense of empathy for the vanquished and those companies that got hit and shuttered, or the companies that had to downsize because of the rise of Amazon. For instance, the likes of Barnes and Noble – which is especially ironic, since it was the coffee shop in Barnes and Noble that played host to Bezos and his compadres, as well as their early customers and investors in Seattle. It's not just Barnes and Noble that hit a brick wall when Amazon started to rise; it was retailers like Macy's and Nordstroms as well.

But it also doesn't just stop at brick and mortar companies in old tech – it's new tech as well. Etsy, for example, has also seen better days.

For those of you who cast Amazon and, by extension, Jeff Bezos as evil and un-American (talk of monopoly and all that), I urge you to think again. Have you played that thought out in your head – do you really think that they are out to destroy the past icons of American commerce because they have nothing better to do? No. That is the genius of Amazon and the brilliance of Bezos. They are out to revolutionize the landscape and take advantage of technology in doing so.

Or maybe you think it has to do with greed at the expense of others? I don't see any evidence of that. What I see is a person who has identified a piece of technology and used that technology in ways others are only now starting to comprehend.

As the book unfolds, one of the things that you will start to understand about Bezos is that there are two sides to him (more actually but, in this instance, these two sides are in stark contrast with each other.) On the one side you have a man who is so tech savvy that he sees their utility in the nitty-gritty of the infrastructure (of that technology) – he is the kind of guy who could tell you why the Starship Enterprise can go into warp and why it maxes out at Warp 9 – by the way, if you look closely, Bezos has a cameo appearance as one of the alien characters in Star Trek Beyond (you should totally look that up). The other side of him is one that is almost stoic in a philosophical way. He is one of those people that reads new-age authors in philosophy like Taleb (Nassim Nicholas) and other technology philosophers. He is one of those people that sees the fundamental thread that runs through things and he can't really understand the perspective of those who do not see that as well. He is highly intolerant of ignorance.

His ability to understand the place for technology in today's world is because of his philosophical mental framework and his understanding of how things play out.

Bezos is not caught up in his money the way we are and, if you really want to understand the secret of his success, you need to leave your preconceived notions of fair play, arbitrary standards of moral right and wrong, ethical standards of business, and antiquated notions of competitive forces right here before you move forward.

When you do that, what I assure you that you will find is the secret sauce that is packed into all things that Bezos touches. It is not for the faint of heart.

The best way to chop up and consume a biography (any biography – not just this one) is to look at the cause and effect of a person's actions as it pertains to themselves and the world around them. When you look at someone like Bill Gates, do you turn around and discount all the philanthropy he has done, all the wealth he has amassed, and all the benefits that have come from his building of Microsoft? Or do you look at the possibly unfair (I don't think it's unfair – but many who judge think that it is) way that he got the source code for the original version of DOS? He did what he did and changed the world in the wake of that decision.

We are all the sum of our choices, as Bezos said in his speech to the kids at Stanford during the commencement ceremony – and rightfully so. We have to live and die by our decisions and how that affects all things in our gravity. How we do them and what we do comes from those choices and those decisions. If we choose to take the path that people like Bezos or Gates have taken, then the outcome will be pretty close to the same. It's like baking a cake – if you follow the exact measurements and the correct sequence and methods, you're going to come pretty close to the same result. The chance of getting that result is also whether you are doing it willingly or just going through the motions. I can tell you from personal experience that if you go through the motions but don't really believe in it, then you're wasting your time.

But if you want to strike at the chance for success and contribute toward the trajectory of this civilization, then you gotta get up and break some eggs and you should watch attentively how some of these masters go about achieving their success so that you can do the same – in your own field. I would like to think that is why you are reading this biography.

That is how it is written – not just to give you salacious juicy facts and figures, but to highlight the junctions and events that brought about decisions that charted a meteoric path. It is a fascinating story and one that has taught me so much. It is a quest that transcends space, time, and person.

To aid that quest, as I have said, it is best not to highlight the negatives, or focus on the subject's errors (in essence, reserve opinion and judgment of the subject and look for the constructive contributions). Rather, it is best to look at the challenges, ask the questions, digest the reasoning, and contemplate the similarities.

We all need direction and clarity to go about achieving the various vocations that we are drawn to. We all need ideas and we all need examples to do the things we would like to do but hesitate to because subconsciously we do not have a clear path ahead.

Not all of us. In fact, only very few of us who read this book, and go on to read other books about Bezos, and books about other men of significant accomplishment, will go out and successfully build another Amazon or build the replacement of Amazon. But that is not what I envision as I write this book. What I envision is that all of you find your own spark and do the things that light up your soul. For Bezos, it was technology (I will come to that in the next chapter). For Steve Jobs it was elegance. For Bill Gates, it was mass markets and technology adoption. For Jack Ma, it was advancing Chinese businesses.

You will not find the answer to your pressing and subconscious questions of life and how to succeed by just reading one book (or many books) about one man. You will come close when you read about many. Ultimately, your success already lies within you. You can't copy another person's success; you can only understand the frame of their mind and see what makes things tick, then learn to bring your own powers to bear in your own life.

In light of this, I hope that you are inspired by the facts, anecdotes, and analysis contained in this book. I hope that you find your own spark that propels you to the next level. I pray that you evolve into your full potential and touch all those within your gravity to achieve the same.

***

Chapter 1 An Overview

"Invention is by its very nature disruptive. If you want to be understood at all times, then don't do anything new."

At the time of publishing, Amazon's share price stands at $1,450 per share, giving it a total market capitalization of 699 Billion Dollars. This puts Amazon in the top 20 largest global companies. As large as it is, it is not the largest company in the world just yet. That title belongs to PetroChina, which is valued at over 10 Trillion Dollars – but things like PetroChina don't count in this calculus as those are state-run companies and, thus, do not detract from the size and achievement of our own Amazon.

In the US, Amazon is the fourth largest with those numbers, just barely behind Apple, Google, and Microsoft. Most people would tell you that Amazon started as a bookseller and that was the goal all along. It's not.

Amazon's first products were books indeed, but it wasn't the founder's idea that that would be the be-all-end-all of Amazon. He knew from the very beginning that it was the juxtaposition of technology and utility that he wanted to exploit – not just books. He didn't think about selling books as his purpose in life.

There are two things wrong with this picture. The first is that it casts Bezos as a simpleton – which he is not; he is as complex as they come. Second, it makes it look like Amazon's success was by accident – it was not. It was deliberate, calculated and chiseled into its present form.

Start with Books

We all know that he started with books from his garage in Seattle – where he had just moved to from New York. Amazon was best known for that, and even still today, Amazon remains the largest bookseller in the world even though it has stopped labeling itself as such, as it did in 1994.

The decision to start with books back in 1994, was because books happened to be the one item in mail order catalogs that lent itself to online purchase and shipping. You will see later in the book that Bezos had thought long and hard about what product to offer in this new world of the Internet and so he looked through all the possible goods and services that could be catalogued and sold; and he found that the reason books were not part of the mail-order business was because there were so many titles that no one could possibly print a catalogue and send it to every household via US Post. The Internet solved that problem, naturally, and it was the easiest way that Bezos could enter the world of e-commerce. He already had the ideal medium, now he needed the perfect product – and he found it.

That is not always the easiest thing to do if you think about it. We get to sit back and say that it was an obvious choice but, if you really think about it, how often can someone say they looked at something and managed to find an opportunity within it? It is the result of a resourceful brain – it's like being MacGyver in the business world.

The Technology

Think about that for a minute and you will realize that, while the Internet has successfully eclipsed the mail order world that preceded it, the mail-order business was a huge industry. Remember the loads of junk mail that you used to receive, pre-90s? Remember the catalogs that used to fill up your mailbox? At the heart of that was commerce. At the heart of that was the seller reaching out to a buyer and letting them know that they had stuff to sell.

When Amazon started in the mind of this young electrical engineer in the offices of a Wall Street quantitative hedge-fund house, it wasn't because he thought mail order was a great business. He did so because he believed that the Internet was a great channel to reach millions of people.

Most companies look at their product then think about the distribution channel. Fair enough. But no one thinks about the channel and then tries to stuff it with product. Yet, that is what Amazon is the result of.

That's all it was - an entry point; a wedge to leverage the new network of distribution. It would be like picking up the latest technology in graphenes and saying, "OK, now that I've got it what can I do to fully take advantage of this?"

By no means was Amazon the first to try selling books online either. There were already a few Internet companies that had started to offer books online. And we will get to that but, for now, just look at the humble beginnings of Amazon and couple that to the fact that Bezos saw the potential of the Internet as a driver for what Amazon can do rather than seeing the product as the driver of a technology.

The reason we should take note of this frame of mind is that we can invoke it at times when we are looking to embark on something. You know those times when we feel like we need to get out on our own and we feel that the 9-to-5 grind is just holding us back?

New Ventures

We tend to take moments like this, look at the global opportunity, think about where our skills intersect with it, and that's what we think we are limited to pursue. That is true for some people but, on balance, that is untrue. The greatest achievers, and the ones who make it as billionaires, do not necessarily look at themselves and say, "What is my passion?" Look at Jack Ma, for instance. Even today, he still has no idea how to write a simple program or hook up a server. His driving force was to launch Chinese businesses onto the world marketplace and he ran with that because he saw the potential. He did what needed doing, not what he felt like doing. You have to create your own passion and create your own luck. You cannot be at the whim and fancy of fate and others. Stand up to the forces that would sway you, and you will see your hopes of becoming successful materialize, just as Bezos did.

We seem to make the mistake that we have to only do what we are good at. That's not always true. Certainly, there are some people that do not have the ability to muster the motivation to do what they are not passionate about. Know thyself. If you are one of these people, then look for the passion. But if you are not one of these people, then don't just wait to find the passion for something. Instead, find the something that you can make the difference with and then fire up the passion. On the same note, don't omit something just because you don't have the technical credentials to achieve it.

If you look at Steve Jobs, it was Wozniak that did the technical work. If you look at Richard Branson, until recently he didn't know how to read a Balance Sheet. And if you look at Trump, he inherited the real estate business from his father. There is no evidence confirming that, to be productive and ultimately successful, you have to only do what you are good at or what you are fond of. You can be inspired by anything if you let yourself be.

Entrepreneur's Dilemma

This is the key difference between how we see the businesses that we hope to start, and the way that Bezos saw Amazon when it started. The vast majority of those who have a notion of coming out on their own think of what they can do and see if they can pull together. They look at what they are good at and hope that it meshes with the market. People are advised every day to find a niche that they love, and do that.

For Bezos, selling books was more of a way to take full advantage of this new technology that could potentially allow one business (any business) to reach out and touch every person on the planet. And to be able to do that, he really did want to sell anything to anybody and everything to everybody. But as with all astute and in-control minds, he knew that he just couldn't do that on day one. So, he picked books and used the perfect product to develop the technology and then launch that into new areas.

There are a number of rumors out there that talk about how he was only interested in selling books, and that the rest was about greed. There is also the other side of that coin, which says that he saw how well the books did and then wanted to sell more. No. He knew that he wanted to sell everything, and he leveraged the Internet to do just that.

The Start

Bezos set up the company in July of 1994 and began his Angel / Venture capital rounds around the same time – in fact, a little earlier. He figured on a $6 million pre-money valuation that originally came off rich to most Angel investors, but Bezos stuck to his guns in most cases. There were some strategic individuals that he was willing to alter the $6 million valuation for and make it $5 million. But he did this with his eyes wide open. Bezos has a stubborn streak that is not easily matched, and you need to have that too if you want to build something.

If I told you that the winning lottery numbers will be ABC123, would you accept anything else when you went to make the purchase? Would you be firm with your demands with the clerk telling you that you should take another number? Or if he told you that the machine was not working? Wouldn't you do everything in your power to make sure those were the numbers you ended up with? Why? Because you were certain of the outcome if you did certain things – in this case, make the purchase of the ticket with that number. You could not be swayed and, for that, you may be called stubborn. Were you being stubborn, or were you just doing what you were certain of? That's how Bezos goes about each and every decision he makes. His certainty makes him adamant about what he needs to do and he does not accept anything less from anyone, much less himself.

This is sort of a recurring theme in this book because it is a recurring theme in his life too and in the way that Amazon was built and continues to operate today.

Stubborn

You will repeatedly see how stubborn he can be, but his stubborn streak is not born out of an oversized ego. Far from it. His stubborn streak comes from knowing exactly what he wants at any given moment in time. He is driven by the picture in his head, and that picture dictates his ability to do what is necessary in the moment. There are many people I've heard of who denigrate this kind of behavior and say that he is mean or has no patience. They say the same thing about Steve Jobs and even Bill Gates.

What you have to understand when it comes to these men is that they are not tactless or arrogant on a personal level; they are intolerant of deviations in today's actions (or lack thereof) because they see that the deviation here causes a deviation in the final picture that they see in their head – and that is unacceptable.

Most of us mere mortals have a vague sense of cause and effect. We know that if we touch fire we get burnt. We know that if we eat junk food we get unhealthy. We understand the superficial aspect of cause and effect but, in the case of Bezos, he is acutely aware of the things he has to do and knows exactly how to go about doing what needs to be done to get it and then realizing that the results are inevitable.

He was not born with that ability. No one is. We have some of it, perhaps, innately available to us, but the bulk of it comes from making mistakes. The bulk of it comes from learning to pick yourself up and then getting back to what you were aiming for. Bezos, just like the other achievers in the world, values the battle scars that he gets from his mistakes.

Think about that for a minute in slightly different terms. Let's say you knew, beyond a shadow of a doubt, that if you get drunk at the New Year's party, and there is a blizzard outside, that there is a good chance that you will not make it home. Some of us skirt those chances and we roll the dice. Those who do this, do it because they either have less than optimal confidence in their knowledge of things or they cede control to 'luck.' The Bezos of the world make their own luck and they do not cede control to anything, anyone, and certainly not to anything arbitrary.

Going Live

Amazon opened for business in July of 1995 and, since then, it has rapidly grown without much need, even in the early stages, for large-scale advertising. Conventional wisdom would have told you back then that massive advertising was required – now it's important that you put on your 1995 cap to think of conventional business wisdom back then.

If you looked at a business and said you wanted to get started, your business consultant will whip out his template and ask you what market you were going to target – and he would mean that both in geographic terms as well as demographic. If you had the unmitigated gall to tell him that you wanted to sell to all of America and the rest of the world, he would pack up and tell you that you were crazy.

That's what doing business in the days that preceded Amazon and the Internet entailed.

For those of you who don't have first-hand experience of the venture capital market in the early 90s, getting funded wasn't a given just because you were a tech company – stories of tech bubbles, cheap money, and the craziness of the 90s notwithstanding. Just because you had an idea doesn't mean you got an investment. And even though the valuations of the 90s were overly enthusiastic, they were for Internet companies and not bookstores – which Amazon, for all intents and purposes, was in the beginning.

The reason I bring this up is to illustrate the ferocity of headwinds one would face when trying to be so ambitious in the eyes of Private Equity executives and the typical venture capitalist. It's a good thing that he was extremely personable and that he was in the business, so he knew people who were willing to lend him an ear.

When Amazon first got off the ground, even at the early stages, and the now-infamous stories of him banging away at a laptop, hammering out the business plan as they drove from Texas to Washington, was about raising the first million. Without seed capital, the idea was not about to go anywhere.

Investor Pitch

When he started making the pitch and talking to VCs, and angels, and even PE firms, it soon became clear that it was an uphill battle. He was talking $6 million in pre-money (pre-money is what they call the valuation of a company before you take into consideration what the company could do with the investment). So, that meant that looking for a million dollars demanded a willingness to part with a sixth of the shares he owned at the time.

But the one thing that many of the investors that met Bezos at the time would tell you is that he was a very nice young man. They thought that he was as smart as a whip and every bit as enthused as one could imagine. Where the split between them occurred was in his opinion on where he was certain Amazon was going, and their perception of things. He, in retrospect, was right.

Well, they were both right. Bezos knew exactly where the company was going and what had to be done to convert potential into reality. What he didn't know was how much money it would all end up being worth. His perspective was not so much the tangible material but the intangible success. Bezos did not make the mistake many do – they mistake reward and money for success. Indeed, money and reward are the tangible features of success, but they are not success in and of themselves – the underlying achievement is. Bezos was always about the achievement.

The outside investor route was not as smooth, and so it ended up that he took most of the seed he needed from friends and family. He turned to twenty of his friends and family, as you will see in further detail later, and raised $50,000 a piece in return for less than 1% of the company each. If they held onto that till now, that $50,000 would be worth $5 billion (that's 100,000 times more over the course of twenty-four years.) I don't think many of the initial investors stayed that long. The company has, after all, had its share of ups and downs. But the comparison should give you an idea of the kind of value that Bezos extracted from a business that started in a two-car garage, receiving and shipping books on an old door that they used as a table. That was 1995.

By the time 1997 came around, the year they went public, this out-of-the-blue upstart was clocking in $148 million in revenue. To put that into context, the average startup, if revenue-positive, takes in between 40,000 and 50,000 in the first few years. 7 out of 10 companies make it to their second anniversary, five out of the first ten make it to their fifth, three make it a decade, and only two go beyond that. When you put that into perspective, you need to realize that the 148 million is a big deal, but it is not the entire picture because, at this point, that was just revenue and, at the bottom line, they were still in the red and burning the original investment they had taken.

You have to see those revenue numbers for what they were. Bezos saw them as a vindication, yet he also knew that they were far from getting started – at least in the vision of his own mind. You can think of it this way, the first few years and the first few hundred million in revenue were really the way to cudgel out the nature of the market that no one had yet tried to understand. There was a move toward online commerce, and there was even a prior bookstore that had started online, but the difference between that bookstore and Amazon's was that the first bookstore wanted to be just about books. They wanted to live and breathe books – like Barnes and Noble in the brick and mortar world; while Amazon was just getting started with books – they were not its end game.

***

Chapter 2 Meet Jeff Bezos

“People who are right most of the time are people who change their minds often.”

Amazon is not about books. It’s not about a marketplace, and it’s not about merchandising. It is all those things, yes. It needs to be. But the Amazon that Bezos sees clearly in his head is about the use of technology to touch the farthest hearts and minds; to cover distance and culture and to be able to use technology to do so.

In this book, we will take a lot of real estate and build the story of Amazon in tandem with the story of its founder. Why? Because a truer understanding of a man cannot be fathomed when you are looking at his creation. You will see the meticulous nature of the man in the care he takes to smoothen the edges; you will see the prescience of man in the foresight he applies to its design; you will see the empathy of a man in the way his creation affects the rest of the world, and you will see the genius of the man in the way he approaches and solves the problems that inevitably arise on the way to success. You can even see the integrity of the man in the mistakes he makes and the way he recompenses.

He said it from day one – that Amazon is about selling everything to everybody and he meant it (you know that smiley on the Amazon logo – have you noticed how it is an arrow that goes from A to Z? – that was no accident).

Crossing the Hudson

By the time he crossed the Hudson from New York to Jersey on his way to Texas, he had already decided that he was going to set up his business in Seattle because of the tax structure there and how it would be beneficial for him as he sold to the whole world. None of this is by accident. Everything that happens to Bezos and around him is scripted, methodically thought out, and acted upon with the certainty of a soothsayer who has seen the future. The only difference is that Bezos doesn't need to see the future; he knows it will happen because he gets up and does something about it.

By no means is this characteristic unique to Bezos. In my quest to understand and chronicle the efforts and habits of successful people, there are a number of traits that have stuck out constantly from each. Every single one of the people I studied had this particular characteristic – they all knew the future – they all knew the chain of cause and effect was always precise and its principles, never yielding. They knew that the intangible inspiration and tangible effort they generated with consistency, ferocity, and certainty would yield exactly what they envisioned. That was their secret sauce.

Think of Edison, Einstein, Newton, and many more – their achievements changed the world. They are no different than Bezos, Gates, and Jobs. All of them had a vision that they pursued and attained.

For Bezos, the one thing that he conspicuously displayed more than most was the clarity and certainty of vision. But then there was also his intelligence in deciphering what he needed to do and then doing it.

It's like having an inspiration to create a spaceship to fly into space because you can plainly see the benefits, then you use your intelligence and resources to make it happen. They are two separate things – inspiration on the one hand; effort on the other.

He may not have been the first to see the use of the Internet to bridge the spatial divide between buyer and seller, but he certainly was one of the most resilient, resourceful, and enthusiastic people to do so.

At the end of 2017, the world crowned Jeff Bezos as the richest man on the planet based on the price of his company's stock. In 2018, just days before this book went to print, his position was further solidified when the tabloids and Wall Street watchers noted that Jeff Bezos is now the planet's richest person in history. His assets exceed that of even Rockefeller, Carnegie, Astor, Gates, and Buffett. Not only is he the richest man compared to all the people today, if you took all the wealthy people in the past, he is richer than them too.

Remember, I mentioned earlier that the purpose of this book is not to marvel at the richness of a man's wealth, but to understand the richness of his soul – the reason he has gone to this point and made the contributions that he did and to have touched the number of lives that he has.

For those of you who didn't know Bezos and where his wealth comes from, Amazon is just the start of the next chapter. Wall Street does not see the current calculation of 700 billion as an inflection point. By the way, my opinion of the stock is not, and should not be taken, as investment advice or stock promotion – I am talking about Amazon in the context of Jeff Bezos and how well he has done for himself from his start-up 23 years ago. You should speak to your broker or Investment Advisor if you plan on any investments. The same applies to any of the other titans of industry.

The early chapters to this point are really designed to lay the masonry for what comes later. We will build the rest of the book on the hows, the whys, and the reasoning so that it gives us something actionable to emulate instead of something hollow to gawk at.

Some of the most successful companies that you can think of, like Google (Alphabet Inc.), Apple, Microsoft, and Alibaba have market caps (the total value of all their stock at the current stock price) of 770 billion, 824 billion, 710 billion, and 480 billion dollars respectively; Amazon is 700 billion. That puts it in context with the other big names in business today. But the thing that is most interesting is that those same five companies, Google, Apple, Microsoft, Alibaba, and Amazon tell a different story when it comes to PE ratios. Now, remember this is not about whether one is better than the other or if Amazon is better or worse than the others. It goes to show the value of the company and if it is back or front loaded. The PE ratios are just the ratio of the price of the stock and the most recent earnings that they have experienced. So, let's say you have a company XYZ that is earning $1 per share and the price of the share is $10, then it has a PE ratio of 10. It is priced at ten times its earnings. You can tell right off the bat that, if the market thinks that this company has a lot of potential and that it will earn more in the future, the stock price will be bid up and, since the earnings haven't caught up, the PE will increase. If I think that all the company has to offer is in the present, then my stock price is going to be so much closer to home. Google is trading at 37 times, Alibaba is at 46 times, Apple is at 17 times, Microsoft is at 62 times, and Amazon is at a whopping 230 times.

Undervalued or overvalued is not the point here. What is, is that that stock price reflects a company that is future driven – just like Jeff Bezos has been saying since day one. He is not the kind of person to sacrifice the future just so he can take some form of stability in the present. When he stood firm with his six-million-dollar valuation, almost everyone he spoke with in the VC community said that it was excessively high. The problem back then was obvious. They couldn't get past seeing it as a book retailer – and a startup at that, years behind the Barnes & Nobles, Waldenbooks, and such of the world. No one could see the true nature of the vision that Bezos had. But that did not deter him. He did not recoil and rethink his plan. On the one hand, he wouldn't do it, on the other hand, Mackenzie would not allow it.

What started out as an electronic storefront to sell books during the early days of the Internet catapulted into one of the world's largest online retail platforms, changing the way every consumer thinks about consumerism and how every retailer, manufacturer, and business owner thinks about the commercial ecosystem.

Bezos was certainly intelligent as a kid but, as the book unfolds, you will realize that his intelligence, or as some call it his 'geek factor,' is not the only element at the core of his success. Sure, it played a part, but it was only one facet of a multifaceted life that he built, breathed, and lived. It's not just the vision he had or the drive he put into it. It was also the things that he had to do to get the public to adopt a whole new way of doing things. His ability to see a vision and to change and wrap the reality around others so that they see it too is also a legendary aspect of Bezos. How else would you convince tech experts to leave California and get to Washington to work in a garage for a startup? How else would you convince people to buy from you? How else would you get a group of people to invest a million dollars? How else would you get cracker-jack smart finance people like Joy Covey to come out west to spearhead the IPO process?

The why is in his nature and effervescent personality – that famous laugh, his unique gait and his total ability to focus on whoever is talking to him. Although you can't really tell that these days –

since he looks like he is carrying the weight of the world. But back then he was gregarious, affable, and smart without being a know-it-all. People who met him liked him, had confidence in him and trusted him. That is how he single-handedly convinced almost two dozen people to part with a million dollars in return for a sixth of a company that sold books on something called the Internet.

I have to leverage this to really make the gravity of the point of his affability and believability. One of the first angel investors to come on board was an investment group that was comprised of a few friends who had no idea what the Internet was. Sure, to us, the Internet today is something that is ubiquitous, and we do not give online purchases a second thought. Last month, my family bought almost all our regular shopping items online. A quarter of a century ago, there wasn't much you could get online as the web technology was nascent. It seemed to be an extension of a mail-order store. If you told someone it was a mail order store, they would understand. They knew that you picked up a catalog, dialed a toll-free number and then made your purchase. Those were the terms they understood.

E-commerce complicated things. To do the same thing, you now needed a computer, and you needed to make sure it had a modem, and you had to make sure that you had Internet service. So, for someone who knew about catalog orders, this was too much trouble. There was so much other infrastructure that a shopper would need to get to be able to be part of the e-commerce revolution. In 1994, America spent more than 60 billion dollars in mail-order products. The first e-commerce sale – where the item was purchased online, happened to be a Sting CD (for the younger generation Millennials – Sting is an artist and a CD is how we used to store music). That happened in 1994 – just around the time Amazon was getting ready to jump onto the e-commerce platform.

Since e-commerce just complicated catalog shopping, there must have been an additional pull that was able to make it seem profitable – if one could solve the inherent resistance given in adopting new technologies. Bezos had to eventually figure out how to make it work. And he did. And if you visit the Amazon campus in downtown Seattle the plaque that hangs there gives you an understanding of his perspective – 25 years later, he still thinks that the Internet and the technological colossal that it is, is still merely the beginning. His forward-looking view and ability to convert that into dollars are why Amazon enjoys a 230-times multiple in stock price.

So, for those thinking that it was an easy decision to get into online shopping – think again – it didn't exist, and its existing competitor was mail order. To take that and try to convince someone to part with money as an investment was an uphill battle. It took Bezos a year of trying to convince friends, family, and strangers to come up with the money. There were two kinds of challenges. The first was that he had to explain what the Internet was and how he could be profitable. This is the group of people that had the same frame of reference as his parents. They had no idea what this was but trusted him. The second group were the kind that sort of understood the Internet but were not agreeable to the 'rich' valuation. He had to manage both, and he had to do it together.

His rich valuation was not the stuff of dreams. He understood clearly that the Internet would change the way the retail world operates. It would allow for better efficiencies and reduced costs. His business plan did take most of this into consideration – but not everything. There are a number of technologies in use today at Amazon that were not yet available at the time they turned on the switch. But still, the raw interconnectivity of the Internet was enough to make Bezos realize that the significant economies of scale and the reduced cost had the effect of changing the retail paradigm, having the effect of improving and bridging the gap between catalog sales and brick and mortar shopping.

He was acutely aware that online retail had a mammoth task ahead of it. It had to make the pull of mail-order shopping that relied on hard copy catalogs, TV promos, and infomercials with the relatively static products that the online store would initially have. But what it made up for in impulse-buy books – which could not viably be put into a print catalog because it would result in a gargantuan volume of information – proved to be larger than the New York telephone directory.

We will get into the factors that contributed to all that as we peel through this book, but stick a pin in this factor as it is a major theme in his life, in the way he sees himself, perceives the world around him, and references his place in it.

One of the blinding factors in understanding Bezos is also the reason we are talking about him. It's blinding because the wealth that describes the man does not define his abilities and his character. It's blinding because the wealth results in publicity and the spread of public awareness bestows a celebrity status. As all celebrity adulation goes, the person becomes what the name symbolizes and the fantasy obscures the essence. In planning and writing this book, I have consciously taken the effort to avoid that inadvertent misstep.

Bezos is a hard man. He is hard with facts and hard with outcomes. He is extremely focused and believes in the power of thinking. He also believes that if you aren't thinking you can't solve the problem that needs a solution, and he is unforgiving in this respect.

There are numerous anecdotes of people who have heard the stories of his temper and naturally ascribe his demeanor to be arrogant. It is understandable to seem arrogant when one is focused or, to seem abrupt when one is in a hurry. Bezos is both of these things. He is focused and he is in a hurry. He is not given to the niceties that many people afford others who do not live up to their end of the conversation.

I understand that trait too well. I saw that every day of my childhood, growing up with my father. What used to drive me insane as a child was his constant inability to accept the slightest fault in others – particularly me. But as I got older, I understood that there are two kinds of arrogance in this world. One is the arrogance that tries to exhibit and instill who is boss – for the sake of ego. The other seems arrogant because it demands only the best. Do you want to know how to tell the difference? You see if they demand that best from themselves as well. If they only yell and scream at others but do not apply that to themselves, then that is fake ability and true arrogance. If however, they demand the best from you and no less from themselves, then you understand that the seeming arrogance comes from the tenacity to get the task accomplished and the job done. It turns out that, not only did my father demand the best from me, but he demanded even more from himself, and I see that same caliber of demands in all that Bezos does.

Looking Deep

To understand the man's success, we need to see it for what it is and, while his rewards and returns are a part of that, it is not everything. That wealth is certainly not front-loaded but comes at the end of choices, decisions, failures, effort, pain, and relentless pursuit. These are the things that made the man. That is what we want to learn. But I can understand that there is an insanely curious fervor that is reverberating through the reading public right now and they all want to know what the secret sauce in the money burger was. I get that. But it happens that there is no secret formula that you can follow like a recipe book and get that sauce to result in the same texture, taste, and consistency. It takes a replication of what's going on inside, inspiration from the universe externally, and sweat and toil of herculean proportions. That's just putting it simply. The devil, though, is in the detail and how you look at that detail, which is what we are doing here. But before we can look at it that way, let's get the glaring bling out of the way.

When we dispense with all the bling, we can then look at him, his decisions and his actions, without the distraction of the distractions.

Looking Past the Wealth

I get it. It's not easy to fathom twelve-digit wealth while we grapple with the various financial challenges and the priorities that we have to contend with because not everything we wish to obtain can fit within our five, six, or even seven-digit income. It almost feels like rubbing salt into a wound. But you should let that pain in. You should let that burn be felt and then you should get up and do something about it. What you shouldn't do is be distracted by it.

We are so inundated by the billions and trillions in the world's financial markets that most of us in this generation can be immune and indifferent to what one hundred billion is. There are many ways we can slice that. One hundred billion dollars has significant purchasing power. You could do almost anything with it. His wealth is larger than ⅔ of the world's individual countries. How's that for size? We are no longer talking about the ability to purchase top-of-the-line vehicles or insanely-large mansions. This amount of wealth is actually useless when you look at it in terms of what you can buy for personal consumption.

After all, how many cars can you drive to work in at the same time? One, just like you and me? How many beds can you sleep in every night? One, just like you and me. How many times can you go shopping in a day? As Warren Buffett said in a recent interview, "Money no longer has any utility for me." When you have so much of it, it ends up being useless in the materialistic, consumer mindset sense.

I remember buying my third vehicle with the thought that it would be a fun thing to have a change of cars and something that I could drive for leisure. After three years, I had driven one of them just twice. The car deteriorated from infrequent use. The same happens when you buy too many apples – what you don't eat, rots. As human beings, we only need a certain amount to survive, a little more to thrive and anything after that becomes a distraction. We need a little to leave our kids as a launchpad. But that's it. Every dollar above that point is pointless. Only the man who has nothing thinks that having billions is the answer. It's not. In fact, if you are not careful, you will indeed lose your soul.

So how do you make sense of this wealth?

The target of our awe at a 12-digit net worth shouldn't be at how many mansions one can buy, rather the amount of impact one has made to be able to amass that amount of wealth. Think of it as a basketball game. The points on the board mean nothing in and of themselves, but they represent the individual achievements that the team had to go from one end of the court and to score on the other end. That's what twelve-digit wealth means – it is a measure of the things Bezos had to solve, counter, and innovate to be able to get Amazon to where it is today. How much easier is your life that you can get online and get whatever you need?

How much easier is your life that you can find things that you can't find in your neighborhood store? How many people has your neighborhood store made into a millionaire? Huh? That's right, you read me. My question is, how many people has your local store, that some of you worry is going to close because of Amazon, made into millionaires? None. Do you know how many individual business owners have become millionaires selling through Amazon? Loads. Ever hear of the Amazon FBA program that Bezos came up with? You should check it out – it's in Chapter 5 – who knows, you may be able to find a new venture.

Back to Bezos.

Hold the Judgement

Understanding what makes the man that makes the business is what I am interested in, and I find that gives me the widest ranging tools I need to explore a better life for myself. I want to watch the game, so I know how the baskets were shot – just looking at the points does me no good. I can't take the points home, but I can learn how to score by watching the game. You see what I am driving at?

Short of being morally bankrupt and ethically indifferent, one's methods of getting to such heights shouldn't come as a surprise when they brush up against our own Utopian niceties.

Be prepared to break some eggs along the way, and don't hold it against anyone who has no qualms about breaking the eggs as they beat a path to the top of the Forbes' list. I have heard the comments and read the mocking sanctimonious judgment against the likes of Gates, Bezos, Jobs, and others. Whatever merit their argument may have, it has no place in this book. Not because of adulation or worship, but because it is hard to learn from someone while we are judging them negatively. And the whole point of this biography – any biography for that matter – is to learn about that person so that we may somehow find the secret to success.

The quantum of his wealth, while stupendous, should be viewed in the right context. When it is viewed as such, then it ceases to be purely his benefit and crosses over this book to become yours as well.

***

Chapter 3 Young Man on a Mission

"If you never want to be criticized, for goodness' sake don't do anything new."

Bezos was born to teenage mother Jacklyn Gise (Pop's daughter) and her boyfriend, who was just a few years older than her. It was 1964 and they were in Albuquerque, New Mexico. That relationship didn't work out and, since this book is more about Jeff Bezos rather than his mother, we are not really going to get caught up with her relationship with young Bezos's biological father.

After leaving Bezos's biological father, Jacklyn eventually married a Cuban immigrant of Spanish descent who arrived in the United States at the age of 15.

Peter Pan

Miguel Bezos was part of the Operation Peter Pan – or Operacion Pedro Pan. Operation Peter Pan was an effort that was carried out in the interregnum period from when Batista left Cuba to the time Castro came in. There was a time when the United States accepted children that wanted to come to America and they did it over the span of a few months. Children were airlifted from Havana airport on multiple flights a day and brought to the US to start a new life. They were housed in Florida, many of whom stayed in temporary hostels that were set up for them and then they eventually made their way to their own lives across the US. This happened between 1960 and 1962. During that time, 14,000 children were brought in. Miguel was one of them.

It was an extremely hard time for all those children who were separated from their parents.

Miguel eventually made his way through school, graduated from the University of New Mexico and went to work for Exxon as an engineer. Miguel Bezos married Jacklyn when little Jeff was just four and officially adopted him, changing Jeff's name to Jeffrey Preston Bezos.

The Bezos family moved to Houston where young Bezos spent most of his formative years under a close relationship with his adoptive father. After Pops, Miguel was the next greatest influence in his life. Miguel and Jeff remained close over the years and played a huge role in the development and work ethic of the already intelligent young man. Between the two larger than life men in Bezos's life, it's hard to say who had more influence, but that really doesn't matter because what resulted was that there was a good balance to all sides that pulled and tugged at him. While Miguel (a.k.a. Mike) came from Cuba and worked hard to get an education then built his career up one brick at a time, Pops came from a line of settlers and, over the years and across the generations, the family bought land and kept enlarging their ranch. Under Pops, the land was a healthy 25,000 acres located in Texas. Pops (a.k.a Lawrence Preston Gise) was the Regional Director for the US Atomic Energy Commission and was a man of science. Science technology, cause and effect, resilience, and resourcefulness were all the buzz words and attitude that arced from Mike and Pops and ran right thru little Jeff. It was just the beginning.

Bezos's natural curiosity and his closeness to his grandfather sparked off a natural consequence of him adapting to science at an early age. From science, the leap to computers was not a long shot and, with his grandfather's guidance, Bezos's interest in computers, electronics, and science quickly formed the core of his character and interests. His dream of getting to know space and space travel was rewarded when he attended NASA's Huntsville Space Camp.

With his grandfather on the one hand, and his father, Mike, on the other, Bezos marinated in science and technology. This made him naturally less fearful of advances in science, and he understood, at the very fabric of his being, that science was a way to advance human betterment: from the way we live to the way we conduct life, technology was there to improve the quality of our existence and to advance us forward in the way we organize our societies, facilitate relationships and experience all this life has to offer.

The two men in his life imparted a sense of adventure in science in the young Bezos, which took root almost instantly. As mentioned earlier, he would advance the house vacuum into a hovercraft. As intriguing as it sounds, and as adorable as it seems, the thing that occurs to me is that making things and inventing new ways was just the way his mind worked. When you combine those Infinite Player attributes to a naturally inquisitive mind, the result is a person who really does change the world.

As his character developed, many of the attitudes and mannerisms that you see in Bezos today had already surfaced as a child. He was not one to mince words or to waste time with niceties. The one thing you can be sure about when it comes to Bezos is that he speaks his mind and, if you have nothing to hide, and you have all the interest in the world for an honest opinion, then you are not going to mind whatever he says. Why? Because he is going to tell it to you like it is.

You may have heard stories and read the anecdotes that pepper the web and the tabloids about how he can be so mean to the people who work with him and the people who work for him. You need to put all that aside and see where he is coming from. This is a guy who has always held himself to very high standards. This is a guy who has put his nose to the grindstone, both mentally and physically. And all he is expecting is that all those that he takes the trouble to hire should do the same. When they don't, his response is natural – it is not mean, it's just direct. Bezos does not know how to be mean, and he has no time to be nice. He just wants to get the point across, and he has learned, over time, and from natural instincts that most people remember, not to be stupid when you yell at them.

Have you ever heard the saying that "nice guys finish last"? There is a reason for that because nice guys aren't really nice at all. They are demure. Nature is rooted in a lot of insecurities and misplaced allegiances. From the perspective of being a nice guy, Bezos fails miserably. He is, however, a good person; someone you would want to have in your corner, regardless of his wealth. Not being a nice guy just shows the level of confidence he has in his own vision. When he was 18, he had an aversion to cigarettes and understood the effects of it. Bezos is not necessarily a health buff, but he does take his health seriously, and he thinks that health is just one of the factor inputs into a person's path to success. His logic is simple. To succeed, you first have to be alive and to be alive and work for success you have to have zero distractions – and health problems become major distractions. Cigarettes lead to health problems, so he has no time for them.

When he was a kid, he had already formed his opinion of smoking and he tried to impart this understanding to his grandmother who was a smoker, but his enthusiasm and earnestness on the matter, which can come across as nasty and tough, made his grandmother cry, instead of getting her attention.

It was not something he expected, neither was it something that he relished since he did love his grandmother tremendously. Bezos remembers the lesson his grandfather gently imparted to him in the wake of that incident: "Jeff, one day you will understand that it is harder to be kind than to be clever."

He apparently has that 'problem' still today because society's definition of kind and his momentum of purpose seem to come to a head each time they meet. He doesn't seem to have time to play or be nice. But he does not mean harm or ill to the person – he really just does not have the time.

In understanding him and his ways, it took me some time to reconcile this and tee it up to the successes that he has made. What I found is that his not being nice and his success are intricately related. Putting aside all that about 'last guys finishing last,' you have to understand that opportunity doesn't wait for you as you gently step around an obstacle. You have to shove your way through, and I mean that as much literally as I do figuratively. A lot of clichés come to mind: "time is money" and so forth. But the actions that Bezos takes are ones that are deliberate and well planned. All he needs is to think about how to execute that plan and then do so. He certainly learned that from his Pops and Mike.

Ranch Life

Bezos spent his early years between the family's home in Houston and his grandparents' ranch in Cotulla, 80 miles south of San Antonio where he operated equipment and castrated bulls – one of the many things that Pops did around the ranch himself instead of calling in expert help. It must have been an amazing experience to do things for yourself.

I can't even get the lawn trimmed.

Bezos spent most of his summers between the ages of 4 and 16 there with his grandfather, busy working on the farm and tinkering in the toolshed. That mechanical side of him was something that he had even as a toddler. There is a story in the archives about him and how he used a screwdriver to take apart his crib when he was just a toddler.

Resources

Mackenzie, his wife of 25 years, sees that as a plus because she had no problems letting their kids, even when they were less than ten years old, to handle power tools. According to both husband and wife, they would rather live with a kid that lost a finger than a kid who does not know how to be resourceful. I don't know if I am of the same opinion when it comes to my kids, and maybe this is one area that I would disagree with, but I do see the merit.

What I find telling about this whole thing is that, in the silence of his meditation and the reflection of his mind, as well as the recounting of their efforts, the Bezos really ascribe a huge part of their abilities and their achievements to being resourceful, and they want to make sure their four kids do not lose out on that.

You can tell that even Bezos himself and Mackenzie see eye-to-eye on a lot of things. You can't forget that she has had a front-seat view of this entire Amazon drama as it unfolded a year after they married. She has also given unparalleled grounding influence and rock-solid support for the man that came face-to-face with so many crucial and critical issues during the development of Amazon.

On a side note, I can only imagine the conversation they must have had in the car as they drove from New York to Seattle.

Let's get back to his younger days.

The Awkward Years

You could just tell that this kid who did well at science fairs and projects was the kind of kid that tinkered with the electronics he could find and the tools that were lying around. With Pop so handy at the farm, and Mike who had built a career in engineering, he was surrounded by men who were good with their hands and mechanically inclined.

Bezos would play with electronics as young as nine. He loved the way the electronics could be calculated and predicted and then eventually, as they got more sophisticated, he could even program the once simple electronics that he played with. He even managed to build an electronic access/denial system for his room so that his brother and sister could not come in when he wasn't around. He certainly loved his privacy even from a young age, and there are miles of papers dedicated to the stories of him being a privacy hound. I am sure all the media attention he gets is the one downside that he sees to the rise in his net worth.

Among the other things that he invented along with the intruder alarm was a cooking apparatus that worked on solar energy, an approximation of a flying vehicle, and numerous attempts at a robot (more on this later). Funny how our youth has a bearing on our adulthood. Everything he played with as a kid, he is playing with as an adult now. Not only does Amazon use robots (more than 15,000 of them in Amazon's warehouses), he even builds space vehicles for travel at Blue Origin.

Age of Computers

He arrived at his teenage years just as computers were hitting the collective consciousness of the country. Bill Gates's DOS and the IBM PC hit stores in 1981, just as Bezos turned 16. Of course, the Internet was nowhere near the public eye, but the use of heavy mainframes and large computers connecting directly to each other using telephone lines was already underway.

In high school, Bezos started to learn about mainframe computers and it so happened there was a company in town that donated its excess mainframe time to the school. No one in the school felt that they knew anything about it, so Bezos pulled the manual and, with a couple of friends, he got to work on it. His industrious nature was also the characteristic that allowed him to advance himself. But the one thing that Bezos was not up for was mundane work.

Mundane vs. Reasoning

Of course, someone's got to do it, and God Bless those who do but, when it comes to Bezos, he couldn't do the things that fall under the category of minimum wage. He strongly felt that it was a waste of his brainpower and his time. When he was in high school one summer, instead of heading to Pop's ranch, he managed to get a part-time job at McDonald's and hated every mundane minute of it.

Within a few days, he quit and started up a summer camp where he charged $600 per kid for a 10-day event for 4th, 5th, and 6th graders. It was called the Dream Institute. Dream stood for Directed REAsoning. Two of the six who enrolled were his brother Mark, and sister Christina. Pretty interesting that he considered reasoning to be a skill that needed teaching and that it was something that parents should get their kids to attend. $600 back in the 70s was quite a bit of money.

When you look at the core concept of the camp, it gives a little insight into the way he thinks – with reason. His powers of reasoning are superior to most, which is the way he arrived at the valuation numbers that he did and the reason the investors that came in at the initial round agreed to the kinds of valuation that he calculated.

When he went in for the second round of funding – this time for 8 million dollars, he had two highly-rated private equity firms willing to come in. He made the choice of who would invest, and it was Kleiner Perkins – now known as Kleiner, Perkins, Caufield, and Byers. In the end, his reasoning and inspiration were the reasons he was able to build the company up to a point that facilitated an easier second round of funding before the IPO, the following year.

Not only does his ability to reason make him a powerful negotiator, but it makes him a powerful problem solver too.

Coming back to that summer.

As part of his course, he offered literature and science. For reading, they were assigned parts of *The Lord of the Rings*, *Dune*, *Watership Down*, *The Once and Future King*, *Stranger in a Strange Land*, *Black Beauty*, *Gulliver's Travels*, *Treasure Island*, *Our Town*, *The Matchmaker*, and *David Copperfield*.

The science component included space travel as well as the use of fossil fuels, fission generators, and other forward-looking inventions. The letters that all the parents got that year described the programs as "emphasizing the use of new ways of thinking in old areas." Funny how that is exactly what Amazon is today – mail order using computers.

Like I said, we can see the silhouette of a man when you see the boy. And you could certainly see the glimpses of what he could do with all the intelligence and that propensity to put in the effort. He was not afraid of a little hustle, and he was not afraid to bring his mind and his back to bear. He just didn't want to spend his time doing mundane things without the prospect of a future.

The thing that becomes evident as you thumb through the catalog of events, ideas, and disappointments in his life is that he has a work ethic that you do not easily find elsewhere, not even along the corridors of the Ivy Leagues and in the towers on Wall Street. The work ethic that Bezos cultivated and made second nature was something that allowed him to labor through the details and see through the bumps. There is no other way to make it to the top. There is no stopping or pausing; there is no time.

Role Models

When you want to understand the motivations of a man, you should look at his role model(s) as a kid. The one thing most men do not realize is that we all look to our role models when we are kids and the tenacity we do that with is under the surface, but extremely powerful, nonetheless. For those of us who have fathers we see often, we latch on to every action, word, and style that we can, and mimic it as the way to guide us. That's internal – we all learn from mimicking.

For boys of single-parent families, they take on a large part of their mother's strength and their mother's innate empathy. For some, the guidance comes from TV, outside friends, relatives and so on. Wherever it eventually comes from, the one thing that you should know is that it has to come from somewhere. For Bezos, it came from his grandfather and his father.

The development of a man is best narrated by the anecdotes of his life. But not everything can be chronicled, for the mundane might render the necessary obscure.

With that in mind, in this book, we take the time to look at Bezos from the highlights of his life, his turning points, and his patterns, in hope of understanding the path and the tools necessary for success.

As I observe his childhood, it repeatedly occurs to me that young Bezos is nothing short of an arduous achiever, whether it was his kindergarten projects, his grade-school homework or his high-school term papers. He was full of useful energy that he plowed back into himself as an investment.

At every turn of his childhood, his teachers recall, in retrospect, that Bezos was different – and not in a weird way. You know how some of the geeky kids can feel strange at times. Yes, they know it all and can recite a string of facts, stopping only to catch their breath, but they don't get the nuance of things or their deeper effect. Bezos differed in that he was not like that at all. He knew his stuff, but he could also be cool about it and not seem like the know-it-all.

He was valedictorian of his high-school class, and a double major at Princeton, graduating with honors and that can't be taken lightly on its own. Sure, a lot of people do well in high school and go on to secure an Ivy League education, but something was here different.

Boundless Energy

He couldn't leave things well alone; he would always go out to make things more than they were originally designed to be, like when he tried to make a hovercraft from the vacuum cleaner in the garage in his parent's home. There were many other instances of things that he would do as a child that had the earmarks of great intelligence coupled with that boundless energy and what always resulted was fireworks.

It was that boundless energy that propelled him through the down times at Amazon. And as anyone who has started a business could tell you, getting the inspiration is just half the picture. You have to hustle and jive to get the vision to materialize. You either have one of two things that you need going for you. You are either super smart and know everything about everything, or you know how to go out and hire the people that you need to do the job that you can't already do. And even if you did know how to do it, you can't do it all. You need someone to do some of it for you and, since you can't micromanage that person, you need someone to be as smart as you.

That's the thing Bezos looks for in his employees, and that is what he was looking for on day one. He understood computers, and he understood the electronics of the game, but he didn't have all the programming skills to put a database and a website together, So, he had to hire the talent to do so.

Delegate

Delegating came easy to young Bezos. Even on his grandfather's farm, Bezos learned to do the tasks that were delegated to him and delegate the tasks that he was not able to do. But he never stood on the sidelines watching while others toiled. He was always in the thick of things, doing what needed to be done and watching with a careful eye of what more could be done without the absentmindedness of a person not in the moment.

At that age, it was Pop's resourcefulness that guided Bezos to the point where there is nothing he thinks can't be done.

Of course, you would think that way too if you grew up watching your grandfather managing the entire farm on his own with little help, and the help that he did get was that of unskilled labor. But most of the heavy thinking came from Pops, who was a deeply resourceful and independent man.

It's funny stories of Pops that litter the Bezos string of anecdotes and, when he tells these stories, there is a twinkle in his eye that accompanies his guttural burst of laughter. One such story of resourcefulness was the time Pop had ordered large farm equipment at a significantly discounted price and had to work on it himself to get it up and running. When they got to it, they figured they needed a crane to hoist it, but they didn't own one. Instead of spending the money to rent a crane, Pops took a couple of days to fashion a hoist from tools and stuff he had, managing to get the equipment off the ground. This was not a one-off. Working out on the farm, far away from conveniences, Pops could handle just about anything once he decided he needed to.

That sort of exposure proved to be invaluable for Bezos and he really began to see things in the same way and work at the impossible in the same way as well. It's hard for most of us that grow up with all the conveniences that we take for granted but, with folks who have to put their noses to the grindstone day in and day out, you find that there is very little that you can throw at them to get them flummoxed.

Pops would undertake these large projects around the farm and he would carry through each one of them regardless of how daunting they might prove to be.

Bezos unabashedly admits that his lessons in resourcefulness came from Pops. That's a good thing because, if you want to make a business go from startup to the top of the world, that would be exactly one of the things that you need. Pops even had to birth cows and suture animals on the farm when needed because the closest vet was too far away. How many of us would do what needed to be done no matter how complex or how undoable it seemed in the beginning. If you are exposed to this kind of ethos then, in time, that grows, and you do all kinds of things to make sure that the objective and not the task is what gets done. And that is the reason that Bezos is the way that he is. There are stories from within Amazon that talk about his ability to focus on outcomes and achievements rather than focusing on tasks. He is not the typical manager that wants to focus on how you get something done; rather he wants to focus on getting it done.

There are tons of business owners who do not look at the objective of the action and look at the processes instead. We fail to understand that, to be innovative, you need to be resourceful; to be resourceful, you need to be results-oriented. Being task-oriented has its place, but that place is certainly not where you need to be if you are trying to build the world's biggest retailer.

The Graduate

Upon graduation, he joined Fitel, where he hung his hat for two years and invested the kind of zeal that is shown by people who own startups. His coding and attention to detail were so exemplary that he was quickly promoted and placed in charge of responsibilities that required him to travel once a week to London, from New York.

It was a huge leap in responsibility but it was one that runs you ragged after a while, and the kind of toll this exacts on a person is not the same kind of toll that a person building a company experiences. This is the kind of exertion that doesn't amount to much and so the whole thing got really old, really fast.

He decided to quit, even though he was employee number 11 and his prospects would have been good if the company made it in the future. After all, this was the company that he gave up the likes of Bell Labs and Intel for.

He quickly found employment at Bankers Trust in New York. It was a different industry but, nonetheless, it added to a skillset that was already diverse at the young age. He was selling software to the bank's clients and, though he managed to put in two years, he found that it wasn't going where he wanted it to either. He was happy to be working with software and he was happy that it was a strong company, but the x-factor was certainly not present.

He was highly focused and knew what he wanted but was not arrogant enough to let the world pass him by without him taking a taste. He started passing his resumes out to headhunters, with the explicit instruction that he was looking for a technology play.

Sometime later he got to know about D.E. Shaw with the warning that it was nothing that he was looking for. It was a new (2–3 years old) hedge fund founded by another computer scientist. Bezos took the meeting with David Shaw, the founder, and they hit it off. Bezos joined Shaw for the simple fact that he thought Shaw to be his intellectual equal and that was not something that he saw in many others. It was now 1990, and Bezos was a young 26-year-old.

At D.E. Shaw, two things happened that changed his life forever and are, to this day, a very large part of his life. The first is that he met and married his wife, Mackenzie, and the second is that he struck on the idea for Amazon.

It's hard to fathom a rise equal to what Bezos accomplished at Shaw. He did his work superbly, and he was noticed for it. When you have someone like Shaw himself thinking that you are an amazing find, that's not usually off the mark, considering that Shaw himself was one of those left-brain-right-brain personalities who was both artistic and scientific all at once – just like Bezos.

By the time the middle of 1994 rolled around, Bezos had clocked in four years at Shaw; he was a year into his marriage, and he was sitting high on Wall Street. The thing you need to know about Wall Street and the firms there is that the biggest part of the year is around Christmas bonus time.

Bezos had already been there for some time, Shaw was doing well, they were already halfway into the year, and bonus time was not too far away. Oh, and let's not forget, he was a family man as well by this point. Then, out of the blue, Bezos finds the opportunity to open a bookstore on this new thing called the Internet. Right there in the middle of all this, he ups and quits his job, flies down to Texas, borrows a car from his father and drives to Seattle with Mackenzie.

He was 30. Mackenzie was 24, their marriage was a year old, and they threw off their bonuses and hitched their 'trailer' and rode west.

Bezos and Women

From high-school valedictorian to Princeton commencement, Bezos had the stable basics that made him a reliable young man those around gravitated toward. The physical characteristic that dominated his persona was not his height, build, or his receding hairline at that time, but it was the gesticulating and guttural bursts of laughter. You could not help feel the gregariousness of character and the fullness of life that he displays when he gets into one of his laughs. It was, in fact, the very first thing that attracted Mackenzie Tuttle to Bezos. She could hear his laughter through the walls at D.E. Shaw.

Before Mackenzie, Bezos – after all a man like the rest of us, even if he does go about it in a way that is different – created a system to meet women. Though he may have had better luck if he was as buff as he is today (wink).

Getting dates was more a science for him than something organic. The typical guy would head to the bookstore, coffee shop, or club; Bezos took ballroom lessons so that he could (in his words) increase his 'women flow.' I am sure that there are some of you who would have thought of that but, as for me, it would have never crossed my mind.

Chapter 4 Launching Amazon

"We can't be in survival mode. We have to be in growth mode."

Amazon was not always the super company that it has turned out to be. You see in the age of the Internet and in the run-up to the Internet bubble in the 90s that the paradigm had shifted from solid bottom-line financials to lofty top-line projections. At a time when valuations were given to technologies that had yet to show revenues, much less profits, Amazon was booking in revenues at levels that Bezos knew they deserved.

When Bezos set out to build Amazon, the thing that he said he relied on the most to get through hard times was the kind of resiliency that was instilled in him as a kid. His Pops was the source of that lesson as well, and he learned it alongside the lessons on resourcefulness.

He also learned that objectives superseded all other events. If you want to do something, you do it before you set out on doing anything else. And if you start it, you are not done until you succeed. It was the Edison-esque qualities of his grandfather that addressed the seemingly Herculean efforts that were undertaken during the course of events that Amazon experienced over the course of its development.

Take, for instance, the way that Bezos raised the first million. It required consistency, resiliency and, even though he gave himself only a 30% chance of succeeding with Amazon, he put 300% into it to make it work. In contrast, if you look at the typical entrepreneur today, if they think that they are going to succeed, then they put in 70%. If they think they won't succeed, they only put in 25%. Guess what happens when you do that? At 25% effort, you end up not getting anything except wasting the effort and the energy that you put in. Remember that the human body is designed to survive. It will hold on to energy, keep playing it safe and never set foot over the horizon of the mind. But to succeed in life and to build billion-dollar companies, that is exactly what you need to do. So, people like Bezos and the rest of the achievers subconsciously expand their minds and go beyond mere survival in deciding to thrive.

Most people don't do that. When he went out to raise that million, it took him the better part of a year to put it together. But for every eventual investor who agreed, there were three who declined for one reason or another. Mostly it was because the risk-adjusted valuation was beyond their appetite.

Sometimes, I wonder how those guys who passed on Amazon bear to watch the ticker and see AMZN go past.

Bezos wasn't really trying to build a web store that looks exactly like a retail store, with a customer display area in the front and a large warehouse of goods in the back. That's not really the model that has come about in this exercise. He was looking to build something that would cater to the droves of people that were getting on the Internet. It's like the old real-estate adage – "Find out where everyone is going and get there first." That's exactly what Bezos did here. The only difference between Bezos and us was that he actually got up and did it.

Pops taught Bezos how to use whatever you have in front of you to make something that your mind can see in the moment. He taught him that all things are fungible and that fungibility can be deciphered if you use your cerebral resources.

Bezos is a great fan of thinking, and he is of the school of thought that relies on the mind more than the collective – quite the departure in philosophy from those of his generation. Which is probably what makes him such a unique case study.

Distractions

One more thing that makes him unique and that comes from his grandfather as well is that, from a young age, he was thought to ward off distractions. That's why, when he talks to you, you know for certain that he is talking to you. That is also the reason he is never distracted by his phone or why you really need only to tell him something once. He is present when the event is happening and doesn't 'arrive later' when you say something that jars him out of stasis. It is a time saver – according to him and according to Pops.

I have seen this characteristic in many of the successful people I have studied. All of them, without exception, be it successful politicians or titans of technology, are always in the moment. They are always alert, and their mind is in the place and time they stand. Bezos was the same way as a kid and teachers that he impressed along the way bear testament to this.

His teachers relate stories about how they never really thought he would be a titan of industry, but they were impressed with his ability to be confident and to be able to compete with ferocity in whatever he undertook – whether it was academic competitions, projects or debates. He could talk his way through anything but not in a smarty-pants-con-man sort of way. He was born to convince people of things that only he understood.

For Bezos, what he sees is not just the product of his inspiration, it is also the product of his intellect putting two and two together. He didn't just trip and fall onto the combination of retail, books, and the Internet.

In high school, his teachers remember him to be someone who had boundless cerebral and physical energy. He would zip around getting things done, yet he would always be grounded in his efforts. There used to be a simple happiness about him that matched his generous laughter and his broad smile

Most of us find that there is a wall between what we are inspired to do and what we eventually do do. We can always see the summit but are oblivious to the side of the mountain. It's also the same when we see the wealth someone has achieved but, for some reason, we forget to appreciate the work that went into it.

There is also a loss of appreciation for the work that goes into the ambition, as well as the reality, the outcome, and the toil. We all have loads of ideas and have plenty of dreams, but only a few of us actually go out and do something about them.

We hear over and over again about how the stars lined up for Bezos, but we need to understand how each crucial step demanded an answer from him and, when we are faced with things like that in our life, how do we respond?

Take, for instance, his time at the New York hedge fund D.E. Shaw. By the way, while he was there, he rose rapidly among the ranks and was the youngest Senior VP in the history of the company. That is also where he met his wife, Mackenzie. While he was at D.E. Shaw, the Internet was beginning its growth and the company was looking for opportunities to invest in – after all, they are a hedge fund. He was making good money and was riding a good career track. Think about it: within a few years of graduating he was already at the VP level on a Wall Street firm, he had just met his wife to be, and he was living the life most Ivy League graduates dream of and achieve.

Then take that event and look at the fact that he graduated Princeton – which means he didn't really need to go knocking on doors to find the dream job. Ivy Leagues have recruitment events for seniors and offers usually come piling in before graduation. It was the same for Bezos, who had received offers from Intel and Bell Labs. But he turned them down and instead joined a startup called Fitel.

Put yourself in his shoes, with all that stability and the possibility of a family in the future. Why would he decide to leave it all behind to jump into a pool of the unknown? It's one thing if he was getting offered an MD position at Goldman Sachs or something, but he was going from a VP, on track for more, to jump-starting an idea that no one had thought about.

Now that you have that picture in your mind, think about how you would act, especially when you do not have the benefit of hindsight. Is it possible he had the vision to do it? Or was he just stark raving mad? Bezos was always a trailblazer, and that's what trailblazers do. They don't jump on a train because they have the foresight of where that train is going, they jump on that train and drive it to wherever they think it can go.

With someone like Bezos and for most of the entrepreneurs who make it to this level of the game, their starting objective is almost never about the reward – it's about a fulfillment that occurs at a deeper level. When you speak to Bezos, you will hear the passion he has in his voice for all the things that he is doing with Amazon and through Amazon. That's when you start to get an understanding of what it means to be someone who builds something that is larger than life and how he could chisel a marketplace of over 300 million people.

It's hard to do something this big when you are focused on trivial rewards. For something to get this big, it is about something so much more. It cannot be about the reward because, if it was, at the first sign of trouble, he would have either gone back to the drawing board or thrown in the towel.

Bezos was playing the infinite game not the finite one. If he was looking for the reward, the best path for him to take would have been the one he was already on. Just remember that he left a pretty secure job to dive headfirst into a startup company within a nascent industry of e-commerce on a platform called the Internet that most people didn't know existed.

Bezos talks about the early days of the Internet in a way that puts it in perspective. He tells us that, in the very beginning, he needed to raise a million bucks and he had to get the money together or else Amazon would have ended before it began. He struck a deal with a diverse group of 20 investors for the money and, in return, gave them 20% of that company. Each person ponied up around 50,000. That 20% is worth almost $90 billion now.

There are rumors that talk about how driven Bezos can be and how his employees pay the price for his drive. On the one hand, there are many who see Bezos as a 'slave driver' while to others his tenacity is just part of his charm. Well, in my opinion, you can't make an omelet without breaking a few eggs. To be able to drive your team to excellence is not just about campfires and awards, you must transmit drive by contact. For those who have no drive of their own, another person's drive can be hard to accept, and that's typically where the friction arises.

When Bezos looked at the mail order industry, two things popped out at him. The first was that he was already in the specific frame of mind required to merge the concept of mail orders to the concept of the Internet. It was an inevitable mash-up. It just needed people like Bezos and some of the other titans of industry to turn the vision into a reality.

The idea was not for the giant that Amazon is today. Instead, the idea was to merge old industry with a new facility. That was the purpose of running through the mail-order catalog and seeing what would fit. But his nature of being laser-focused was already on full display here. He didn't decide to take the entire mail-order catalog and make a company out of it; he decided to just focus on books, simply because it was at the near-bottom of the list. We discussed this earlier.

You see a lot of Bezos in the way Amazon came about and in the way it runs today. The best biography of Bezos is the contents of Amazon's history. By starting up with books, Bezos's goal was to be able to ship things anywhere in the US and around the world so, for that, he had to choose something that could be easily mailed. Books worked out great, and the upside was there because the reason it wasn't doing well in the mail order business is that there were just too many titles to make a decent collection. So, the point is that the strength of the Internet and the computer could be brought to bear on an existing endeavor. By putting in all the books he could find (randomly settling on the one million number) he created a store that would sell books alone.

Unlike today, almost two decades into the new millennium, the late nineties did not have apps and software that you could pull off the shelf and create a company. So, Bezos had to get together with a software designer to build a place where he could catalog the books and people could make the purchase.

It took fifteen months of work to get the website ready. Employee number one, Shel Kaphan and number two Paul Davis were winging it during the first few moments of Amazon's beginning. The net was there and web pages indeed had sprung up, but no one really knew how to make the most of them.

Bezos is the kind of person to jump into things whether he knows the technicalities behind it or he doesn't. He is driven more by the vision in his head than by the arsenal in his inventory. The idea is to get started and then do whatever is necessary to make it happen. But once he gets started he goes full tilt.

However, don't get the idea that anything he does is random. Just because he gets started and then works out the details, that doesn't mean he doesn't think about his actions. Take, for example, his decision to move to Seattle and set up Amazon there. That idea was because the US Supreme Court had ruled two years earlier in Quill Corp vs. North Dakota that there would be no sales tax collected from a company that didn't have a physical presence in the state the sale was made. Bezos narrowed his choices down to Nevada and Seattle, eventually settling on Seattle in part due to this benefit and also because he wanted to be in a state that had a smaller population. Why a smaller population? Because that would mean a smaller part of the revenue would be paid toward sales taxes. The remaining 49 states would not be able to collect taxes and would represent the lion's share of the market. That same line of thinking persisted in the decisions to eventually set-up warehouses. The next warehouse was set up in Delaware – no sales taxes to think about; and the third was in Reno, Nevada, also with no taxes but easily a stone's throw to California, which is a huge Amazon market. Nothing in Bezos's actions is random. Everything is deliberate, everything is with purpose, and every purpose has an infinite horizon.

The Reflection of Amazon

To understand Bezos the Titan, you need to understand Bezos the person, on the one hand, and Amazon, his creation, on the other. Any narrative that addresses one and not the other is going to fall short of the mark. It's like trying to understand Shakespeare without reading any of his works. In the interest of that, the next chapter is designed to give you a little insight into how Amazon works, looking at its most vibrant operations so that you get an idea of what exactly Bezos set out to do and what exactly he accomplished.

If you want to understand any piece of art, if you want to appreciate the content of the symphony, you have to build and understand the context around it. In most cases, that means you need to understand Beethoven from the work he did and appreciate the work he did from fully understanding him. If you've ever sat down and listened to Beethoven's Symphony No. 9 from beginning to end, you will come out feeling elated and in awe. If you then go on to realize that Beethoven was deaf at the time he composed it, you will suddenly have a renewed appreciation for the work that is deep and inspiring and be able to get a clearer understanding of the man's genius.

A man's true biography isn't in the words that biographers pen, it's in the product of their own hands. They leave their fingerprints all over their creation, they leave their DNA, and they impart a little of their soul. Just as Bezos has with Amazon.

Chapter 5 Understand Amazon – Understand Bezos

"Position yourself with something that captures your curiosity, something that you're missionary about."

Bezos is a giant in the world of e-commerce, especially when you consider that Amazon has over 300 million users and growing. To put that in perspective, that is almost every man, woman, and child in America.

For some, Amazon is a shopping mall on steroids. For others like the hundreds of thousands of small sellers on Amazon, it's an avenue to make money. More than 100,000 sellers made more than $100,000 in 2016. In 2017, visitors spent $200 billion on Amazon. It holds more than 40% of all US e-commerce activity. That is the largest market share by far.

What you must understand about Amazon and the size of the market and following is not limited to just the awe the numbers invoke. What those numbers should tell you is that there is critical mass in what they do, which drives the value of the company and the value of Bezos to that company's bottom line.

He created an avenue not just for him to sell books, but for you (anyone out there) to sell just about anything to anyone. That's what most people don't get. They see Amazon everywhere, and they see it as just another brand. Amazon is not just another brand. Amazon is the bridge to 300 million users worldwide (and growing) who, together, present a wide variety of tastes that you can fulfill. For a retailer, that is a dream come true.

The rest of the world sees, in 2018, what Bezos saw in 1994. But he didn't just see it, he actively went out and made it happen. We sometimes mistake the true value of a company, just as we underestimate the true value of a person, by ascribing a number that we can associate. It is typically arbitrary and is used to convey with limited scope how good, how great, how bad, how awesome something is, or its potential, its contribution, and its worth. On Wall Street, we use terms like PE, EBITDA, Stock Price, Bond Rating, and Margin. On Main Street, we use things like market growth, market penetration, mindshare, and market cap. For the person, we are caught up by the awards they receive, the title of the office they hold, and the wealth they possess. In and of themselves these metrics are fine. But we should not obscure our own perspective of the true contribution and worth of the company or the person based on these limited numbers. We should remember that they merely scratch the surface. Instead, we should look at the kinds of challenges they overcame, the kinds of experiences they faced, the kinds of responses they afforded. If the former could be categorized as the quantitative measure of contribution, then the latter would be categorized as the qualitative measure of contribution.

In pursuing a qualitative measure of a man, we instinctively turn to biographies, just as we turn to analyst reports for a company. When it comes to Bezos, we do both because the qualitative measure of a man can be found in the anecdotes his life generates and the contribution Bezos made and continues to make, is described in part by the story of Amazon, and also the other companies that he has created.

Take Blue Origin for that matter. He is funding Blue Origin from the sale of his Amazon Stock. In the last couple of years, he has taken a billion dollars' worth of Amazon stock – at whatever price they were at the time and then liquidated his position so that he could inject the cash from the sale into the development of Blue Origin. His last sale was in November of 2017.

Since that first year in Seattle, Amazon had grown to over half a million employees – second only to Walmart as America's largest employer. That number would be significantly higher if it weren't for the large force of robotic arms and the level of sophisticated technology and computing power that Amazon employs to run its business. Just five years ago, America's Top Ten Employers list did not include Amazon; now it occupies the number 2 spot. A testament to the ferocity of Amazon's growth rate. This has yet to include HQ2 (their widely reported second Headquarters) which is set to open this year and is anticipated to employ approximately 50,000 workers at all levels. This is also not including the worldwide expansions that Amazon has planned for some of the overseas operations and another 50,000 across its currently existing facilities. When it is all said and done, not only will the headcount pass the 600,000 mark, but it will also include a higher number of robots and automation to keep up with its rapid growth and expansion plans.

So, on the one hand, you see him as a job creator in the communities across America that host the Amazon operations. But what you should also take note of is those robot arms. I know it is sometimes overwhelming to peer through all the different ventures that Bezos penetrates into, but there are significant numbers of them and, while we won't touch on all of them, I will highlight those that have reached a certain threshold of interest.

Robot Arms

Remember all those things that Bezos built when he was a kid – the electronic gizmos and intruder alarms, solar cookers, and stuff like that. Well, among them there was a distinct interest that young Bezos had harbored from all his Science Fiction books – it was the robot. He was fascinated by the robot and the electronics, computing, and technology that went into it. Remember too, that Bezos is an electrical engineer by training which gives him insight into the hardware. Alongside his electrical engineering degree, he has a computer science degree also, so he also understands the coding and software side of technology. Put these together with his interest in robots as a kid, and what you get is a man that scoops up one of the world's leading robot arm/automation technology companies.

They bought it, then renamed it Amazon Robotics. But at its heart, it is a company that is rapidly developing factory automation and logistics streamlining in a way that is revolutionary. The reason you don't hear so much about it in the news is because, as large and significant as it is, it doesn't reach the levels of what Amazon has grown to become. But the essence of ingenuity and foresight still characterize Bezos, and his decision to purchase the company was not only to save costs for Amazon, but also to push the technology so that it advances the causes of Amazon and locks out other entrants. His strategic perspective keeps him one step ahead of other players, and I imagine it would take at least a decade for someone to surpass Amazon or the entire basket of accomplishments that Bezos has made in this industry, assuming he is no longer around.

The true greats - the ones who deserve the accolades and the wealth that rewards them don't just have a premonition of where to be when the market makes a run. The true greats not only know where the market is going, but they also steer the market to the vision they have. Bezos not only left a mark on Amazon; he has left a mark on retail, publishing, and lifestyle too.

Amazon is such a robust platform that not only does it allow millionaires to be minted here, but it has also created other sites that have turned into moneymakers as well – think Alibaba.com. Alibaba clearly acknowledges that the concept of its marketplace is one that observes and emulates Amazon. There is nothing wrong with that. I think mimicry is the greatest form of a compliment. Don't you think? And it worked out great for Jack as well. It was a win-win for both. There are large numbers of sellers on Amazon who take from Alibaba and sell on Amazon.

That effectively means that not only is Amazon selling goods that it stocks, but it creates a marketplace for others to find goods from anywhere and everywhere to sell on its marketplace.

There are numerous niche sellers that even go to Walmart, load up their cars with items on sale, then get home and sell that stuff on Amazon for a profit. Something like that would not be possible without Amazon.

Others go to Aliexpress.com and buy goods, made in China, for pennies on the Dollar, then sell it back home on Amazon at market price. Some of these companies in China are even willing to place your label on it so that you can create branding and then ship it to the warehouse that Amazon owns, then Amazon will ship it for you to your end customer – it is the FBA (Fulfilled by Amazon) program. Also one of Bezos's ideas.

He has taken every aspect of Amazon and optimized each facet of it so that it creates value and long-term benefits for an array of participants. He has even managed to monetize the value of the brand. Take, for example, his FBA program.

If you are a niche that uses white-label products and drop-shipping supplies, then FBA would be an avenue for you to reach Amazon's 300 million customers. If you own your inventory, either by virtue of manufacturing or by purchasing it and taking ownership, then the option to get your items Fulfilled By Amazon starts to make a whole lot of sense.

The Amazon Customer

To understand Amazon, you need to understand their customers and the way Amazon interacts with them. The typical Amazon customer can be divided into two groups. The first group is the one that comes under the Amazon Prime label. These are the customers who have paid an annual fee for priority service.

The second group of customers is the one that falls outside this umbrella. Marketing may not have been his major, but he definitely understands how to extract value from differentiating with his customer base. He doesn't spend a cent more than he has to and he monetizes even the intangible.

As of the end of 2017, there were more than 32 million Prime customers. Amazon spent $1.5 billion on shipping across the board in 2016, yet 32 million Primes paid in almost $3.3 billion. How smart is that?

What that means is that, even though the Primes are getting free shipping, their membership pays for all of the shipping that Amazon does even to regular members and then there is still a balance left over of $1.5 billion. Everybody wins. The

Primes get a load of free stuff and priority shipping. The company covers all its shipping costs and that drops straight to the bottom line. If you are not a prime and you buy stuff and pay for shipping, that falls straight to the bottom line as well.

While Prime members only represent 10% of the total Amazon customer base, they spend an average of $1,600 annually versus the other 90%, who average about $600 annually.

Amazon has been online 24-7, 365 days for the last 24 years. Part of the algorithm that is sorting out what you buy and getting it shipped to you is also studying how you buy, what you buy, and when you buy it. There is a huge customer intelligence algorithm running in the background and it is gaining a wealth of information each time you visit, each time you buy, and each time you browse. Bezos made sure of that.

Understanding Bezos Through His Employees

In the research phase for this book, I came across numerous instances of complaints of the work conditions at Amazon – specifically its HQ. I wasn't going to include anything about it in the book but then, as it started to seem that the gripes that were talked about related directly to working conditions of the cerebral kind rather than the Health and Safety kind, I decided it would be a good way to understand Bezos and his way of doing things. What I found only gave me a better understanding of the facets that defined Bezos and his ethos toward work, as well as his singular focus on achieving the stated goal.

The first thing that you realize when you want to work at Amazon is that everyone is very clear about how much work you will have to put in. This is not a regular 9–5 job. This is not where you set yourself up for life to walk in the door when your 24 and clock out when you retire after spending 30-odd years doing the same mundane task, and then collect your gold watch. No. This doesn't work that way, and I wish I had known this when I was just coming out into the job market all those years ago – this would have definitely been a place I would have thrown my hat into to be considered. Of course, when I graduated, the only Amazon that existed was flowing in South America and had nothing to do with my major.

I would have loved to work here as a kid out of college, not because it would have been easy work but because it would have been one of the hardest things that you ever do if you were coming straight out of graduate school.

Why?

Because it is run by a man who doesn't see things in shades of hard or difficult; he sees things as do or don't do. Almost Yoda-esque. There is no measure of try, and there is no measure of driving the task. It's about delivering the result that has been planned for, not the attempt of doing it.

What the general public has failed to understand about the Amazon culture, just like everything else at Amazon, is that it is a reflection of Bezos himself. They have one driving force, and that is to be the best at online commerce. And that really is an extension of Bezos himself, who wants to be the best that he can be in everything that he is a part of. If he can't give it his entire attention, he won't do it. If he can't be his best at it, he won't do it, and if he can't give it his 300% then he would rather find something else that he can do.

Typically, business consultants would look at this and say that it is too vague, you need to cut that down and focus it a little more. If you don't have the focus, you are not going to be able to communicate it and you are not going to be able to execute it. These are the guys that have no idea what they are talking about. Amazon and Bezos are not about processes and targets, they are driven by objectives and doing whatever it takes to get from concept to outcome. To do whatever it takes to get that Christmas gift to your doorstep a little faster, to get your lawnmower to you earlier than you expected, and to make your trip to the store less painful and more convenient – all the while fending off and hitting off competitors who are trying to emulate and reconfigure the market in their image.

To this end, just like Pops did, Bezos sets these seemingly insurmountable goals and expects that those he has around him can meet the challenge by applying their minds and efforts. He is not the kind of person that reacts well to excuses or reasons that something didn't work out.

But if you are about to go work for him, the one thing that you can find solace in is that he may push you till you feel you are about to break – then two things happen. One, you find it somewhere in you to make it happen and you grow as a person, or you do break and you find the limits of your ability. Either way, working for Bezos is not for the faint of heart. Consider yourself warned. But if indeed you do take the challenge, be prepared to climb as far as your spirit can take you.

***

Chapter 6 The Bezos Mindset

“It’s not an experiment if you know it’s going to work.”

There are two kinds of mindsets when it comes to leaders in the corporate world, academia, and politics. There are also two kinds of games that they see themselves playing.

These games are not really things that we think of when we think of having fun. These are games that represent the way we approach, handle, and compete. These ‘games’ are more about the competition than they are about the playing.

Games describe a process of interaction between players. Buying a car from the dealer is a game. The players in that game are the purchaser and the salesman scouting the lot on that day. The game can be seen as the transaction, the interaction, and the communication. The game is intangible.

On the other hand, the players are those who play the game. They initiate the force that defines and moves the game while being the vessel of its results. In the vehicle purchase example, the players initiate the purchase and the seller agrees. When the sale is concluded, the buyer owns the vehicle – the owner of the vehicle's value – and the seller holds the cash – the owner of the cash's value. Each is a recipient of different values – values that they wanted to obtain.

There are two kinds of games when it comes to the corporate world and even politics – the infinite games and the finite games.

To play the infinite game we have the Infinite Player, and to play the finite game we have the Finite Player.

So now that we have all the ingredients to this thought experiment, let's get started and show how it all fits in with Bezos and Amazon.

Finite Players

Finite Players look at one common focal point. This focal point is that there is a quantifiable, definable, and impending end. It is either this financial year-end, this end of a quarter, this cycle – whatever, as long as it is finite.

Whatever your timeframe, there is a finite and definable end-point to focus on. These players, the finite ones, have a certain mindset that is totally opposite from the Infinite Players. When you see the moves they make, the decisions they end up with, and the kinds of choices they make typically, you start to get a sense of the way they see the game in their head. Look at the quotes at the beginning of each chapter and you will start to get an idea of the mindset that Bezos has and the kind of game he is playing. Does it sound like a finite game or an infinite one? Keep reading, as you will start to make sense of it.

Finite games are the ones where you clock in at kindergarten, go all the way to high school, get to a university, get recruited as an executive, get a few promotions, retire, then move to Florida. There is a goal at every stage, there are rules for what you can and can't do, there are mindsets to make sure you follow the rules.

Infinite Players

The thing that is part and parcel of an Infinite Player's character is an incapacity to cheat. If you meet someone who is an inherent Infinite Player, you will realize that they are the kind that you can trust without hesitation. Bezos was such a person. On the trip to Seattle, he had stopped to meet three future employees and Shel Kaphan, one of the three, just fell into a trusting relationship with him, so much so that he packed his bags and moved to Seattle. That's not an easy thing to do. You can't fake that kind of trust and you certainly can't fake it with people like Shaw and Kaphan, and each of the 20 initial investors that forked out an average of $50,000 each to get Amazon to the next level.

Infinite games, on the other hand, break the molds and have no rules except to keep the game going. You play the game over and over again.

Here is a good way to think about it. If you play a game of chess with one person and you know that the game is going to be just a one-off game and, after you play with them, you will never see them again. Would you play differently? You also know that the winner takes the titles, then you will do anything you can to beat that person. You don't care if they never play with you again after that game because the second game is not your objective. Your objective is to win the game at hand.

If you take the Infinite Player and place him in a finite game, the results will be suboptimal. The reverse is the same.

To get the best outcomes, you need to place the Infinite Player in an Infinite Game and a Finite Player in a Finite Game. When you match the player to the game, the results are spectacular. Especially if you have the Infinite Player leading a revolutionary company and his finite-player managers hitting the goals and tasks he sets.

Remember how Bezos could not find his satisfaction in hedge funds (at D.E. Shaw) – the quintessential finite game. Players who play the infinite game don't recognize rules and the status quo. It's not that they don't follow the rules, they just don't see how the rules apply to their world and their thinking. Infinite Players inherently only see the purpose of keeping the game alive and continuously progressing.

If you are a Finite Player playing chess, then you just throw all you have at the game in an effort to win. If you are an Infinite Player, then you take each game as it comes, you study the opponent's moves, you keep the game going gradually one after the other, and understand that there are higher levels of interaction than just the physical game.

There is an entire branch of philosophy that is propping up on this whole finite and infinite game. It is also one of the elements of Nash's game theory. The reason I bring this up here is so that we can get an idea of how Bezos thinks, what his motivations are, and the real relationship between him and the things that he does.

Using the Finite-Infinite Framework

But there is a more important reason for us to look into this framework. Of course, we get to understand Bezos better and we get to apply that framework to a host of other achievers but, more importantly, we get to apply it to ourselves. If you look at the achievement of a person like, say, Bezos, and you look at yourself and find that you are more of a Finite Player, then the last thing you want to do is try to emulate someone like Bezos who we believe is an Infinite Player. Finite Players are people like Tiger Woods, Alan Greenspan, and Jack Welch. Finite Players make great CEOs and drivers of goals and outcomes.

If you are, on the other hand, an Infinite Player, then you need to ask yourself the ultimate question, and that is if you are happy where you are and in what you are doing. Bezos was never happy at the few jobs he landed after Princeton. Even at D.E. Shaw he wasn't happy, and he was looking to satisfy his tendencies as an Infinite Player.

The next biography you pick up, read it with a mental framework of the Finite and Infinite game and place it in context. That will give you a better point of reference so that you can see where you can emulate and where you can just observe.

Chapter 7 - Beyond Amazon

Now, don't forget, Amazon is not the only thing that Bezos is responsible for creating. He also founded Blue Origin.

The whole point of this biography is not just to chronicle the who, what, where and when, but to peel back the layers and try to understand the why and the how. Between Blue Origin and Amazon, what do you see?

As for me, I see that here is a man that looks across the horizon and has a clear picture of what needs to happen. You and I may look at the nascent e-commerce industry and say, well, that is unproven, and we are not going to take the risk on some new fancy idea. But, that's not because we are not risk-takers, but because we only see the risk. The risk obscures our perspective of the goal.

As for Bezos, he sees the goal and, because he is an Infinite Player, he doesn't see the risk as risk; he sees it as part of the package. I've spoken to numerous risk analysts and they all say one thing clearly; that if you calculate the risk of a startup like Amazon then, based on risk alone, there is no plausible reason to start it up. There have been other men like these in history. Christopher Columbus, for one. In his case, he literally could not see what was over the horizon, and in a world that believed that if you get to the edge, you fall off, he either couldn't see the risk or he was so brave that the risk of falling off the edge did not bother him. These are Infinite Players.

Another aspect that points conclusively to Bezos being an Infinite Player is, as mentioned a few paragraphs above, his involvement with Blue Origin. Blue Origin is a company that initially started with the building of rocket engines, quickly outgrew the initially stated goal and started to build vehicles that would go into low orbit. Their purpose was to be able to take the commercial customer into space.

Do you see any demand for people going into space? It's almost kind of like seeing if people would buy a dishwasher online 35 years ago. But Bezos sees these things because he is an Infinite Player. He is not limited by desires to fulfill this quarter's returns and next fiscal year's budgets. His vision takes a longer arc to fulfill and a greater return on any possible investment. Remember what the return was on the first group of Angel investors, who took 20% of the company in return for $1,000,000.

What about Amazon and Blue Origin? How do you fit them into this framework of finite and infinite games? The evidence makes it so abundantly clear that they almost seem self-evident. Bezos is playing an infinite game in both. So, what you have is an Infinite Player playing an infinite game. He took some of the rewards of the first infinite game that was spectacular and invested it into the second. He is extending the entire game into the future.

He knew exactly what he was going to do even when he was a teenager. For his valedictorian speed in high school, he talked about building space stations and creating a better human environment. In part, this is what he said:

"...to build space hotels, amusement parks and colonies for 2 million or 3 million people who would be in orbit. 'The whole idea is to preserve the earth' he told the newspaper... The goal was to be able to evacuate humans. The planet would become a park."

Jeff Bezos is the quintessential Infinite Player, not only because he sees what's beyond the horizon, but also because he plays for more than the reward. He plays for purpose and he plays for betterment. For people like him, success comes easy in his own mind but they are not the same standards that spectators view him with, so what happens is that they misunderstand his actions, motives, and energies.

The closest thing to thinking about an Infinite Player and comparing that to a Finite Player is to think about a long-distance marathon runner and a 100-meter sprint athlete. You have two very different people and you can't put one player on the other's track.

The marathon runner is looking for distance, and his job is to stay in the moment but keep moving. He is not interested in where his competitors are (this is just an example to stress the point). The sprint athlete, on the other hand, is constantly concerned about where the competitors are and how he can keep moving forward faster. But that's just from the outside. The point that is really at hand is that the physical build of a long-distance runner is significantly different from the sprint runner. Everything from the way the energy is managed to the muscles that develop and to the way they breathe are all different.

It is the same way with Finite and Infinite Players. They are built that way and they play that way. The problem is not the game or the player. The problem arises when you put the Infinite Player in a finite game, just like Bezos was when he was at his hedge-fund job; and when you put a Finite Player in an infinite game.

It is worse for Infinite Players because this world and the mindsets of the world, in general, advocate and promote finite deadlines, and finite milestones. From kindergarten to high school, to colleges and beyond, the entire system is designed for inherently Finite Players because of all the measurements and valuations. Those evaluations and structures force the game to be played as a finite game, and that usually messes with an inherently Infinite Player. Most times, people are surprised to hear that a kid that didn't do well in school suddenly leaves school, drops out and goes out on his own, only to become extremely wealthy. Gates and Zuckerberg come to mind.

However, there are many of the Infinites who stick it out, and even do well in the finite environment but are constantly not satisfied with whatever they have to contend with. They either find the point in their life where they get to what's real, or they stay in the finite world and struggle in mediocrity their entire life. Bezos knew exactly what he wanted and he just sailed along in the finite world until his opportunity to play the infinite game showed up. That's why he was able to make the jump from his day-job when most people would have passed and stuck with the status quo.

The one thing that comes naturally to those who play the infinite game is the art of making mistakes. Making mistakes and not getting stuff right is something that many people loathe, and others fear. For whatever reason, they find that mistakes take them back a notch or they see themselves in the light of the finite world, so they see a picture that is less than what they know themselves to be. Think about that for a second. What this does is give them the strength and the visualization needed to weather through mistakes, errors, and failures. Because to them, these are not mistakes, errors or failures, these are just the way the infinite game is played. There are no winners and losers when you play the infinite game and, therefore, you have no worries about making mistakes.

In the long-term, Infinite and Finite Players serve different purposes. Neither is good or better than the other; they are just different. But when you are true to who you are and play the game you were built to play; you extract value from your contribution. Just as Bezos did with Amazon, and just like he is doing with Blue Origin.

When you look at his other investments, you can gain insight into his thinking and into his view of the world around him. He is very practical about his present moment but also cognizant of the potential we all face. He is a named investor in a number of startups that happened around that time. For instance, he is one of the early investors in Google and was nearly one of the early investors in eBay.

His investments are managed by a company called Bezos Expeditions. Bezos Expeditions has been actively investing, primarily, in companies and industries that have strategic synergies with the interests in the areas that Bezos himself is involved in. His investments are not purely designed to maximize financial returns without strategic benefit.

His investments parallel his beliefs closely and are typically made when they have a greater purpose. His initial investment in the rocket-engine company was not just an investment but something that was close to his heart. Eventually, that investment gradually turned into something more. To understand Bezos, this is how you have to see him: there is nothing random about his actions. As with the case of the rocket engine companies, it's very easy to jump up and ask what on earth does a retail, e-commerce titan have to do with rocket engines? Well, if we look at it superficially, then the answer is "nothing," but if you look at the investment based on the person, you can see that the rocket-engine investment was merely a detailed piece in a vast puzzle in Bezos's mind. He knew very early on what he wanted to do and where he wanted to go, he just kept collecting the prices he needed to get there.

As we look at the other investments he has made through Bezos Expeditions, there are just some that should strike you and reaffirm the fact that he is an Infinite Player. Bezos Expeditions (BE) makes an average of between 5 and 7 investments a year.

His recent investment in biotechnology is one of the most curious because its main research and stated purpose is to extend the length of the useful life, or as they call it, 'extending your healthy life.' That's one way to refer to a company that is doing research on aging and prolonging.

There is always a method to his ways. In the run-up to his announcement of making an investment in rocket engines, Bezos used a number of shell companies to make the purchase of land in Texas. Between the amount of land he personally purchased, and the inheritance of land that he received from his family, Bezos is one of the single largest landowners in the state of Texas. His actions, again, were not random; his purchases were for the purpose of setting up the launch site for Blue Origin and the space program. While the actions may not have seemed evident at the time they were made, they eventually fell together.

***

Chapter 8 Mindset Manifestation

"If you decide that you're going to do only the things you know are going to work, you're going to leave a lot of opportunity on the table."

We ended the last chapter talking about Blue Origin in the context of finite and infinite games. If nothing else, you should start getting an idea of what the two games look like and you should be able to see the investments and businesses that Bezos makes to get an idea of who, and what, he is. Many of the things in his life strike me relentlessly in proving that he is indeed an infinite character. Even when he is intolerant of people who make mistakes, his quips are "Why are you wasting my life?"

Now think about the psychology in that for a second. He is not saying what people usually say, which is "Why are you wasting my time?" Instead, he is talking about his 'life.' He sees his time in the context and with the perspective of so much purpose. There is so much that he knows he has to do that he is not fooling around. Most people who work for him cannot always take that. They are either Finites in an infinite environment or Infinites who are used to the finite world and are getting something they didn't expect. In either case, it is normal for those around someone who is on a mission to be unable to keep up.

That's typically why he is there, and they are still trying to make it in the world. Many of his employees attribute his nature to being someone who is in a rush and someone who is highly ambitious. That is an assumption that should not be trivially accepted. It's not about ambition in the traditional sense of "Hey, what do you want to be when you grow up?" His ambition is not really an ambition; it's about purpose. He doesn't see himself as someone who needs to dream big and visualize it into existence. He sees himself as someone who is already destined to make it happen.

How many people talk about building space colonies and actually grow up to invest over half a billion dollars into it and make it work. Yep, that's right, Blue Origin is so far ahead of the curve, that it looks like they will keep their mark and hit the first customer in space mark by 2018.

Another thing about Infinites is that they don't see things as big dreams or audacious goals. They see it as the next progression to wherever they may be at the moment. They don't parse these goals in their head into deliverables and milestones; they see the whole picture. This is exactly how Bezos does things. Most people get confused about his ability to see grand ideas and, at the same time, to micromanage the deliverables and tasks assigned to staff. This is one of the things that Infinites do, and the same thing happened to all those who worked with Steve Jobs as well. When they see the whole picture, they see the whole nine yards and every inch in-between. There is no difference in the micro or the macro picture; there is no forest for the trees, it's all at once.

He is able to do that because, as many of those around him have repeatedly observed, Bezos has unbounded energy. He has tremendous resilience in his pursuits, and he has no intention to stop. Successful people believe in their vision and what they are doing. Bezos doesn't stop at belief; he knows what he is supposed to do and he just gets up every day and he does it. Then, when he gets there, he has more inspiration to go on to the next thing. And so he went from books to everything. As the motto for Blue Origin so eloquently reflects

Bezos's ethos, *"Gradatim Ferrositer"* loosely translated to mean "Step by step with ferocity."

Most ambitious people want to get there in a single leap. That's the thing; he seems to follow the adage, "Rome was not built in a day." Unlike many of the people who have graced the list of the wealthiest people, or the list of the most accomplished, the thing about Bezos is that he is easy to observe and understand if you look at his motives.

Bezos's motives have always been clear, and he has always been open about them. He goes after each goal relentlessly, but he is not concerned about failing. If he does, he just picks himself up and keeps going.

Throughout our history as a country, and our history as a civilization, we have seen men of greatness carved from the stone of the Infinite game. Churchill, the Wright Brothers, Steve Jobs, and much more. These men of the Infinite game have all the same characteristics and the same perspectives. You can see their patterns across the board regardless of the age in which they made their impact. There are a number of people in our lifetimes that have been obvious Infinites. Bezos is but one of them.

It is a common fallacy among academics who think that CEOs and chairmen should not concern themselves with the minutiae of the company. They say that the founders and the leaders should concern themselves with the strategic direction of the company and the big ideas. They should not waste time with small matters. But that is absolutely not true and that is not how Bezos does business. He is, as they say, a hard ass. He knows all the details, and he understands them acutely. He also knows the big picture. In his mind, who could you possibly know the big picture if you do not know the details? And he is right. The reason this trait is misunderstood is that those who are typically Infinites have the capacity to handle both strata of any business – the details and the big picture. That's one of the reasons Bezos is who he is.

Bezos's obvious power of resilience comes from his absolute dedication to his purpose in life, which from as much as we can gather from his actions and words is that he wants to improve everything he touches and that includes making the world a better place. There is a sense of largeness about him that transcends everything he does and how he thinks. It's how Infinite people navigate this world.

***

Chapter 9 - A Parting View

"Maintain a firm grasp of the obvious at all times."

With a better understanding of Bezos and the accomplishments he has made over the course of the last quarter of a century and, really, over the period of his life, there are many instances on which we can look back on to understand that he is, after all, human. We can never forget that. He is neither superhuman nor is he gifted. He is by no means a prodigy.

Bezos is just someone who is driven. His intellect comes from pushing himself and from the desire to fill in the gaps. He just can't seem to let anything go without understanding what it is and solving the puzzle before moving on to the next thing. He also wants to get in the game and fix whatever needs fixing and, if it doesn't need fixing, he wants to get in and be the catalyst for it to evolve.

He just can't leave things alone – and in this case, it has proven to be a good thing.

What would soon occur to anyone who studies Bezos is that he is inextricably linked to Amazon, and I don't just mean that in a natural cause-and-effect sort of way. Their link is more than that. Amazon is almost a perfect reflection of him – focused, fair, driven, yet completely on the ball. You see, Bezos can be altogether a really pleasant person to deal with, and yet, at a flip of a switch, can be hard as nails.

After leaving Houston in his father's car, Mackenzie drove while he kept pounding away at a business plan and running the numbers on his laptop. They stopped in California to meet Shel, then drove on up to Seattle.

When they got started, it was just the three of them: Mackenzie, Bezos, and Shel. They were working out of the garage of the Bezos home to keep overheads low and they were constantly on the move – taking meetings with book suppliers, meeting with shipping and trucking agents, meeting possible new hires. There was also a lot of coding going on as they needed to set up the database to hold the millions of books that Bezos had set his sights on.

They also needed to set up the website, so Shel kept piecing that together. Not long after that, they took on the second hire and then both Shel and the new guy, Paul, kept working on the simple user interface for what would eventually become Amazon's main home page that you see today. But remember, back then, they were just selling books.

It was not as easy to start up as one might think, but it also wouldn't have been as hard for others to wing it and get it up and running. There was a tremendous level of work ethic on display, along with discipline and belief in the idea.

Resources were tight, as you have seen, and they stretched it by doubling up on whatever they could; coffee shops became meeting places, doors became tables, homes became offices. You get the point. It's not different from what most people would have done when they kickstart a business from the garage of their homes.

The things that were different was how deliberate each action was. I can't help but see all of Bezos's fingerprints on how things were set up and structured. There was some form of irony in sitting in the Bellevue Barnes and Noble Starbucks and plotting the rise of a business that would someday soon stare Barnes and Noble down. I wonder, if the managers had known this, would they have still allowed Bezos, Mackenzie, and Shel to use them as a second base of operations.

When the time came to infuse cash into the business, it was almost touch and go at the time.

Bezos, who was in charge of the business end of the idea, started shopping for VCs in Seattle. There was a sense of trying to keep everything close to home. He shopped some of the funders and he got a bite. It was a VC firm in downtown Seattle that finally agreed to take on the entire $1 million in equity, but the talks went down in flames when they halved Bezos's valuation, and wanted to take 50% of the equity of Amazon in return.

Bezos turned it down without any hesitation and all the deliberateness that you would imagine. As you already know from an early part of the book, he finally convinced friends, family (his parents among them), ex-colleagues, and everyone he knows to come together and fund that first million. They only took 20% in return.

Bezos doesn't downplay that event and is very sober about the fact, that if that million dollars hadn't come through, Amazon would have never been able to get off the ground.

Here's another reason that Bezos as Amazon's embodiment is an absolute fact. In the wake of Amazon's success, principles of the VC firm that kept the risk premium high on Amazon and demanded the lower valuation were asked about that decision. The thing that was most striking to them is that they should have seen Amazon as an extension of Bezos and not just as a basket of risk. They were certain that Barnes and Noble would trounce them the instant Amazon came into view. They did not count on Bezos's resilience and tenacity, not to mention his ability to think his way out of a corner.

The server was finally completed and the website was ready – simple, but functional, the database was also completed. Paul and Shel had managed to do a decent job of things. They turned the lights on finally on July 5th, 1994. There was no pre-opening advertising – remember this is the early 90s and there wasn't Google PPC. There was Netscape browsers and little else. No doubt the Internet was ringing up online users rapidly, with over 300% growth annually, but the infrastructure was still pretty thin. There was still a bridge you needed to cross between brick and mortar and e-stores. By the way, there was no Facebook or even the hint of social media at that time. The crossover companies needed to accomplish was the ability to get existing customers on the web to their site, or to be able to use conventional means to advertise their presence, and then get them to visit from there. A purely online play was still unheard off for the most part, and Amazon was indeed headed into thick jungles as far as the challenges to get people to key in the URL and make a purchase.

Bezos and Shel rigged the computers to chime whenever a sale was made, and it did soon after going live. Every time a sale would come in, it faithfully chimed away. Within the first month, it was getting distracting as the volume of dings increased rapidly. So much so, they had to turn it off.

By the time fall rolled around, they were doing around $20,000 in weekly sales. None of it was taken out. It was all plowed back into growing the business. This was Bezos's hallmark. Even as an alter ego, he behaved on behalf of Amazon the same way he carried out his own life. He used the money to reinvest and remained frugal. For a startup to be revenue generating in the 90s, being a tech company was almost unheard of. The burst bubble of the Internet revolution in the nineties is littered with stories of failed companies, lofty valuations on the backs of zero revenues and negative profitability. Companies at the time were always headed to VC alley to rack up findings based on a promise and a smile.

Amazon, on the other hand, was making real money and putting it back into the business. Bezos's pitch to existing and future investors was to reinvest before dividend. They all agreed. The thing about the initial angel round of investments that raised a million bucks that one needs to understand is that it was given purely on the relationship. Let's clarify that. It wasn't money given to a friend; it was money invested in a business that someone highly trusted was promoting. His parents invested a few hundred thousand dollars – the lion share – even though

Mike's first question to Bezos was, "What's the Internet?" – that question apparently was echoed by all the other friends and family that invested in Bezos. We have to be clear about it, without Bezos, that investment would not have been made. Bezos could have backed selling toilet seat covers and that first group would have still backed the endeavor. This is another reason why Amazon is Bezos.

In 1999, Bezos went to Kleiner Perkins and successfully raised $8 million in a Series A (a company's first significant round of venture capital financing). Two years later, Amazon went public at $18 per share. Two years after that, Bezos was named Time's Man of the Year. This was well deserved because Time correctly recognized Bezos's contribution to the Internet and how he had popularized the e-commerce aspect of it.

What most people do not get about the Internet is that it is a world where knowledge and commerce coexist and it's no accident that Amazon feeds off that relationship. The modern iteration of Amazon, the one that quickly ascended into being able to sell anything and everything to anyone and almost everyone, is based on the ability to get information on products and the underlying problem it solves. Bezos was directly responsible for the structure and form the Internet took when he designed Amazon and its current form.

Bezos fits both roles easily and comfortably – the role to lead and blaze trails into the unknown and to follow and learn from other leaders. That is really the mark of a true leader.

His leadership skills were not that of typical managers; it was more. There is an air of intensity in what he demands from an employee, which is by no means a one-way street. He demands the same from himself and, in fact, probably does so to a higher degree.

The brand of leadership that is ingrained in the fiber of his being is one that understands that perfection is not unattainable and that the status quo is only temporary. You can either change it to fit your vision, or someone else is going to change it to fit theirs, in which case you become the follower, and they are inaugurated as the leader.

***

Chapter 10
Philanthropy

Bezos's arc of career and accomplishment is still ascendant. Philanthropy for major achievers doesn't typically come until they start to step back from the world of accomplishment and doing, fading toward their own retirement and silver years.

There is no single standard reason for this, but it is typically because philanthropy is not just writing a check to your favorite cause and being done with it. Philanthropy is more than charity and a tax deduction. Philanthropy is really understanding what means a lot to you and understanding the cause behind the giving. This takes significant time and singularity of focus and, Bezos being Bezos, he is not the kind of person to be able to do something with less than 100% of his attention and interest.

Having said that, even though he hasn't gone full bore into it yet, he has donated to some charities over the last couple of decades. Recently, he even sent out a clue to what his eventual charitable foundation may focus on, and it looks like it is going to have to be something to do with current utility – meaning he would like his charity to have an instant impact. Maybe not all of his charity and not right away, but the first round of his ideas looks like it is going to be ideas that focus on creating assistance that could be used in an immediate situation and in an urgent fashion.

But for the immediate past, the charitable donations that have been conducted thus far have been in areas that involved immigration, education, and healthcare.

Their total donations at this point, to charity in the healthcare field, has been predominantly in the area of cancer research as well as in the area of neurology. Specifically, the area of research that they have sponsored is one that is a new field and taps into the collection of data so that future research in this field can be more meaningful. This suggests to many research and philanthropy watchers that the eventual philanthropy organized by the Bezos family, which includes the funds coming from Jeff and Mackenzie, also includes charitable donations from the stock of Amazon that had been donated to the Bezos Family Foundation by Miguel and Jacklyn Bezos.

Conclusion

The soundbite that keeps playing in my ear is when I heard him say, "It's not an experiment if you know it's going to work." In that moment, Bezos and his actions up to this point crystallized and gave me the sense of clarity and the thread to stitch the whole narrative together.

Here is a man that set out from the stable cradle of a career in New York – the exact place that thousands of eager graduating seniors from the halls of Ivy League schools and thousands more from business schools and other graduate disciplines place their allocated bids and pin their hopes of working on Wall Street. He got it. He attained the goal and he was in like Flynn. No one would have thought any less of him. In fact, the level of his achievement was still the highest of his family. I know what that feels like because I reached the highest level of education in my family too, and there were no shortages of kisses and hugs from adoring grandmothers, exuberant uncles and aunts, and gleaming parents.

But that was not enough for him, and that is not because he was greedy or didn't know how to stop reaching. It's because he was fundamentally not at peace with all of it.

His lack of peace inside was not because he wasn't happy with what he had already achieved, it was that it didn't go far enough in the direction that he wanted. When he made that decision to jump from Shaw and set out in the development of Amazon, he did indeed see the future and the result that he wanted.

Bezos does not fancy himself to be a teacher. He doesn't think that is his responsibility nor his place. But he is the quintessential philosopher. His perspective on life and how to handle its fleeting nature are things you would expect Stoic philosophers to extol, and it is possible that he reads new-age philosophers in parallel with classic philosophers. It certainly does seem consistent if that is indeed the case, because of the way he frames the grand scheme of technology and computing with the ability to apply advances that may happen tomorrow to problems that people face today.

He is the same way with his philanthropy, and he is the same way with his delivery. In fact, he is the same way with his ideas of space travel and his efforts in medical research. It feels almost like tomorrow can't come fast enough for Bezos and that he is rushing and headed somewhere in a hurry.

As we come to the end of our introduction to Bezos and the understanding and analysis of his actions and anecdotes of his life getting to where he is, we see that the arc of success doesn't necessarily start when you are an adult. All the things that you accomplish as a child and develop in your pre-teen years coming into high-school then leading up to college serve to form the foundation that predicts where you go as an adult.

Let's be clear, we all can't be the richest man on the planet – by default, there can only be one person. Even a dollar short and you fall to second place. On the other hand, if you set the bar to achieve based on what he has achieved, then you come to a path that leads toward different levels of accomplishment. You have the cerebral accomplishment of facing challenges and overcoming them; you have physical challenges that you have to muster up to; you have inspirational challenges that you hone with meditation and focus, and you find that the moment you decide you want to get somewhere and you stand resolute in your decision, only two things remain. The first is to know that your limitations are temporary, and the second is to remember that all problems have a solution and all solutions are a function of the degree of your resourcefulness.

Bezos just turned 54 this year. That's a relatively young age, and he is still at the top of his game.

When he got started, when he made that trip across the country, he was a young 30-year-old who had less than a decade's worth of real-world business experience. He certainly had no experience in merchandising or website development for that matter.

From this one point alone, as we have also talked in the book, you can be sure in your own life that you do not need to be totally caught up on what your training is and what you think you can do. The real key is whether you are a person with a Finite Game or an Infinite one. Once you can figure that out, choosing the stories that will most benefit you become so much easier. But that is also not meant to dissuade you from reading books of men and women who are not the same players as you. If you are an Infinite Player, by all means, read as many books about Infinite Players as you can get your hands on, but do not neglect the Finite Player. Doing so further removes you from a balanced equation.

In other words, read more about the type you represent and then read about the ones that you are not. Guess what that does for you. It gives you insight into how the other half makes decisions. So, the next time you meet a person who is your opposite, you know where their pressure points are.

When you realize that Bezos is the quintessential Infinite Player, you start to see the writing on the wall and the earmarks of his actions. You start to see that he is not the type to be placed in the straitjacket of routine, but he is also not one to be concerned with processes as much as he is concerned with outcomes that are superior. Although that is not to say that he is not interested in keeping the processes strict – he knows that, in a large organization, there is only so much freehand you can afford at the organizational level before things start to get out of sync. But at the higher levels and as far as delegation of responsibility goes, solving the problem takes precedence over keeping the process.

Infinite Players essentially see the larger picture. That's why they know that life is not limited to this quarter and this financial year. It's a lot larger than that and Bezos is no different. That is the anchor that allows him to stay true to a long-term goal of constant improvement. If he were to have developed Amazon as a Finite Player, then there would have been a very different outcome. An interesting comparison would be someone like Balmer at Microsoft and Tim Cook at Apple. Neither are the founders, but the culture of the company that was left to them by the key founder dictates the culture that overtakes them and creates the parameters of the game.

Jobs left behind a company that played the Infinite Game; Gates left behind a company that, for whatever reason, played the finite game. Microsoft has always, in recent history, been about the quarter, the year or the next two to three years, at the most. And what happens to that sort of a company is that it shows in the products that they come up with. Look at the Windows phone that didn't last long because they conjured the phone up as they were trying to compete in a market they did not develop and conjured a device just so they could compete in this quarter. The result was catastrophic. But if you look at Apple, on the other hand, you see the Infinite culture becoming ingrained in every single one of the hands on deck. In my upcoming book on Steve Jobs, I dive into this a lot deeper, but the reason I bring it up here is that the comparisons are significantly relevant. The Infinite Player always wins over the Finite Player. Look at the battle between Samsung Phones and the iPhone. Samsung is fast to come out of the gate with products that capture the market's attention, and their price points are enough for the mass market to adopt easily, but then Apple doesn't rush to catch up. They bake their technology and, when they are good and ready, then release the product. Now, mind you, I am certain that there will be a number of you who are not Apple fans, and believe me when I say I am not an iPhone user, but I do appreciate the way they approach the market and the way they handle design innovation, as well as the way they introduce disruptive technology every once in a while that sets the trend for others to follow – case in point – the iPad.

Back to Amazon.

Amazon is a trendsetter too. It was Amazon that AliExpress followed and it was Amazon that the likes of Lazada in Germany followed as well. Amazon is no doubt a trendsetter, and they will continue to be. When you are at this level of the game, your job is not to think about the small stuff, but to think about how to set the trends and have others follow you. If no one is copying you, then you're not doing it right.

Another of Bezos's poignant sayings that I will take with me for some time is (allow me to paraphrase) that we are all the sum of our choices. It is one of those things that pulls right at the strings that makes me remember I am human, no different than the men I write about. No different than Gates, Jobs, and Ma, and no different than Bezos in the endowments that result in this form and this function. We are all connected; we all assume the same content of our biology. Where we differ is in the choices we make, the content of our intentions, and the consequence of our actions.

Those that stand up to achieve do so with the certainty of cause and effect. They know that doing nothing, on one side of the spectrum, results in obscurity. Doing something gets you by but doing the best of your ability gets you far.

If Bezos is indeed to be believed, and he is, then we, being the sum of our choices are a work in progress. We can change the calculus of historical choices just by making new choices – if that is indeed what needs to happen. Or we can just read about these men of accomplishment while sitting by the river and watching the grand riverboats steam by. The choice is ours – there it is again: choices.

Bezos was not happy in the jobs he took on not because he didn't like working, but because he was tired of mediocre achievement. That bell rings in all of us. We just misinterpret it, or the sound of it tolling is muffled by our fears and laziness.

We are happiest not when we are rich and famous. We are happiest when we are at peace and progressing. We are happiest when we solve issues that no one else can come close to. We are happy when we build something.

Bezos is happy not because he gets to play with rockets, robots, and technology. He is happiest because he is able to keep his mind sharp doing something that no one else can and build something new every day.

Elon Musk:

Moving the World One Technology at a Time

Elon Musk:

Moving the World One Technology at a Time

Insight and Analysis into the Life and Accomplishments of a Technology Mogul

JR MacGregor

Elon Musk: Moving the World One Technology at a Time

Insight and Analysis into the Life and Accomplishments of a Technology Mogul

Published by CAC Publishing LLC.

ISBN 978-1-948489-44-7 paperback

ISBN 978-1-948489-42-3 eBook

This book is dedicated to those innovators that dream of one day changing the world for the better. To those who are always a step ahead of their time and often misunderstood for it. Keep innovating, keep thinking, and never give up until you've accomplished the task.

Chapter 1 An Overview

"When something is important enough, you do it even if the odds are not in your favor."

— Elon Musk

I am part of a generation, as is Musk, that grew up in a world where man has walked on the moon. Born shortly after the Apollo missions where all the jocks with the right stuff had launched the imagination of a planet. But that is the extent of our affinity to space travel – stories of the glory of histories past.

Therefore, there was always this thing in me that has seen our generation as lacking in the kind of tenacity that it takes to innovate big things – not just innovate social websites to share photos from the last family trip (which really, no one wants to see) and porn. These are all really wussy innovations – and by then it's been some time since we've had some really good kick-in-the-pants kind of innovation and collective reaching for the stars.

We haven't done much in a long time. Sure, we've got the Internet – but so what? Aside from shopping and posting pictures?

Then came the shuttle years when I was in high school. And since then there have been events here and there that didn't quite match up to Armstrong's first step, or Lovell's thirteen days of valor. Until this afternoon.

I hadn't planned on taking time off my already jammed schedule to watch what would be a frail attempt at a webcast of the Falcon Heavy being launched. The experience reminded me of the numerous live webcasts that were anxiety-ridden between the delayed telecasts, dropped transmissions, poor sound, grainy visuals and pressing matters that occupied the reality of my day. But against all intents to the contrary, I was late and checked my YouTube feed only to find that either I had the time wrong or the launch was delayed. Eventually, the live cast started with a couple of enthusiastic SpaceX employees and a whole bunch in the background. There was a vibe I had not recognized. It was invigorating, and I stayed.

The moments to the countdown moved at pace and as precisely as a Swiss watch – or should I say, with the precision of Musk. It was fairly flawless; the countdown started and the next thing I know spaceman was in his joyride pose in the Tesla convertible on his way to Mars. I was surprised, exhilarated, and full of appreciation for the steps that had been taken. Even if launching a car into space has got to be one of the most brilliant PR stunts ever concocted, planned, and executed, it was a testament to what we can do as individuals, as a team, and as a species.

But the thing that I thought was ironic was the fact that it was probably the world's only electric car to have used kerosene to get to its destination – and lots of it. It got me to think about the dichotomy of Musk's mind. On the one hand he is constantly talking about environmental issues and why we need to buy electric cars and use solar – all of which are spot on; but then, on the other hand, he lit a match to a kerosene rocket – the biggest one ever, and that will be the first of many. So, the dichotomy of his intentions and his mind are apparent. He swings from one state of existence into the next without effort, and you see it even in his views of AI. Or maybe it is just the way we humans advocate ideals but partake in necessities (even if the later does go against the former). Musk is no different decrying the ills of AI while using it in his products smacks of hypocrisy but, let's face it; human beings are complex. We tend to roll with the punches and we have different opinions on different things based on the circumstances that surround those events.

To the layperson who is not an adoring fan (disclosure – I am neither a fan who thinks he is the next Jobs, Edison or Tesla; nor am I totally aghast at his actions, words, and deeds) Musk comes off as a bit of a kooky character, from the way he looks to the way he speaks. I give him a pass on that, but I do want to make a lesson out of his life.

He is obviously aware that he comes off as a little crazy, and far be it for me to label him as such since I am not qualified in any way to make such proclamations – but the fact that he can ask others if they think he is crazy shows that he either believes it, someone has told him so, or he is holding on really tight. I don't begrudge him one way or the other because I strongly believe that, to change the world, you have to walk the fine line between mediocre and insane – every once in a while tipping over to the side of crazy. And that is what, with all due respect, Elon Musk is.

But I am not here to judge. We all have to balance our ideals because we live in the real world. But that just brings me back to the first point about Musk – the dichotomy of his mind. He sees things in two dimensions. And sometimes what you see in one dimension can be totally at odds with what you see in a different dimension. This is the point of departure we want to make with this book and the look that we take into the perceived motivations and life of this larger-than-life mountain mover.

I chose Elon as someone to write about because it's someone that each and every one of us can relate to and, if you decide to make it in life, no matter which corner of the world you come from – and this includes the corners of the world that go beyond just first world countries, but the ones where kids grow up surrounded by things that most of us can't even imagine. Musk grew up surrounded by Apartheid in South Africa, and that's not the most conducive places for kids – especially smart ones. It was also a place that was marinated and drenched with racism – with effects unlike what our typical views of racism look like. It was a whole different brand of racism that was mixed with ungodly and evil acts and outcomes. That sort of environment breeds contempt for all creation and creates a social environment that you can't imagine.

There are countless stories that you can easily Google about what life was like in Apartheid South Africa. Two great men – long before Musk was born – have sprung from the clutches of this past – India's Gandhi, and South Africa's Mandela. Both these men were in the midst of the atrocities and cruelties of a mindset that was based on the color of one's skin.

Let me just give you an idea of the mindset in South Africa before Musk was born and through the time he was there.

There were three classifications of race: European, Colored, and African. Whites were European (a term of social and legal privilege – not necessarily to be associated with the continent), of course, coloreds were those of mixed heritage and Africans were black. And they had tests for these classifications. These tests for race were as arbitrary as they could get. For instance, your race was determined by such things as the moons of your fingers. If they were off-white, then that meant you have Black blood and that resulted in your being either colored or out and out black. People from Chinese heritage were referred to as colored, yet those with Japanese ancestors were considered white. Go figure.

Caucasians were obviously white, and so referred to as Europeans – and if you were blonde and blue-eyed, all the better. There was another interesting, yet albeit random test, and that was the test of your hair. If they put a pencil in your hair and it rolled off then, even though you looked dark skinned, you could be considered colored – a promotion of sorts. On the other hand, if the pencils remained in your hair and didn't fall, then you have knotty nappy hair and that made you African.

By no measure, in any civilized world, can this be considered remotely amusing or innocuous. This was institutionalized and systemic racism of the vilest kind and, while this book is not about race politics in South Africa, it goes to show the mindset of people in the country that Elon Musk spent the early part of his life with.

In the cities, Africans (remember, that's the term for those with black skin) were not allowed access after dark, and there was one of two ways for them to be in the city. They needed to have permission and they needed to be placed in housing that was adjacent to the Whites that they worked for. The way it was known, if the African had permission to be in the city after dark, was that it would be stamped in their Passbook – something that all Africans (blacks), and only Africans, had to carry on their person at all times. Europeans had no such burden.

Violence against Africans was widespread. Europeans could abuse and mistreat Africans with impunity, and the bravado that was part of the collective mindset was prevalent. Long train rides were not safe – for anyone, much less road travel. These were the kinds of conditions that were daily realities for those who lived in South Africa. The narrative here and in the rest of the book really doesn't even come close to scratching the surface to the deplorable psychological stresses it places on a person, especially if that person is already empathic in nature and one who is not naturally given to illogical biases of race. Such was the basis of displeasure that Musk faced growing up.

Africans were not allowed to attend school, but coloreds were, so many people tried to change their race by doing the pencil test, and tens of thousands were successful. But the gang violence did not abate. There was an ingrained hatred of those of colored skin and there was a misunderstanding of the value of life among all. Even those who were colored or black in South Africa were convinced after some time of their place in the works. About thirty years ago, I was traveling with a teenager of colored classification. We rode to the city together from Heathrow Airport and, along the way, the city was going about its business, among which were garbage collectors putting trash bins by the side of trucks and emptying them in there. My new friend was in shock to see 'white men' do the work and he said that this can't be – it's not right. The notion in him that was ingrained so deeply was that it was unnatural for a man of white skin to do jobs of labor. It took a few years before he realized that all men were indeed created equal. But if he felt that way imagine how the white population of South Africa felt and how much of that dictated the way they behaved to the people around them. A sense of entitlement and a bullying sense of bravado. And even though Musk was neither colored nor African, he too felt the tip of the bravado's whip.

His experience during high school was more than just that of a school nerd getting trashed at the hand of the neighborhood bullies. It was a mix of personal animus they had for him and the typical bravado of a country that had trickled down to the youth of the city – and that was something that did not look at the equality between men, rather it was always White over Black, Strong over Meek, Brawn over Brains.

There was a stretch of time in high school when he was literally stuck between the devil and the deep blue sea. The only difference was that it wasn't a choice so much as a timeshare. He split his days between time at school where he attended classes, talked to friends, and either got beat up or spent the afternoon running and hiding from those who had marked him as quarry; then he packed up and went home for the second half of his day and there he would read, do his chores, read some more and deal with the difficulties of a father that was the cause of so much pain and anguish in his and his sibling's lives. More on that part of his life in the chapters to follow.

Then there is this third factor – National Service. Serving in the military during National Service is something every teenager does. A number of countries have this in place, although it is not something that we have here in the US. It's tantamount to a draft, but it is more of a compulsory perpetual thing where every person, by the time they reach a certain age, have to enlist and serve a mandatory period of time where they are trained and deployed if need be. This is supposed to serve two purposes. The first is that it is supposed to provide the country with able young men to take part in military duties, which include domestic control if need be. The second, and the reason it is so in many countries, is that it is meant to enhance the character and personalities of young men in the country. It has been proven that a two-year stint in the military increases the person's ability to succeed in the world at large and to be able to learn the necessary discipline to be part of a workforce that is effective.

This thing about having to join the military was not something that Musk was too keen on. In fact, he hated the idea of having to get into an isolated environment where he would be exposed to more bravado and the possibility of more ragging and bullying – probably something that would be worse than what he had faced in school. The second thing about joining the military, even if it was just for National Service, was that there was a lot of brainwashing going on in what they needed to do and the politics of Apartheid had a lot to do with that. He would have to be forced to listen to that propaganda – and what's worse, he would probably have to enforce it when deployed. The beating of blacks and the unnecessary abuse inflicted on them by the military was not a secret. If creating a life and advancing his interest in electronics and software were the 'pull' he felt in going to America, then the fear of joining the military was the 'push' to get out of Apartheid South Africa.

There are stories abound all across the internet – so many in fact that I was initially not planning to include it in this book. But no matter how much I tried to put it away, it is not entirely possible to give you an accurate picture of the man or the forces that shape a man – and in this case the forces that shaped Musk – without going into the brutal beating he took as a kid and the one that brought him within inches of his life.

The forces that existed around him as a child, from the break-up of a happy home to the violence he was treated with in the schoolyard on a daily basis, and the harsh environment of the paternal home after his parents' divorce would have been daunting for any other kid. Even if I had to go through that, I think that I would have found myself going crazy and, I suspect, Musk is also very cognizant about how he acts so that he does not come off as being crazy.

But when you add these events to the fact that he was subjected to some of the harshest conditions one could imagine, but yet he kept his intellectual ability intact, it shows the resilience of the human spirit. I define the ability that all of us possess, to varying degrees. It defines the cache of strength and mental ability that we can turn to when things get tough and when hope is hard to distinguish from pipe dreams.

It has always been my understanding, and all my books on famous figures in history and commerce reflect this, that biographies are not just about names, dates, places, and salacious fragments of information. Biographies are about how successful individuals made it great and made it beyond what we sometimes admire – and, let's be honest, sometimes loathe.

For biographies to make sense, we need to see them in context and we need to look at the content with understanding instead of judgment. When you judge a person, the lessons they have to offer are wasted. Everyone has lessons to teach us. Churchill or Hitler, Gandhi or Lenin, the lessons in life and the path to our personal growth are there if we just look without judgment and malice. The same goes for the likes of Gates, Jobs, and Branson – all of whom I've written about, and it certainly goes with Musk.

The reason I decided to write about Musk is not because of the wealth he has managed to amass – I certainly don't see his wealth as something that is that amazing. There are richer people than him after all. But what I do really appreciate is his ability to apply focus and attention to the things that his mind conjures and then he is able to make it happen.

There is a known cycle that happens within each of us and that cycle is either a death spiral or a leap to the top. That cycle is about the ability to have potential but lacking the belief that you can make something happen without losing too much.

Many people tend to have ideas but never actually make it because they think, "What's the use? It probably won't work." Or "What's the use? Someone else would have already thought of that." Or worse "What's the use? It's not going to be worth very much." And these kinds of thoughts feed into our psyche and we end up either not doing that which would put us on the path to greatness or it would put us on the path to saying, "See, I told you so" when it won't come to fruition. Normally, when you do not go all out, that's exactly what happens. You end up proving your doubts right. I see Musk as someone who never, even for a moment, thought that it was not possible. But what's more important – he never worried about the payoff. Once you take the payoff out of the equation – you have nothing to fear because there is no downside.

All too often, we read material that disguises itself as motivational rhetoric and feeds us with notions claiming that focusing on the reward is all the energy you need. There have been some who have evidence to point to, but I assure you that any evidence that suggests reward as the primary motivation is evidence that is ill-contrived. In Musk's case, he was hungry for contribution and achievement.

Chapter 2 Maternal History

"I'm not trying to be anyone's savior. I'm just trying to think about the future and not be sad."

— Elon Musk

Maye Haldeman, Musk's mother, was born in Regina – the capital of Saskatchewan, Canada. Even from a young age, Maye was extremely attractive in appearance and vivacious in personality. Her energy was undoubtedly compounded by a family who didn't know the meaning of kicking it back or taking it easy. They couldn't necessarily be labeled as overachievers – a suspiciously pejorative term, but they were a high-impact and high-energy lot. They were always on the move and always doing things that were not typical of the average Canadian family.

Maye's parents, Winnifred and Joshua, were trailblazers even if it was just the start of the fifties in North America. History looks at the fifties in southern Canada with the same lens it looked at James Dean's America – wild, successful, and rebellious. That typically characterized the Haldeman family. They were financially well-positioned – enough to pack up and move their entire family across the world to almost wherever they wished. And, because the Haldemans were pretty adventurous and they could afford to buy their own aircraft, they packed up the family, loaded them up into that plane and flew halfway around the world to South Africa.

As the bird flies, in a straight line, that is about 8,000 miles. But if you think about it, that aircraft would not have been able to fly straight across; it needed to puddle jump and head east before coming up on Europe then flying south toward Pretoria, and that made it more like 10,000 miles. So think about that for a minute. It's not like getting on I40 and driving for three days from Nashville to Flagstaff. If you think of driving from Tennessee to the Grand Canyon in the summer, it is a brilliant experience with the kids. Try making this flight with four kids, two of whom were just two years old (Maye and her twin sister were two years old when the family made this journey.)

Maye's twin sister is someone you would have probably heard off: Kaye Rive. Yes, that's her married name. Before that, she was Kaye Haldeman. (Interesting set of names for the twins – Maye and Kaye.) Maye went on to marry Errol Musk and became Maye Musk while Kaye became Kaye Rive, mother of Peter and Lyndon Rive of Solar City. Yes, Peter and Lyndon are Elon's cousins. Small world, ain't it?

Well, back to the cross-continent excursion that the Haldeman's took when Maye and Kaye were just two years old. It must have been one interesting flight to cross the Atlantic and the only way that a single-engine plane could do it without running out of fuel over the Atlantic would have been to hug the New England coast up the Nova Scotia then cross over to Iceland before heading over to Norway and down through mainland Europe, and from that point on it would be all overland flying except for the crossing of the Mediterranean, unless they crossed it near the Nile in Egypt and continued down all the way across the African continent until they got to South Africa. This route is good for two reasons. First of all, it is the best route to take when crossing the Atlantic in a single-engine aircraft.

You can't just plug the lats and longs into the GPS and make a straight line from Regina, Canada to Pretoria, South Africa. Well, first of all, there were no GPS satellites to transmit data, no GPS receivers to receive the sat data, and no database of maps to make sense of it all. It was, after all, the fifties. But even if you put all that aside, remember they were flying a single-engine (piston engine, nonetheless) and in the event of engine failure you need to be able to glide forward or backward, or left or right, toward land for a safe emergency landing. So, for this to happen, you always have to have land within a glide path based on your altitude. The only way to do that would be to fly at a certain altitude and hug the coast in a way that, in the event of a problem, you'd just have to glide to the coast. As safe as that is, it makes for a very long trip because you need to stop every three to four hours and fill up on Avgas. What made the trip even more interesting was that it was done by dead reckoning all the way. That means no electronic or radio navigation equipment, just good old maps, rulers, compasses, and protractors.

Grandpa Haldeman bought his aircraft and obtained his Private Pilot's license while working as a licensed chiropractor in Canada. By the way, Musk is a Private Pilot as well. Just after the sale of Zip2, around the time he bought the McLaren, he also bought a single-engine aircraft.

Back to the Haldemans.

Dr. Haldeman was a popular and well-respected member of society and had a thriving practice when he decided that Canada was not politically in lockstep with his ideals. So, he packed-up, picked-up and moved to Pretoria. Curious choice of cities but the Haldemans were looking for answers to life and nature. They were also looking for a break from the monotony of the West and the romance of the African bush. The Haldemans were of Canadian citizenry even though Joshua was from Minnesota. Maye and the other Haldeman children were born in Canada. You will see later that Elon Musk found his way to North America forty years later thanks to this fact.

Once the Haldemans got to Pretoria and got situated, it didn't stop there for the flying Haldemans. You see, Grandpa and Grandma Haldeman were looking for the lost city in the desert and they made a dozen flights crisscrossing the continent of Africa with that objective in their small single-engine plane.

But that wasn't the extent or limit of their flying. The Haldemans also flew longer journeys and navigated their way – family and all – across the globe and down toward Australia. That was approximately a 14,000-mile trip to basically travel back up to North Africa, then across Asia Minor, over India, and then down through South East Asia, down the Malay Peninsula across to Indonesia, and along the islands of New Guinea and down to Australia – all this with kids in the backseat. "Are we there yet?" takes on a whole different flavor under those circumstances.

The Haldemans were a tremendous influence on the Rive and Musk kids as they grew up close to each other and heard stories of their grandparents who took South Africa by storm. They were brave souls that were up for a good challenge.

Maye and Kaye raised their children close to each other and with a good relationship between the cousins who, as you can tell by this point, are all strong entrepreneurs in their own right. Between Elon's tech endeavors, Kimball's green adventures, and the Rive brothers' energy and so on, what you have is a family that has taken this world by storm. That is one launchpad that you should keep at the back of your mind as you size up Musk and, more importantly, try to understand him so that you can find the light in your life and make a difference, finding your unique way just as he and his siblings and cousins are doing.

Vanity Fair calls them the 'First Family of Tech.' I have to agree.

There was a lot of intellectual wattage in the Haldeman strain. Both Maye's and Kaye's kids – the Rives and the Musks – were an amazing bunch of kids who were close-knit beyond just the binds that tied them from their mothers. They had another similarity going for them beyond genetics, which was the fervor of intellectualism. Imagine having discussions with your siblings and cousins about the efficacy of banking at the age of twelve? Not exactly what I was talking about at that age. How 'bout you?

But that just goes to show the caliber of their grain. In another famous story of his youth, the cousins got together when Musk was still a teenager and they decided that they wanted to get a business up and running.

Musk was an advanced coder by the time he was twelve years old and was able to code a game that found enough interest that it was published, *and* he was paid for it. There is no doubt that he is industrious and he wants to earn a buck. But earning a quick buck is not all that interests him.

He and his bunch of siblings and cousins got together and decided they wanted to open an arcade near a school. He understood marketing very well and he understood it from a functional perspective rather than an academic one. This group of industrious kids did everything that they needed to do. They got the documents and got the lease, then put in for licensing and did everything that went along with that. A significant amount of thought and work went into it and they were on the home stretch when they came upon municipal documentation, which needed an adult over 18 to sign it. None of them had seen this coming and were totally taken aback. They didn't know where to turn to. They tried Maye, but Maye was too busy working two jobs to be able to take the time to come downtown to sign the documents. They tried Dr. Rive, but he was not only not willing, he was absolutely upset that all this had gone on without a shred of permission from any of the parents. In the end, it couldn't get off the ground because there was no adult to sign-off.

This says a lot about this group of kids. There is a lot of energy and imagination. They didn't just start down this enterprising path when they were teenagers either. This goes pretty far back to even before they were having conversations of banking and commerce amongst themselves. They put rubber to the pavement when they realized that there were so many opportunities in different layers across different dimensions – and that is how they saw it.

In one incident, they realized that chocolate was a cheap commodity in comparison to most of the other candy. It was easily affordable and this was the good chocolate, not the candy that is made to look like chocolate that you see on shelves now. The chocolate that they could get was fairly easy to find but fairly good quality. They also realized that there was a huge disparity between the cost of input – the chocolate – and the price people were willing to pay if it was in a different form. That was the first dimension.

They decided to change the form of the easily available chocolate and make it into Easter eggs and, that way, what was once just pennies could now be sold for much more. But they didn't stop there. By the time they were done, what could have sold as Easter eggs for a Rand (the unit of South African currency) they sold for ten Rand. Remember, the chocolate was just a tiny cost, melting it and shaping them into eggs demanded skill, but they could now turn around and sell it for 1 Rand – a huge profit. But they didn't just do that. Instead, it was Elon who decided to sell it for 10 Rand and, instead of just going anywhere and selling it, they went to the poshest neighborhood in Pretoria and knocked on doors, sporting their cutest smiles and smartest outfits and demanding 10 Rand for something that you could get at the store for 1 Rand. Most of the times, the differentiated clientele paid the asking price, but if in the rare event, they were asked why it was so expensive, the kids returned with a well-rehearsed line that they were enterprising and that they should be rewarded for such. They made a killing from that endeavor.

Does that sound at all familiar to you?

It should, as it's exactly what Elon did when he started selling Teslas. He peeled back the layers of commerce and understood that the wealthy will always be willing to pay more in appreciation for some things. You could then take that increased margin and reinvest it into other cars. And that's how he positioned the Tesla brand, and that's how he financed the development of production runs – by going to the rich consumer first. I have no doubt he will do that with SpaceX and their first shots to space. More on that later in the book.

The significant intellectual ability among the kids was in no small measure due to the way the Haldeman twins raised them. Both sisters have three kids. The Musks included Tosca, Kimball, and Elon, and the Rives included Lyndon, Peter, and Russel.

The one way to describe the kids was the same way you would describe their mothers and the same way you would describe the Haldemans – energy. They had pure energy coursing their veins in such abundance that they could take on almost any project and then make it happen.

I remember during the Presidential debates in 2016 – don't worry I am not going to talk politics here – Candidate Trump talked about low energy candidates, and he was right. Low energy people move slower than sloths. But the Musk and Rive family were all highly energized and, thus, had all the motivation in the world and the energy to make something happen.

There is a genetic aspect to this because, if you look at all the boys in those two families, you see the same energy that Grandpa Haldeman had in the way he made his practice a success and the way he was a popular figure in politics in his neck of the woods. You can also see that he was gung-ho in finding the lost city of the Kalahari Desert. Grandpa Haldeman passed in 1975 in an air crash chasing after the elusive lost city – Elon was still a toddler when it happened, but that same exploration-adventure gene Joshua Haldeman had was certainly passed down to his grandkids.

Maye Haldeman was an attractive young woman, just as Kaye was. She started modeling early in her career but she wasn't just one who stepped toward a life of glamor as a model like many do, as she also had a good head on her shoulders. She was as sharp intellectually as she was charming personally and Errol Musk couldn't take his eyes off her from the first time they met. She said no many times and obviously, as history tells us, his tenacity won the day. Errol was a handsome young man at the time as well and, what's more, he was equally as smart as the stunning Maye. Errol went on to become an engineer and Maye completed two Master's degrees.

Once they were married and the kids were born, Errol's business was doing well and they lived in one of Pretoria's finest neighborhoods. Errol was a civil engineer who specialized in building homes and was a strict father. If you gazed at him and just blurred your focus a little, you would look in Errol's direction and think you were looking at Elon. Elon and Errol look more like each other than Kimball and Elon do or even Kimbal and Errol.

But the similarities in looks and the ability to turn on the focus of their minds is where the similarities between the older and the younger Musk start and end. Everything else is night and day.

There is a big family secret about the way that Errol treated the kids and no one really wants to talk about it. They keep a really tight lip and that alone speaks volumes, I feel. I will get to that a little later. But, for now, what you should place at the back of your mind is that Errol, for all the stories that you may have heard, is not a bad person or a bad father. He was not even a bad husband.

If you want to take this a step further, just think about it in these terms.

Once they moved to the larger house in Pretoria and when things were going really well for the Musk family, the cracks between husband and wife started to show. The couple who were very much in love with each other, and electrically attracted to each other, had hit a few bumps and grown apart. Nine years into the marriage, the Musks separated and the children followed Maye.

But that didn't last for long because, about a year or two later, Elon asked to go live with Errol. When Maye enquired as to the reason, Elon's only reason was that a boy's place was next to his father. Soon after that, Kimball followed and, soon after that,

Tosca did as well. All three kids went back to their father and stayed there for some time.

Money was not a problem in the Musk home, and the fact that they were European in an Apartheid rule meant that they had a fairly good life. Errol took the kids on long journeys within South Africa and even abroad. They flew to countries that showed Elon and his siblings that a world outside South Africa existed and that it was abundant and amazing. One of the motivations that Errol had for doing this was the conversation Errol had with a three-year-old Elon years earlier where Elon asked his dad "Where is the whole world?" For some reason, that question and the tenacity in which Elon undertook all things made Errol want to show his son more of the world than what one could see around Pretoria.

The fact that the kids went back to their father says a lot about the dynamic that existed between them and this has been misunderstood. There is a lot of online stuff that places Errol in a bad light and that is not entirely true. How bad could he have been if the kids chose to stay with him? Think about that for a minute and you will realize that the reasons that they wanted to stay with him and the difficulties they had growing up are not even close to what is said on the internet and what is insinuated. Errol himself is a charming man with a deep intellect and an interesting sense of humor. He is full of energy and he obviously needed it because, without that, he would not have been able to keep up with Maye, who was energetic, as mentioned earlier.

Chapter 3 Paternal History

"The idea of lying on a beach as my main thing just sounds like the worst. It sounds horrible to me. I would go bonkers. I would have to be on serious drugs. I'd be super-duper bored. I like high intensity."

— Elon Musk

Errol Musk and May Haldeman divorced when Elon was nine years old. As young as he was, he was fully aware of the event, although he may not have been fully aware of the conditions precedent or the full consequences of it. From his perspective, the happy family that he saw with his pre-pubescent eyes had come to an end and he was now leaving the home he was familiar with and moving away with his mom and siblings. He still stayed in contact with his cousins and, of course, Kimball was next to him even if Maye wasn't. She was busy enough – handling two jobs to raise three children.

This part of his life had an impact as days rolled into weeks and weeks became months. As much as he loved his mother and his brother and sister, he had this deep longing in him for his father. It was unbearable and the tears that he had at that time, even though mostly in private, were tears that even he didn't fully understand.

There are two areas to note when it comes to Musk's sudden separation from his father. Although they were not that far away from each other, the fact that his presence was not under the same roof made a huge difference to a young boy who had it hard in the outside world and relied a lot on family. The second area to note was that boys – all boys – have much to learn from their fathers. It is a genetic fact, and the ones that usually feel that are the ones who are immensely in touch with their feelings or those who have hypersensitive personalities.

Elon Musk certainly lives up to his reputation of being hypersensitive. That hypersensitivity was the core reason that he retreated from social engagements and it is the same reason he was able to attach himself to the pursuit of knowledge that was presented to him. When you are hypersensitive and empathic, your only source of solace comes from the source of enjoyment that is predictable – in Musk's case, that was reading. Reading gave him a sense of certainty of calm. What he read could not hurt him or harm him but, most importantly, what he read would not overwhelm him in the same way people and events around him could.

Indeed, the world around him did overwhelm him constantly and deeply. When you have a hypersensitive personality, you tend to take in more than others do. Think about it this way; imagine your mind and senses as a water tank. And this water tank is connected to a larger water tank that contains the water. For now, just assume the smaller tank is the psyche of a person and the larger tank with the water is the world around this person.

Now, the way the two tanks are connected is via a conduit. A normal tank will have a conduit that is maybe an inch in diameter and, with this one-inch conduit, the water from the outer tank flows at a moderate pace to fill up the inner tank. So, you get that analogy, right? The stimuli from the outside world enter your psyche at a moderate pace – sight, sound, smell, and all the events that are going on around you. At this moderate pace, you can manage the incoming information stream.

For a hypersensitive or empathic person, it is like taking that same water tank set up and, instead of having one external tank draining to the internal tank via a one-inch conduit, it's like placing a dozen larger tanks and attaching it to the inner tank and connecting each of them with a conduit fifty inches in diameter.

When placed in identical surroundings, the average person and the empathic person experience very different events. The empathic person absorbs more of the surroundings while the average person doesn't. So, the average person is able to process what he perceives in a way that is manageable while the empathic person (who is not used to his power) gets overwhelmed. Empathic people who are not used to this usually retreat into themselves or do something that cuts out the rest of the streams of information. They learn to focus just so that they don't get overwhelmed. Musk was this kind of kid.

Chapter 4 The Early Years

"I came to the conclusion that we should aspire to increase the scope and scale of human consciousness in order to better understand what questions to ask. Really, the only thing that makes sense is to strive for greater collective enlightenment."

– Elon Musk

By the time he was three, Musk's parents started to notice consistently and frequently that he would withdraw into himself. They were quite concerned. Being a kid from that same generation, I can tell you that psychiatry was not what it is today. We didn't think we know what it was and so he was not diagnosed with ominous sounding ailments. They just let him be.

It turns out that Musk was empathic and he would not withdraw. Instead, he would counter the stream of input by focusing his energy on one thought or one event and he would give it his entire effort in contemplating or understanding.

The human mind is an interesting piece of work – for some of us more than others. Musk's mind is one of few living specimens that reaches a level of ability that is fairly rare and surrounded by unique circumstances. Einstein's genius came from his ability to imagine; Newton's genius came from his ability to observe things and finding ways to explain them; Edison's genius came from meticulous tracking of errors and hypothesis – a sort of meticulous process of elimination. Jobs' genius came from recognizing order and aesthetics. All the great men and women of the world have a specific brand of genius that they capitalize on. In Musk's case, his genius was rooted in his ability to direct his attention, aim his focus, and not come out of it until he gets to the point where he has fully assimilated the knowledge that he was focused on, or finds the solution he is in search of.

If you have read anything about Musk online, you will probably be in possession of the same impression that he is a genius with a photographic memory. That's true. If you know that, then you would also know that he is an avid reader. Well, calling him an avid reader would be like calling the Pope holy. His reading has been the hallmark of all that it means to be Musk. But we need to look at that ability at a microscopic level to understand these powers of reading, memory, and assimilating data to make sense of it.

When he was a kid, his father used to notice that, more often than not, Musk would stare off into space. But the thing to note was that his eyes weren't vacant and glazed over, they were intense and alive. Nevertheless, he would have no connection to the rest of the world when he was in the midst of one of these episodes. And this happened pretty often. This was before the time he could read and it was not clearly understood why, but it was taken to be a related phenomenon that was unique to just Elon among his siblings.

There are three areas that you should understand about Musk. The first is his ability to apply intense focus on whatever he was paying attention to. The second is his ability to not get distracted from that event, Finally, his ability to memorize every aspect of the event. This was certainly applicable to reading and diagrams, but not limited to them. It applied to everything his senses witnessed as long as he was paying attention.

A person's memory is fairly intuitive to understand if you pull on the right strings. In the case of memory, it's all about making neurons in the brain and then associating those neurons with other existing neurons to form associative memories and then building on top of that. We won't go into the details of memory creation or memory recollection, but a brief visit to the way Musk processes his is in order.

When you see something in passing, your mind records it. In fact, recording the memory is not always the problem. If you were exposed to a sequence of flashcards, it all gets recorded in your brain, and there are three things that happen in particular. The first is a chemical reaction that stores short-term memory in chemical format. You can think of this as the staging area. Once this is done in the hippocampus, the part of the brain that stitches events in your mind and directs the recording of the memory has to decide whether or not this memory is something that you will recollect frequently or otherwise. If it determines that you need to access this memory frequently, it will store the memory in a way that is easily accessible – in your conscious memory. If it determines that you do not need to access it often, it gets stored in a sort of subconscious memory. I say 'sort of' because the kind of memory we are talking about here feels like it is subconscious because it is not consciously accessible and you need to go to great lengths to retrieve it. There are at least two ways to determine if your brain stores it in conscious memory or in subconscious memory. The first is the manner in which it was recorded. If a lot of attention or sensitivity was applied to it, then that memory is what we say "makes an impression" and it is stored in conscious memory. If it is just absorbed in passing, then there is no intensity to it, and it then gets stored in subconscious memory and, when you need to access it, you need to get someone to hypnotize you to access that memory or you need to put a lot of effort into it. When most people find that an event is not readily accessible or still unavailable to them after a little effort, they typically give up and say they have forgotten the event. But, actually, it is still there and just takes longer and more effort to access.

In Musk's case, he remembers everything because he is super-present wherever he is and whatever he does. His intensity is unparalleled so his mind records everything and records it in the conscious memory. So much so that he seems to have a photographic memory.

Out of the three things that categorize his cerebral abilities, the part that is most important is indistinguishable from the part that we would normally categorize as less relevant. You see, all three parts of him, the undeviating attention and the intense focus, coupled with the third ability to not be distracted – meaning it's almost like you can't wake him up from a dream because none of his other sensors are connected.

Think of it this way; if I were asleep and you tried to wake me up by calling my name, when I respond to that call and wake up to fully awakened consciousness, it's only because there was a part of me that was listening to the outside world while I slept. If there was no listening going on then, no matter how loud the alert, it will not reach my mind and that will mean I can't respond and, thus, I can't wake up until something internally releases me from that slumber and I wake up on my own.

In the same way, a typical person's ability to lose themselves in a focused effort on a task is usually about 4–6 minutes and then they are internally shaken out of their state so that they can view the world around them. This was the way we evolved so that we are constantly alert about our surroundings. It is a feature that keeps us safe. We are designed to jump to alert in the event that a new stream of data comes along. But in today's world that new stream of data that takes us away from whatever we are doing is called a distraction. And the best way to focus is not to apply more energy to it, but to rather just disregard distractions. Some of us have the ability to inherently not regard distractions and others have to build it by force and discipline. In Musk's case, it came naturally.

As he started focusing on the things around him, distractions never phased him because he could not really perceive them, so he would stare and focus on something till it was done. It was the same when he saw something new, or it was the same when he was reading a book – fiction or non-fiction.

When he read fiction, as he would so often do, he could not put the book down like how the average person reads. He needed to get to the end of the story and, between his curiosity and his ability to not be distracted, there was just no way of pulling him off a book until the intervening event was so great or he finished the task. And, because his focus was absolute, he stored everything he consumed in conscious memory, and that gives him the ability to recall all that he has laid eyes on. That is really the secret to his genius. The secret to his success, however, is another matter.

It doesn't end there.

Elon Musk has superior powers of analysis and understanding the subject matter for what it is. When he was in Queen's College, as well as the times when he was at Penn's Wharton School, his ability to just memorize the facts were not in doubt, but his ability to understand the fundamental nature of the knowledge that was being focused on was never really understood by his peers or teachers until they started to see his creativity and understanding come into focus.

When you have the ability to memorize, what does that get you? Well, nothing much really. You just mimic others' conclusions and you parrot others' words. But when you take superior memory and add it to the ability to understand and contextualize, then what you get is a step in the direction of genius. When you then take that and add it to the ability to imagine – which can, of course, be related back to memory, then what you have is the makings of a genius that is unlike any of the other towering successes that we have come to know. Musk is such a person. He has powerful memory, recall, understanding, and imagination.

During his college days, whether it was physics or economics, the intellect that his classmates say he exhibited was not one of just memorized and regurgitated facts and data – anyone could do that. His intelligence came in at two levels. The first level was his ability to understand the concepts he was focusing on in human terms. That means, if we look at a simple economic study of supply and demand, for example, he understood that concept beyond just the charts of sloping supply and intersecting demand curves. He instinctually absorbed the information enough to understand what it meant in practicable, actionable, and accurate human terms. The knowledge was real to him and, because of that, he was able to apply what he learned to what was already percolating in his head.

When he was at Penn, he was enrolled in two separate programs. On the one hand, he was doing physics in the School of Arts and Sciences and, on the other hand, he was doing business at the Wharton School of Business – both faculties of the University of Pennsylvania. By the way, these are both tough programs to get into, being as Penn is an Ivy League university and Wharton is the top undergraduate business program in the country.

So, he was sharpening his skills on both sides of the equation. On the one side he was looking at technology and on the other side he was looking at commercializing that technology. One of the papers he wrote for one of his classes was actually a Business Plan that talked about creating a business that would harvest solar energy from the sun. I know everyone has grand illusions of the idea but here is where Musk distinguishes himself from everyone else.

On the one hand, he was looking at it from the Utopian physics side, where there is a cleaner and more efficient world based on clean energy. That's great, most people dream of that but, in Musk's case, the physics behind his plan was spot on.

Then, on the other side of it, was the business plan that talked about the way to make it commercially viable. And that too was spot on, according to the professors that graded his paper. They looked at it and asked him to defend the science, which he did, and they looked at the business principles which were all sound. He obviously got an A for the paper, but the thing to note is that it wasn't a pie-in-the-sky kind of endeavor. It showed a depth of thought and he knew one thing for certain – he knew that to make it work, no matter how much it benefited society, the practical matter of the whole thing was that it had to make money. And it did. That's how he is with all his businesses. Look at Tesla and look at PayPal. All the businesses that he started, no matter how complex, were technically sound and financially viable. That was his winning stroke and it remains so today.

Musk's early years were not defined by the events of his childhood as much as they were corralled by the intense dataset and understanding that he had accumulated in his head. His intellect gave him the cloak he needed to shield himself from the bullying in school and the imagination gave him the wand to wish away his troubles at home. It was the perfect storm of greatness, but I am sure that, during the time he was enduring it, it seemed excruciating rather than uplifting.

His life was not a bed of roses, as you have seen to this point. From the split of the family home to the treatment he received in school from the bullies to his inability to understand the social environment around him, he could not get a grip on the only reality he knew. The beating he received in school that put him in the hospital for two weeks and made his face unrecognizable to his father was the result of the incessant bullying that he stood up to – or ran away from – depending on the odds and the situation surrounding the encounter. It got so bad that the bullies got together and gave him a good thrashing, kicking him down the stairs. This bullying thing was a systemic problem in South

Africa, and his father's report to the police didn't result in much except the police saying basically, that 'boys will be boys.' No action was taken and no charges were filed, even though his father repeatedly pushed the cops to do something about it. Even the school, Bryanston High School in Pretoria, looked the other way. Years later, under the current Principle, however, they were sorry to hear how much misery their indifference had been the cause of.

That episode of the beating has been told and retold countless times across the web. The narrative of the event has taken on various shades of intensity and almost diluted its real effect and influence on Musk's life. But it was not the only event and it was not the last one. He recently revealed that he had to have surgery to correct a nasal anomaly that resulted from that particular episode. He had, until the surgery, trouble breathing because of the hindrance the injury had caused all this time later.

That single event, while having an effect on his youth, was not the driving force of his decisions, but it was the visual representation of the taunts and conditions he felt all through his school years – and that was indeed the fuel that drove him to better develop the strengths that were inherently within him. You see, bullying has a specific psychological effect on the victim. It creates a simultaneous feeling of incapability and fear. In

Musk's case, it caused him to worry about his safety on a daily basis, and it told him that he was powerless. Two very negative aspects of life to have baked into a boy while he is growing up.

The national culture in South Africa is very different from the culture of the West – Canada and the United States, or pretty much the whole of Europe. What the Apartheid nationalists call European is in physical appearance only - skin color, hair, and eye features. But it has nothing to do with European values or cultures. The Apartheid South Africa that existed back in the day viewed success very differently from the way the rest of the world viewed success, and Musk instinctively understood that from a very early age. How he picked this up is not clear, but it must have been from an amalgamation of his reading and his travels, and in no small part due to his instincts telling him that there had to be a better way.

I make it a point to distinguish Apartheid South Africa from today's South Africa because the culture has completely evolved. The Apartheid South African culture that prevailed during Musk's childhood and early teenage years was a foreboding force in the lives of all that country's people and the negative effects were undiscriminating, even though government policy was.

One of these side effects was the way that success was viewed. We take it for granted that success in the United States and much of the Western world is seen as a uniform benchmark. But success is pretty much an individual's definition even if it does have national influences and cultural bias based on social norms and national conversations. Success in the United States means a lot of different things and it is very different from what it means in Tibet. For instance, success in Indonesia means something totally different than it does in Australia. Although Hollywood's pervasive influence has all but leveled the playing field today, thirty years ago definitions and corresponding actions differed.

In South Africa, entrepreneurial success was not revered; it was questioned. When someone in South Africa makes it big and makes lots of money, back then they would ask "Why do you have so much money?" In the US, the question is 'How did you do it?"

It may not seem like much, but it was part of the culture that did not appreciate or promote entrepreneurial endeavors. If the country does not promote entrepreneurship, then it is not going to be geared to providing the psychological infrastructure needed to develop and motivate budding entrepreneurs. When that is missing, those who have entrepreneurism in their blood instinctively look elsewhere for this element. That was in part what drove Musk out of Africa, as much as all the other stuff that was happening in his life.

Moving to America is not something that you should take lightly because not everyone agrees with its politics or cultural values. Errol Musk certainly didn't. When the time came for Elon to spread his wings, his father was not interested in spreading them to America. In fact, Errol reneged on a deal he made with his son to accompany him to America. It even got to the point that Errol threatened him by cutting off his funds if he were to choose to go to America. Instead, he was told that all of his educational needs and expenses would be met if he attended a local university in South Africa.

Most people that age have one of two things going for them. They either have their parents pay for college or they live in a country where financial aid for college is easily obtained. But for someone like Musk, none of that was available to him. Whatever he set out to do, he needed to do it on his own and without any aid from friends or family. Well, friends were almost non-existent and, as for family, the only one in his family that could afford to help him didn't want him going to America and so withheld the funds; and those who wanted to help him, like his mother and siblings, didn't have the funds to do so. So, he ended up relying on himself.

He could have given up and taken the easy road, but he didn't. And so, by making that choice to face the world alone at that young an age, the positive lessons of hard-knocks were backed into the fiber of his being. He matured with the skillset of someone who had adapted to fend for himself and that strengthened him, emboldening his attitude, and giving him his cloak of invincibility.

Chapter 5 Coming to North America

"I think it's important to reason from first principles rather than by analogy. The normal way we conduct our lives is we reason by analogy. [With analogy] we are doing this because it's like something else that was done, or it is like what other people are doing. [With first principles] you boil things down to the most fundamental truths... and then reason up from there."

– Elon Musk

I wish I could tell you that Musk's decision to come to America and the subsequent events were easy and that he traveled a path that was comfortable, but I can't. What Musk went through in the years following his decision and ability to get out of South Africa were some of the more difficult events I have heard of. It almost reminds me of the 1992 Cruise/Kidman movie, *Far and Away*, about a couple from Ireland who come to America during the time of the Oklahoma land rush. As hard as they had it, when you look at Musk's journey to the US by way of Canada, it almost feels harder and, if you want to appreciate what it takes to make big dreams come together, then this is something that you have to look at more than just the events and the anecdotes that you read online or in books. I mention the movie because, in Musk's case, reality was harder than fiction.

As difficult as his relationship with his father was, Musk always loved him, looked up to him and, most of all, respected him. The South African culture of bravado and macho behavior is not something that is academic, but something that is real in daily life – between friends, between family, and certainly between father and son. It was obviously worse among rivals – which is one of the reasons he was taunted and bullied. But as for the father-son relationship, it was a national bedrock principle that to teach macho, you have to be macho. And so that defined many filial relationships. That is the redeeming feature of the whole story.

There was a filial obligation that Musk was not willing to abdicate, and that was obvious throughout his time in the paternal household. But to be clear, and this has everything to do with his jump to North America, there were four distinct stages of his relationship with his father.

The first stage was the time when he was still a pre-adolescent, and this covered the period before his mother left. The second was the time when he moved out of his father's house when his parents were divorced. The third is the time that passed when he had returned to his father's house. And the last was when he left South Africa and his father behind and headed for his new life – this last part being when he saw the final fraying of their relationship. He is at a point now in his life where he has no intention of introducing his children to his father.

That decision will undoubtedly change as he matures to a point that he understands the actions his father took and, if he is able to step away from the pain, then the natural state of his being would choose to reconcile and bury the hatchet.

You already know that there were no less than three reasons that he wanted to come to the United States. On the one hand, there was the South African military conscription that he really wished to avoid. The second was that he needed to extricate himself from a life that had been horrible to him and, with such levels of psychological and physical abuse, he associated all of Pretoria, and by extension, all of South Africa as one long bad nightmare and wanted to change the view. Finally, and this was the pull when compared to the first two pushes, was that he wanted to develop his software and technical IT ability. For the man that the world now calls the next Thomas Edison, South Africa was not cutting it.

After Waterkloof House Preparatory School, followed by Bryanston High School and then an eight-month stint at the University of Pretoria in 1988, he boarded a plane, against his father's most strenuous objections, and landed in Canada. If you think his life in South Africa was tough based on what you've read thus far about Musk, then you've just scraped the surface.

What I ask you to consider is that Musk is empathic, as mentioned earlier and, if you consider the course of his life in South Africa to be painful, think about how he must have felt facing it first hand, and being an empathic who magnifies his surroundings and the events around him by a significant factor. To say that he was leaving emotional baggage behind would be an understatement. But whatever pain he felt at the time was not something that he allowed to distract him, nor did he ever feel sorry for himself.

One of the things about Musk that jumps out at a number of people who study him, his words, and his actions, is that he is, above all, one of the most resilient people you will come across. There is an old saying that comes to mind when I see him and that is 'strong trees are the result of strong winds.' Which is to say that much of what he endured as a kid was responsible for making him resilient and it also created a path for him to escape into his own mind.

The one thing that was, without a doubt, his father's contribution to his whole equation, aside from the obvious parenting, was that he took the kids with him on travels in and out of Africa. This gave Musk the idea that things were different outside his homeland and that gave him the hope he needed. He sought his father's approval and got it when he asked if his father would take him to America and make the move so that they could emigrate from South Africa. His father had the financial ability and the knowledge to pull it off, but he changed his mind at the 11th hour.

Not only that, he forbade Elon from leaving as well and incentivized him to stay by telling him that he would pay for Elon's college if he stayed in South Africa. Errol was a smart and hardworking man who did not want their wealth to tarnish the mettle of the Musk children and, in the course of doing that, came across as a hard and stubborn man. But in essence, he was doing what he thought was best for his kids.

There were numerous fights and arguments between the stubborn Elon and an even more stubborn Errol. But, in the end, the bottom line was that Errol would cut him off if he chose to go without his father's permission. Since his father had turned him down, he elicited his mother's help. He knew that he wouldn't make it to the United States, which had strict immigration laws, but he knew he had to get started in that general direction. He had known since he was a kid that his grandfather Joshua was American by birth, but because Grandpa Haldeman didn't pass that down to his children and Maye was born in Canada and had taken up South African citizenship, he lost the ability to seek any sort of familial immigration from the INS. But he was able to find out that his mother would still get her Canadian papers and, by extension, he would be able to do the same.

He realized that was as close as he was going to get and he had to do what was necessary, so he went to the Canadian High Commission in Pretoria. He met the necessary officers, obtained the necessary paperwork, filled it all out and did all that needed to be done. His mother just had to sign the prepared paperwork and, in a few weeks, she got her papers and her passport, which he then took and started on his paperwork. In a few more short weeks, he got his Canadian paperwork as well and, the day the passport was issued, he got on a plane with less than $300 in his hand.

And so the adventure of a lifetime began, fraught with uncertainty, hardship, hard labor, little to no food and, at times, no place to sleep. You could say that it was a time in his life when Musk had nothing but for the shirt on his back and bag on his shoulders, with no roof over his head and a future that was so uncertain that the only thing that he had to look at was the dream of how it might transpire.

But in spite all this, he felt free, and he felt that he was on his way. None of the typical comforts of the world that most 19-year-olds crave were at the top of his mind. None of the worries and need for certainties that most adults crave distracted him from his current predicament. All he had to do was stay back in Pretoria and his father would have taken care of all of it. The bullying had stopped; just a couple of years in the military and a South African degree would have meant that he would have been hired with next to no difficulty and he would have been able to continue the father's business if he so chose. It would have been a cushy and easy life. But it would have been hell for him. He liked where he was, even if it did mean sleeping at the bus station or riding in a bus on unending journeys so that he could stay warm.

Of course, he didn't plan on doing all this when he left Pretoria. He hopped on a flight to Canada with the hopes of locating an uncle that lived there. Common sense today would dictate that you get in touch with this uncle before departing Pretoria but Musk was in a hurry and all he had was a phone number. However, his mother did write her brother and told him that his nephew was making his way up there at some point after he got his passport. But they never heard back until the day Elon boarded for Montreal. When he got there and called the number, the line was dead, so he called his mom back in Pretoria, from a pay phone. Letters had crossed while Musk was en-route and his uncle had responded that he had moved back to Minnesota and was no longer in Montreal. That now meant that Musk had nowhere to live.

What does a 19-year-old do in a strange city that he has never been to with very little cash in his pocket – and no plan? Well, Elon headed over to the nearest youth hostel and spent the night, recollecting his thoughts and regrouping. He found out that there was a bus service in Canada where you could purchase a month's pass and you could take the bus across any of its routes at any time in that period of a month. That was the cheapest housing you could get if you think about it. You hop on a bus, without any care where it was going, and what you have is a comfortable seat and warmth. You could sleep and, whenever the bus stopped, you could get food.

Not many people would think of that. What that also did was make it possible for him to scour the entire country for any relative that he could find. Every time he stopped at a town that he thought there might be family, he would get to the pay phone, pull up the directory (in those days payphones had directories; today you hardly find payphones much less directories attached to them) and start looking for all the last names that he could relate to his family. Talk about resilience and resourcefulness.

So, Musk gets on the bus and spends a few days crisscrossing the country, stopping to check payphones and cold-calling possible relatives out of the blue. Let me ask you this at this juncture, how willing are you to pick up the phone and randomly call strangers with a specific last name and ask them for a favor? I certainly couldn't, but Musk had no qualms doing it. That's why he is worth about 20 billion dollars, and counting, I guess. The will to do what is necessary.

But nonetheless, he kept trying and, after trekking about 2,000 miles from Montreal on and off buses, he got to a town called Swift Current, which was just off Highway 1. Swift Current is a small town of 15,000 residents (back in the early 90s); today the population is over 16,000 and it continues to be a wholesome, laidback Saskatchewan town. Just as he'd been doing, he got off the bus, found the telephone directory and scoured it till he found the name Teulon. It turned out that he'd hit the jackpot – it was indeed his cousin, Mark Teulon, and Teulon had a grain farm just outside of Swift Current, in a village called Waldeck, just 18 miles northwest of town.

He hitched a ride out to the farm where his cousin lived, introduced himself and asked for work if there was any. Considering he was family, even though they had never met, they found stuff for him to do. He was still seventeen (a few weeks short of 18) and eager to do just about anything.

He was happy to be off the bus and in a home where he knew that there was some measure of protection and some semblance of normalcy – a job, a bed, a roof, and homecooked meals. It was a place where he could pay his way for the basics in life without having to worry about his dwindling reserves.

He stayed in Waldeck for about a month and a half before moving on, but while he was there, he did two things. First, he worked hard moving stuff and cleaning stores and barns. The second is that he made an impression on his cousins – an impression that this kid was different from any other kid. He was indeed brighter than most and was hardworking as well – a rare and prized combination.

Chapter 6 Tending the Barn and Shoveling the Furnace

"In terms of the Internet, it's like humanity acquiring a collective nervous system. Whereas previously we were more like a [?], like a collection of cells that communicated by diffusion. With the advent of the Internet, it was suddenly like we got a nervous system. It's a hugely impactful thing."

– Elon Musk

While Musk was in Waldeck, working at the grain farm, he celebrated his 18th birthday with his new-found family. It was one of the good times that he remembers fondly and it proved the starting line in a sprint that would see him accepted to the University of Pennsylvania with a scholarship and admittance to the prestigious Wharton School of Business.

This period was also the time in which he was waiting for the rest of his family to emigrate from South Africa. His father was certainly not coming, but there was a good chance that his mother and siblings were going to follow the path that Elon had taken.

It was just a matter of time before they would make the decision and they would make the journey, but for now, Musk was on his own. He was in a new place at a new time in his life, and he was like a fish out of water with the mannerisms and the local culture. On the other hand, for those who are slow on the uptake, being thrown into a new situation may be a little difficult to handle because they are not used to the new surroundings and that makes them incapable of responding correctly. However, for a person who stores everything in the conscious part of his brain, he is quick to adapt and quick to take on the new attributes of his surroundings, melding into the fabric of his new surroundings and then excelling at doing what he was meant to do. He is the quintessential definition of being adaptive.

In archeology, there is a well-known theory that describes the survivability of a species along evolutionary lines. This is the existence of three facts in survival. It concerns when the environment changes – and by environment, I mean your physical surroundings and your circumstances. For us human beings, we have two kinds of environments that affect us significantly. The first kind of environment is the physical environment that we are subjected to. A person living in the North Pole will find it excruciating and, in some cases, deadly to migrate and live in tropical conditions.

The other environment is the cultural and cerebral environment. If we have cultural practices that are significantly different from those surrounding us, it becomes difficult to thrive because we are a species that lives on a community consensus. We live on the approval of others whether we realize it or not. Of course, there are a few of us who are contrarian in nature, but contrarians are few and far between.

The bottom line is that in order to advance our own objectives and promote our own aspirations, we need to be able to adapt to our surroundings. As much as Musk was enthusiastic about leaving Pretoria, he was also born and bred there and, as much as he didn't like their politics or appreciate their mannerisms, he was still dyed in the wool with it. The change in the new surroundings was very much real to him when he arrived, and he had to adapt to make sense of it all and make it work in his favor.

If you want to understand Musk and you, by chance, want to learn from the path that he took, then the thing that you need to come to terms with is the ability to adapt. That is one of the three things that make animals survive in the event that a change in the environment occurs. Because, when your surroundings change, you can do one of three things. You can die because you are incapable of recognizing the change and doing something about it, or you can move to a place that agrees with you, or you can adapt. The dinosaurs either perished or adapted when the environment around them changed. Polar bears will either adapt and become grizzlies as the ice of the poles recedes, or they will sink into the waters that displace the ice. What you do depends on how you see those changes and how you adapt.

Musk is a master of blending in with his surroundings – be it the physical surroundings or the cultural ones. Whether that blending in uses subterfuge and camouflage to disappear in school when hiding from bullies, or else adapting to cultural and geographic changes when he first arrived in Canada. But that ability to blend, to adapt, and to not just survive but thrive, is something we all need to take a good look at and understand how he does it because it is one of the central beams in his foundations of success.

Until Waldeck, Musk had not spent a single minute tending barns, or agricultural machinery. Until

Waldeck, he hadn't known how to wield a ho, fork, a rake, or maneuver a truck. But he learned quickly, and he did so with enthusiastic fervor. It was not as though this was to be his chosen profession. It was not as though he came to Canada to learn the farming business and set up a farm, but you wouldn't be able to tell that by looking at him and how he went about his work. He was still razor sharp and smart as a whip so he blended in by learning how to do what he had to do, and he did all of it well.

Some have analyzed this part of his life as a strict work ethic, meaning that he would do whatever he has to do while he has promised to do it, regardless of how he feels about the nature of his work. You will see this as he moves on in Canada and as we unfold the story of his job history before he gets to college again. But what it could also be, and this is what some of the analysts think based on personal knowledge of his drive and habits, is that he is the kind of person who does a job well and is automatically good at it because he can be. He has the extra capacity in his head and the fact that he is empathic allows him to have a much wider field of appreciation for the facts that come his way, whereas with the normal person the facts lay dormant in front of them rather than flying at them the way they do with an empath like Musk.

The times he spent with his cousin and the family spanned just six weeks, in which time he became fairly close to them and imparted an impression on the family that this young man would one day make something of himself. But even they, in their wildest dreams, would not know how far and wide his achievements would stretch to influence this generation and the world at large. It tickles me to think what they must have been thinking or what they must have been saying to each other as they watched the launch of Falcon Heavy.

The Teulons and Musk made it a practice to sit back after dinner at the table after long days of work in the field and talk about all kinds of things, to which Musk had much to contribute. They talked about space, electricity, pollution, and a number of ideas that were close to the heart of this young man. It didn't bother anyone that this boy was a farm hand by day and intellectual prophet by night.

What seemed to lend him credibility was that the things he learned and the rate that he learned them at was beyond more than what most people could accomplish in weeks. This gave those who watched him pick up things by day the confidence that what he said in the evenings had to be credible. That's human nature as, if you can build credibility in one area, you will slowly build credibility in others. Just as his ability to develop an online payment mechanism was enough to lend him the chops needed to get credibility behind his idea for space exploration.

Musk is acutely aware of this. He understands very well that performance and reputation in one area lends itself to others. That is one of the main reasons he has staked out a very powerful niche in his life. He has crafted his public relations persona to be that of a genius, and it works. Don't get me wrong, he is indeed very smart, and he does have a photographic memory and is able to do quite a bit, but the thing that you must know is that he is no Einstein.

There is a caveat that I have mentioned in passing across the length of this book and will continue to do as you traverse its pages. As much as Musk has a lot to teach us, he is not the prophet that he makes himself out to be. He is smart, he has a photographic memory, and he works hard. But he is not the Einstein or Hawking of this world. The ideas he has developed are not earth-shattering or groundbreaking – but they are inspiring. He didn't build a new spaceship to launch into space, and he didn't take new technology to build an electric car – he took what was already available and tinkered with it. It's not like what he did with PayPal – that was an original idea but then, again, that idea was also percolating in the mind of another company that was eventually in direct competition with PayPal.

The point that I am trying to make is that, before you go ahead and jump all in trying to be Musk, you should know exactly what and who he is and what he has done to get to where he is today. When you know the truth, then you know what to emulate and what to leave out.

To those who are watching and observing, he comes across as someone who is intelligent and grounded. To those who aren't paying attention, they see a crazy man rambling incoherently from one subject to the next at the speed of thought. But here is where he makes the difference. Most people who ramble at the speed of thought live in their heads – just as Musk does. But the difference between Musk and the man that lives in his head with all the bright ideas is that Musk comes out and makes it happen. He converts inspiration and thought into tangible reality.

If he chooses to play up his intellect and genius, so be it. But for us, we will be best served to emulate his ability to absorb and his willingness to do.

If you look at his time at Teulon's farm, or if you look at his time in school where he had to hide from bullies, or if you have to look at any of the other things that have materialized in his life, you will start to realize that he has definitely and defiantly not played the hand he was dealt but rather worked to escape his status quo and create the reality his mind longed for. He is worth every red cent of the twenty billion he is valued at (based on December 2017 valuations) because nothing he has done came easily.

When a month had passed, and he was still in Waldeck, his instincts started to stir. He felt stronger and more adept with the Canadian ways, and he was still not done with his quest – which, if you recall, was to find his way into the United States. But, for now, the opportunity had yet to present itself, so he knew he had to keep moving and keep working. His family had still not joined him, and he was still all alone. He saved what he could from the wages he got at Teulon's and then began his trek westward.

If you understand Canadian Geography, you will realize that trekking from Swift Current to Vancouver is like going from Billings, Montana to Portland, Oregon. They're about the same location longitudinally speaking and work out to be a 1,500-mile westward road trip to the Pacific coast. That slow bus trip lasting days to get to his destination is a long cry from the fast private jet he flies these days that gets him to DC and back overnight.

Speaking of private jets, Musk recently took delivery of a top of the line Gulfstream 650 Extended Range. The plane typically costs 65 million dollars, in addition to the cost of maintaining a flight crew. It also emits more carbon dioxide on the ground waiting to taxi for take-off than all his Teslas do in a lifetime. Just one of the interesting contradictions in his life that I thought was rather funny.

When he got to Vancouver, the only job he could find was cutting logs. It was a good thing he had learned to use a chainsaw on his cousin's spread and so, with a little bit of training, he was able to wield the chainsaw and got cracking with a new job that paid a little more. Make no mistake about it; this was heavy work. It required a lot of intense physical labor and it required the stamina to keep pushing from one task to the next for an entire workday. Musk was not scrawny in his teenage years for long. He had soon broadened out and built up in his late teens, and his job now, carving timber into logs, presented a significant upper body workout.

When I look across the terrain that is made up of all the successful people who have made it in their life, I see that there are two factors that drive people to do what they do. They may go about doing it differently using different parts of their endowments, but the same characteristic seems to always appear when I analyze men of substantial achievement. The first one is fear. The second is ego. Musk has plenty of both. If you have them, don't let anyone tell you that they are a harbinger of failure; they are the stilts to success – if used correctly.

Mind you, this is not a matter to judge or a matter to ridicule. This is human nature. When we tell our kids to do well in school, what do we do? Many parents instinctively instill the fear of failure and the consequence of not doing well. How do the kids respond? Well, they respond by trying harder, or they get stressed. Why? Because they now fear the consequences. Fear can be a powerful motivator. Fear unlocks the hidden strength that we have to go the extra mile and squeeze the extra Joule of energy. It is not just psychological; it is visceral and, more importantly, it is chemical. If you can bring your fear online and extract the energy that derives, then you are going to be able to push harder, overcome internal hurdles and insulate against fatigue and laziness.

In The Batman trilogy's, *The Dark Knight Rises*, there is a scene where Bruce Wayne contemplates escaping from the subterranean prison. At this point, he has tried and failed and, when asked about his fear, his answer is that he fears nothing. Seems like a heroic answer, but the advice he gets in return is that to be able to push himself to squeeze out that incremental level of energy that will launch him to where he needs to be, he needs to embrace the fear. Fear unlocks the edge you need to succeed.

Think about that for a minute. Fear is the reason we have fight or flight responses. Fear is the reason we push for survival. Fear is one of the drivers that pushes Musk. But before you go around calling him a scaredy cat, I urge you to read on and get a full grasp of what we mean when we refer to Musk's fear.

Based on his words and deeds and by parsing some of the things that he says and the way he says it, you can detect that there are certain issues that have an irrational bearing on him. For instance, most of what he is extremely fearful of is what other people think of him, and he goes out of his way to make sure that he shapes that narrative. When Ashley Vance wrote the book about him, he was not inclined to green-light the book. But when he realized that Vance was going to write the book one way or the other, he decided to meet with him and place the condition that the manuscript required his approval. When Vance didn't agree to that he finally gave in but wanted to proof the manuscript. Vance didn't budge on that point either. So, a lobster and half a steak later, Musk agreed to relinquish control of the book. But today, Musk and Vance are no longer on speaking terms (after meeting frequently and religiously to discuss the book over the course of the project) because one part of Vance's narrative didn't sit well with Musk. He had ceded control of the narrative and while most of what was said was within his construct, what was outside was painful for him.

His view of himself is not just about ego for the most part. There is that too. But it is mostly borne out of fear that people won't see him as a genius. Musk needs that to thrive. That is really important to him, just as Donald Trump needs everyone to see that he is a 'stable genius' who invented the art of deal-making. It's not about over-compensation. It's about how they see themselves. They see themselves through other people's eyes. So, if other's see them as a brilliant mind, then they see themselves that way too, and seeing themselves that way helps to support their own view and raise their levels of confidence, which then allows them to go out and accomplish things.

These are all personas that we create, and we want the facts to support this creation in our mind. We tend to go to great lengths to make sure that we keep this up so that we can derive strength and, subconsciously, we fear the breakdown of that personality to the outside world and, to a large extent, the ramifications of how we see ourselves in the mirror.

His view of his own narrative feeds him to push himself and excel even more. He also has the energy to do it and the bravado to feel that he can do more than anyone else. You can see his ability to push himself no matter how tough the circumstances get. Here are two instances that come to mind right off the bat when we think of Musk along these lines. The first is the job that he took after his logging job in Vancouver.

After some time logging, he decided he needed something that paid a little more and so he went to the employment office and put in for a job.

He asked the clerk to show him the list they had and asked which one paid the most. He was in luck. He found a job that was paying almost $20 an hour and the company still had vacancies to fill.

I can tell you this though; not many people would take this job. I know I wouldn't, but Musk went down to the company and spoke to the guy in charge. He was warned that he should know what he was getting into. The company was skeptical of hiring Musk because they know that a lot of people typically apply for the job, but most of them leave in short order. It was a demanding job and had an attrition rate of about 90%.

The manager took Musk to the plant and brought him around to the furnace, then asked him again if he was certain that he wanted the job. Musk was not even the least hesitant. He wanted a higher paying job so that he could save more and get on with his life.

They hired him and 29 other people. The job was not only tough, but hazardous. It entailed him crawling through a furnace conduit and entering a small space where the furnace was ejecting hot molten gunk. His job was to shovel that ejector molten out through the passage that he came in through. Someone on the other side of the conduit would then shovel that out onto containers for disposal. No man was allowed to be in that space for more than half an hour because the heat, between the furnace, the ejector material, and the hazmat suit that they were wearing to be in there, made it uninhabitable. Most people couldn't even take it for 20 minutes. Within the first few days, only 3 out of the 30 that were hired remained at the job – Musk was one of them. Resilient!

The story itself is an interesting anecdote. It shows a person who is not afraid to get down and dirty as long as it served his purpose and contributed to the endgame. The fear that we talked about in Musk is not a fear of bodily survival but the survival of the ego that is more important.

The second anecdote that speaks to his fears, and a comparison to the misunderstanding, is the fear that he had when he had run out of cash and his companies were burning $4 million a month without an end in sight and without a solution to overcome.

This was a period in his life, during his first marriage, when everything that could go wrong was going terribly wrong. He was borrowing money wherever he could, and the fear in his eyes was easily recognizable. He had lost more weight than he had even when he was working in the furnace, and he was looking haggard with sunken eyes and pale from lack of sleep. The fear he felt here was more than he felt at any other time in his life because what was at stake was not just his life, but his narrative – and by this I don't mean to mock him or deride his priorities, I am merely showing how Musk is the kind of person who cares more for his cerebral achievement and what people think of that than he does about his personal safety – and that is why he achieves things most people can't. We are afraid of the wrong things. We are afraid of losing our life but not afraid of wasting our minds.

The time he spent roaming the lands in his new home came to an end shortly after this experience. His mother and family, minus his father, arrived in Canada and the Musks were reunited. Musk and his younger brother were always close and the two fed off each other and drove each other to succeed. Kimbal was the counterpoint to Elon's demeanor and energy. Think of Kimbal and Elon together making the perfect individual. What one lacked, the other made up for and together they could do anything. That was known to them as well. They felt an uptick in their own energies once they were next to each other. It was obvious to anyone close to both brothers. Both were smart, but the older was sharper and the younger was vibrant. Both were business minded; one was practical, the other excelled at theory.

It's easy to get the wrong idea about Musk when you read the stories and anecdotes that are out there about him. So, let's clear some of that up right now. He is definitely a resilient person, but he is not the innovator that the narrative suggests. His inspiration comes from the times reads about and the comics he grew up on. But that does not make him any less of an achiever, and that is the point that all you folks out there need to realize. You don't need to be an Edison, or an Einstein, or a Nash and come up with an original idea that no one has thought of. You can even come up with ways to do things with existing elements. Just shuffling what is on the rack gets old products to do new things.

When Musk decided he wanted to reach for the stars, he didn't decide to design his own rockets. Instead, he went to Russia and looked at the old ICBMs. He then looked at the engines that were already in existence in the US. From those, he picked out the Apollo designs and then used the core design to build the Merlin engines that powered the Falcon and the Falcon Heavy. I am not saying that he poached technology or copied. I am saying that he used off the rack items, made modifications and used software heavily to accomplish cost savings. That is a special kind of intellect in and of itself.

So, my point is that we all don't need to reinvent the wheel, but we can use the same wheel to create something better. That is Musk, in essence.

Chapter 7 Queen's University

"It is important to view knowledge as sort of a semantic tree – make sure you understand the fundamental principles, i.e. the trunk and big branches, before you get into the leaves' details or there is nothing for them to hang on to."

— Elon Musk

As the academic year rolled around, Musk made plans to head back to school. He had two options to choose from. He had to decide between the University of Waterloo and Queen's University. Both were a stone's throw from the US border and located on either side of Lake Ontario. Queen's is located in Kingston, Ontario, east of Lake Ontario, while Waterloo is located on the western shore of Lake Ontario. Musk had the good sense to visit the schools before deciding which one to attend, and he was planning on enrolling in the engineering program in Waterloo. At that point, Queen's was not his first priority. What he saw when he visited was that Waterloo was populated predominantly by guys, while Queen's had a healthy mix of good-looking women.

So, it is no surprise which one he chose and for what reason. His own words described his choice in an interview just a few years ago when he admitted that he was desperately looking forward to the opportunity to be in the mix with a target-rich environment and, if nothing else, why else attend college?

Queen's is considered to be one of the top schools in Canada, constantly achieving top-ten status in nationwide rankings. Its economics program is one of the best, and major companies typically scout for future employees here. But Musk was a technical person, in most part, until this point. In fact, if he had chosen Waterloo, his intended major would have been physics and engineering. So, what gives?

The decision was primarily made because Queen's had a better economics program than an engineering program, and the factor that tipped the scale was the fact that there were more women at Queen's then there were at Waterloo. (Note to the Admissions officers at Waterloo: you might want to rethink your admission policies and get more women.)

Musk's time at Queen's enhanced his life in a number of ways. The first was that it put him in the mix with a new culture that he had not yet experienced. Remember, all this time he had been in Canada and was close to the earth – meaning he was working with his hands and muscle, toiling away and that is a very different surrounding and very different experience from exercising your mind and imagination. Therefore, the culture during that time was much different from the culture at Queen's. For one thing, the average age at Queen's was much lower than the working world outside. The second, there was a mix of genders and he was finally able to set his eyes on the opposite sex. The third was that he could move his mind from the tangible chores to intangible inspirations. It was something that Musk had wanted to do but the reality was still not complete.

Think about this for a minute and this will help you with your aspirations as well. His idea to move stateside was not for nothing. It was not a Hollywood-driven, job-searching itch. It was because he wanted to alter his surroundings to include people that could move him deeper in an area that he had significant interest in – technology.

At heart, Musk was a technocrat, from the time he picked up science fiction comics, and still remains as such today. Much of his visions and ideas are really manifestations of the comics he poured over as a kid. He sees technology very differently from most people around the world – certainly more than his contemporaries in South Africa did at the time, and he sees it very differently from the way most people do today. But that is changing as Millennials have moved the needle in the appreciation of technology and how it is used in this day and age. Nonetheless, that's beyond the scope of this book.

Coming back to Musk and his developmental years.

There are two ways you can see college. One way is to look at it as a trove of resources conducive to the development of your own thoughts. If you look at the likes of Einstein, Nash, and other towering academic luminaries, what you find is that their time in academic institutions is not spent going to classes and slogging through homework and assignments – the true greats rarely attend class (kind of like what Bill Gates and Steve Jobs did as well) and spend their time in other pursuits, only stopping to get homework and assignments from their roommates to make sure that they do the absolute minimum to get through classes.

Musk's engagement with Queen's was no different. He rarely attended classes but still managed to ace those that he felt were important to his development. The quality that he started to display during his freshman year at Queen's was that he could understand topics beyond their academic descriptions. Take, for example, his economics classes and his introduction to supply and demand curves. He didn't just see them as mathematical graphs of lines positively and negatively sloped and met at the point of equilibrium. That's what most students to. But for Musk, he understood the human nature behind it and the reason the demand curve sloped the way it did, going lower as it moved to the left. He also understood the propensity for the supply line to rise at it moved to the left. Not only did he see it from the mathematical and theoretical positions, but he related the underlying concept to human thought and behavior patterns.

To say that he aced his economics would be an understatement – he more than understood the principles, he internalized them, allowing him to develop his own theories and his own thoughts on any given matter. You don't always find a student with the same frame of reference or the same level of understanding as Musk. Even his younger brother, as smart as he was, couldn't hold a light to the older Musk.

Universities are a great place to develop in many ways – academic and otherwise, because they put individual intellectual and inherent ability in competition with others. A campus ground serves more than just a venue for buildings, but rather they serve as an arena to pit one's thoughts against others. These competitions of cerebral matters etch out the truth, showcasing the development of humanity and technology alike.

Musk was easy to get along with in college. He still is these days, but there is a palpable difference in how he makes new acquaintances. He has come to experience the duplicity of human friendship; the same deficiency in trust that could be expected in those you call friends. His view of friendship has grown and altered in time as has his view of family. He went from trusting both friend and family alike until his friend betrayed him in outing his location to the bullies that beat him within an inch of his life. From that point on, things started to change a little. He didn't trust many people outside his own clan.

He was also severely disappointed by the actions of his father in changing his mind about moving to the United States. His frustrations as a young teenager shone a light on a determination to make himself self-sufficient and to be able to do for others what he had hoped others would do for him.

Take, for instance, the way he feels about public school. Public school, unlike university, has two major issues for Musk. The first is that public school does not create a fertile ground for the installation of knowledge or for the development of the mind. The second is that primary education mixes too many different elements that are not always good for the development of the mind. Look at how he structured the development of his own children. Instead of leaving them in regular educational institutions, even though they were private institutions that were top dollar, he was still not happy with the way it was conducted. In pursuance of that line of thinking, what he did was to pull them out of school and built a new school according to his philosophy of learning. It is very evident that he had significant thoughts of primary learning in this present frame of mind, but that frame of mind was fostered and advanced during his time in college, both during his time at Queen's and his time at Penn.

He doesn't trust the system to develop the minds of his children, and he does indeed have a point. You see, Musk is the quintessential innovator. This means that he is not one to come up with something mind-bending and far-reaching – he is no Einstein. But he will come up with something that is far enough off on the horizon that makes sense to the imagination of the masses. He takes that and finds a way to make it work. That is the construct of his mind and, since the time he has been a kid in Pretoria and with what he sees in schools today, he understands clearly that the concept of mass education robs the student of truly innovative thought.

The mind of a child is like the development of a computer program – the way Musk sees it. It requires the necessary structure, framework, and libraries to get the program to work well. The schools provide the set of libraries that the student needs to be able to handle life in the life after they graduate. And in Musk's opinion, the schools today are not doing a good enough job of providing the right algorithms or the right libraries to make that happen. As such, he decided to create his own. He has been this way even since college.

If the class that he was taking didn't provide him with the right set of 'libraries,' meaning that it didn't give him the resources to understand the subject matter in totality, then he would just extract himself, go out and find a place that would provide him with what he needed – he usually found that at the library.

There are significant trust issues that Musk has and it showed in college. As romantic as he is and as intelligent as he is, the thing that worked out in his mathematically precise mind was the fact that human beings cannot be trusted. He really doesn't trust anyone. Not his wife (first and second), not his friends and, to a certain extent, not even his own family.

He had a small group of close friends in college, but he kept away from too much socializing. He did seem to be on a mission to get a girlfriend, and he was definitely the kind of person that looked for a trophy as well as a confidant.

Let me explain.

His choice of women, and mind you, he was not even 19 at this point, were the lookers. The ones that looked really good and knew how to carry themselves. You would think that someone like Musk who was so intellectually inclined would be on the lookout for someone who would match his intellectual ability and fervor. But it turns out that Musk is not that kind of a guy when it comes to his choice in women and his choice in life partners. There are some who say that he has tried to suppress his tendencies to be gay, but that is just conjecture and unproven. But if true that doesn't imply that he is gay; it just implies that he is uncomfortable with the thought that there is a possibility that others might think that he might be gay.

To compensate, Musk has always been the kind to want to be seen with the best-looking women with the best-looking presentation. Other books have chronicled how he met his first wife, who was also a student at Queen's and I won't go too much into that except to say that he pursued her relentlessly, and she was fascinated by the romantic streak in him.

He spent two years in Kingston, most of it outside the classroom. He showed up for exams and handed in papers and still beat everyone else in the class. He had made considerable strides in his development, but the metamorphosis was not yet complete.

While at Queen's he made money on the side by building and selling computers to his dorm and classmates. If they needed to upgrade their computers he would do it for them, or if they needed to fix them, he would easily accomplish that as well. The specialty he engaged in was building game boxes for his friends and everyone around campus new that Musk was the kid to go to when they needed a computer or needed it to be fixed. He made it a point to charge prices based on the rarity of the problem. If it was an easy problem to fix, the price was low. If the problem was not common, then it got expensive. If they wanted to build a new machine to play games, then he would charge them for the build, plus he would scalp the price of the parts. He managed to save up this way with a lot of what he did and, that way, he was able to have a lifestyle that was comfortable without having to rely on anyone. He was supporting himself ever since he landed in Canada – now was no different.

Even though he was Canadian, Musk lived on the International floor at his dorm residence in Victoria Hall. It was there he met Navaid Farooq. There are two ironies here. The first is that Musk, while being Canadian, had never lived in Canada and so found the benefit of living around other International students. His to-be best friend Farooq was also on the International floor but, unlike Musk, Farooq was a natural-born Canadian, though lived overseas all his life. So, both men were Canadian but had no idea what it meant to be such. And so, that became the bond that bound the two of them. Farooq was no lackey either. His ability to be academically advanced ahead of his classmates was well documented, but he was no match for the unbeatable Musk. The irony extended to the point that the two were paired because of their life experience. One was a Canadian all his life while the other was a new Canadian and both had no idea what that meant.

Farooq was in the Faculty of Arts and Sciences while Musk wasn't, but they did share a couple of classes together and, whenever possible, Musk would lean on Farooq for his notes and homework. But in the end, Musk would still beat him out in exams. Musk would score in the high 90s while Farooq would score in the low 90s. Even Justine and Musk would be in competition along with Farooq, and there was a time when Musk beat them all by scoring a 98 on an exam. Even though he beat them, he wasn't happy with the score, so he went and spoke to the professor and debated his point till he got a hundred.

These days, Queen's still looks back at him favorably and keeps a kind nickname for him – Rocket Man.

Musk left Kingston at the end of his Sophomore year to take up the rest of his education at the University of Pennsylvania. He was accepted with full scholarship to the Faculty of Arts and Sciences to pursue a degree in Physics. He went on to get a double degree in Economics as well from the Wharton School.

It only took two and a half years from the day he landed in Canada in hopes of meeting his uncle, and now he was making his way into the United States. From grain farms to toxic furnaces, to girls and books, he was finally making it across the northern border and into the United States. His journey had just begun.

Chapter 8 Justine

"I could go and buy one of the islands in the Bahamas and turn it into my personal fiefdom, but I am much more interested in trying to build and create a new company."

— Elon Musk

This part of the book starts with a look into Musk's personal life as it relates to the loves and love interests of his life. It is not intended to spread gossip – salacious or otherwise – but it is intended to describe the part of the man that is more personal. How you find a man in his natural state in these shadows is a good measure of the true nature of the man. How he pursues, treats, and leaves the women in his life reveals a lot about how he thinks of himself and the people around him.

It's fairly easy in today's world to sculpt your own PR and to lay the trail for the public to form an opinion of you that conforms to the way you see yourself. If you are computer savvy and have a vision, it is easy enough to do. Both these things we know Musk has in abundance. So, to really get an understanding of him you need to do three things. You need to pour over volumes of data going back to the time when he was a kid. Then you have to take that information and filter it through your own senses – sort of a way to pass any smell test. Then, finally, you have to balance what those close to him say with what those who are apart from him say – but, even more importantly, we need to find a pattern of what is uttered versus what is performed.

It's like deciphering a coded message. If you find that the message reads C but actually means A, and a little while later it reads K and actually means I, then you know that you need to spring back two letters to get the real story. In the same way, when a person says A but does E, and says E but does J, then you can get an idea of what to do and how to tweak the words into a credible prognostication of the action to come.

How Musk sees himself is a function of how he wants others to see him, and that in turn is a function of the vision he has in his head. That vision is highly detailed and specific all the way down to the color of the hair his wife – whomever she may be at the time – should have.

Justine was Musk's first wife whom he met at Queen's and pursued to the ends of the earth. He was the exact opposite of what she was looking for in a guy, and she was exactly (short of being a blonde) what he pictured in a woman – strong, smart, and attractive. They say that men eventually marry women that resemble their mothers. Freudian psychobabble aside, you can see why Justine fits this aphorism. Maye Haldeman is smart – a woman with two Master's degrees and a self-made nutritionist. She is also a model. I can't say 'was' a model, because, even in her late sixties she just recently appeared as a cover girl for a famous top-shelf magazine. So, in saying that he saw in Justine all the things that his mother was – strong, smart and attractive – wouldn't be too much of a stretch. What's even more perplexing is that he divorced Justine as well. Just like how his parents had.

Much of Musk's persona when it comes to women seems to be stuck in a loop that begins with his mother. Maye had brownish-blondish hair as a kid that darkened in her life then became more blonde over time. The older she got, the more blonde to platinum it became, and it really suits her. It is a color that imparts a distinguished and elegant look. Musk definitely defines those qualities with the measure of his mom's hair as he insists on the women that he is with to ever increasingly dye their hair blonde to platinum. He tends to show these glimpses of living in a loop by these actions.

There were many parallels between Musk and his father in how they sought and found their life partners. The immense effort that Errol put into his pursuit of Maye was bested by the effort that Musk put in with Justine. In her own words, Justine was totally set up to go after the bad boy. She liked significantly older men for their intellect and stability, and she had just been in a long-term relationship with a much older man – a sort of James Dean meets William Shakespeare kind of guy. Musk is none of that, but he was persistent. The one thing that Justine brings to the table in an effort to understand Musk better than anyone else is that she had a front and center view in that point of his life where he blossomed from the repressive days of Pretoria to the exercising and blossoming of his mental acuity. She saw him rise to towering heights academically, and she saw him fall flat during the troubled days of Tesla and Space X.

She caught his eye across a room once. Justine is tall and has long wavy hair – or at least that's how she was back then. She was certainly the most attractive soul in all of Kingston – undoubtedly so to Musk. She was also a Freshman when Musk was a Sophomore. The year difference in class was totally made up by the fact that she was far ahead of her peers when it came to literary talents. She was well aware that the kids at college were attracted to her slim waist and long sultry hair. There were more than just a few potential suitors who made their advances, but she easily brushed them off without a moment's hesitation.

He didn't have much experience with this kind of thing, and the only thing that he knew to do was to walk straight up to her. But he didn't do that before getting some background on her. The one thing Musk was good at was gathering intelligence. He got most of the story and how most of the guys failed to before getting even a word in; he decided that his attack strategy would be to play on the possibility that they had met before. Sly, but effective – or so it seemed.

He had looked around and, while he flew reconnaissance, he found out which were the parties that she liked going to. So, he waited for his chance and what he did was catch her on a supposed chance encounter while she was coming down the stairs and he walked up to her and reminded her how they had met at a party, and asked her if she remembered him. Of course, she didn't remember him because they had never met. And she told him so, but he persisted and tried to remind her of a conversation that they never had. And she was still not remembering, but she did think that it was an original way to get to know her. As I said, he was not her type. She was looking for seasoned leather, authentic and aged; he was freshly sawn lumber, green and straight cut. But the thing that caught her attention was his accent. It wasn't something from around there, and that spark in his voice provided the necessary mystery and intrigue to keep the encounter going.

This whole thing with Justine ran hot and cold for years – even after he moved to Philadelphia. They communicated but nothing serious ever ignited; it was always touch and go. The interest never really died, but it never really reached critical mass.

Some of the deepest insights we get of Musk comes from Justine who eventually married Musk and together they had five children – twins and triplets. But that wasn't after almost a decade of this on-and-off courtship.

But that aside, Justine constantly recollects, till today, the way that Musk treated her and how he was as interested in her intelligence as much as he was interested in her physicality. In the beginning, he was persistent, but he didn't smother her. There was this swinging pendulum in how he pursued her. As he turned up the charm, he would also give her room to breathe and give her space to grow. Girls in college aren't looking to get married, and neither was she at that point – there was a lot of things he needed to accomplish, but he did see her in a few different ways. There was no doubt about her being his conquest – it was something he wanted to win. It was something he wanted to possess – and by 'it' I am not referring to Justine, but rather the relationship and the conquest.

Those who know him closely, seem to believe that Musk has the ability to read minds or at least has exhibited numerous instances of extrasensory perception. This is not uncommon for people who have high empathic activity and intelligence. In one display of this ability, Justine talks about the time that Musk called her at a moment in her life when she had decided that, if Musk were to try again in pursuing her, she would relent. Within days of that decision, Musk called and, from that point on, the two became an item – officially.

From the time that he pursued her in Queen's, the friendship had been on and off. She had other intentions, but she was intrigued by him, yet not enough to actually spark the chemistry she saw as the prerequisite for a full-blown relationship.

This went on for years. It started the second year Musk was attending Queen's, and it went on to the point when he had left Penn and moved to California. All this time, there was no relationship but friendship. They spoke often, and they even dated other people. Not only was Justine interested in other men at the time she completed her Journalism degree at Queen's, but Musk was also dating various other women while he was at Queen's during his Sophomore year and on to Penn. He was also dating other women at the time he moved out West.

Even though they were separated by a few hundred miles at first when he was in Philadelphia, he would continuously send her roses. That gesture kept him vivid in her memory so, even if he was out of sight, he certainly wasn't going to allow his presence to be out of mind.

But until they got married, or at least until they started to get on the same page about spending life together, she had swung like a pendulum from love to conquest and back again, numerous times, for him. For her, the relationship was different. Each time was a build-up. Slow like the building of a fire in a castle's hearth. It took her close to a decade before she got to the point that Musk became her soul mate. It took him a look across the common room to decide that she should and would make a good trophy.

The one thing that is clear from the actions Musk took across from the time that they met, the time they dated, the time they remained as friends, the time they were engaged, the time they were married and her time after the messy divorce is that his intentions were always clear – he wanted someone to fit the role he had structured in his mind. Justine happened to be the one that came close and so he took what he could and then tried to cosmetically alter the rest.

Take, for instance, the thing with her hair and hair color. He wanted her to color her hair blonde and she was not a blonde but a pretty brunette. She obliged – this was the first phase of the objectification of Justine. As the years passed, his desire for her to be more blonde became more prevalent. She obliged with each additional tint. How she looked, what she wore, and even what she said was subject to Musk's choreography.

After graduating Queen's, Justine left for Japan while Musk wrapped up his second degree at Penn and then spent some time brainstorming with brother Kimball. He had originally been accepted into the Stanford doctoral program – got there and attended it for a few days and decided that it was not where he wanted to be. He and his younger brother set about getting their heads together on a project that could get them to make money with what they knew how to do. All this time, Justine and Musk continued to communicate, but the flowers stopped while she was out East.

Justine had constantly thought of Musk in her time away, but she hadn't fully reached the place she needed to be. Justine, you see, was and till today remains a die-hard romantic and, as many dates that she may go on, she has always needed to feel her man and she was not there yet.

By the time she got back, Musk was accelerating in his endeavors. In his mind, success was fait accompli; in her mind, the future was uncertain. Not knowing what to do next, she started bartending. Back in Canada, she started to think of Musk even more, and she came to the conclusion that she had missed her opportunity at happiness. Absence certainly does make the heart grow fonder. Her instincts of Musk and him not being the right one for her had faded into the background and what remained in the foreground was her loneliness and the yearning for the attention that he knew how to dole out in abundance. That's when he called, out of the blue, and she stayed true to her utterance. They got together.

By the time she got down to California, Musk was living in a loft with a couple of people and plugging away at his endeavor of Zip2. Zip2 was the online directory that he set up together with his younger brother. When he left Stanford, he shot straight up to Canada and hung out with his brother while they brainstormed an idea to move on. What resulted was Zip2. Remember this was the early 90s and anything you developed that could reside online and provide a service was probably going to make a bit of money.

So, when Justine got to California, Musk was plugging away at Zip2 and trying to make it work. It took some time, but she watched him in his new element, a far cry and a long distance in space and time from the boy that relentlessly pursued her against her polite wishes to the contrary.

They got reacquainted at this time across a number of trips that Justine made, shuttling back and forth between Canada and San Francisco. The conversation didn't rest on platitudes for long and they jumped straight into talk about marriage and kids. Both were on board and they gave themselves two years to put their lives on track. As this happened, Zip2 became a hit and, overnight, Musk went from budding entrepreneur with promise to a multimillionaire. It was a culture shock that Justine had no idea what to do with. Soon, the rented loft turned into a purchased apartment, and the meager transportation they used turned into a McLaren.

Then it was off to the next endeavor, and X.com was born. It was the precursor to PayPal, and this is around the time things started to get a little strange. Aside from the McLaren, the condo, and a couple of small things, most of the money he made from the sale of Zip2 was reinvested into X.com. By November of 1999, just two months before the wedding, Musk had lined up legal representation to put together an agreement that looked, read, and sounded like a prenup, but wasn't a prenup. It wasn't a prenup because Musk said it wasn't. As uncomfortable as Justine was on hearing that the appointment was already set and she just had to show up, she brushed it off as something that Musk was capable of and something that didn't mean that his heart wasn't as far along the spectrum of 'soulmateness.' She let it pass and acquiesced into signing on the dotted line.

Just so we are clear – there was no prior discussion and there was no separate attorney present. There was no heads-up or explanation – just an assurance that it wasn't a prenup and that she had nothing to worry about.

He apparently told her that it wasn't his idea but the requirement by the board of PayPal that was requiring that he did this. That made even less sense to her, but she did not have the slightest inclination to not trust him or not take him at his word. Of course, now when she looks back she feels that none of that was genuine. Whether it was or it wasn't is not up to us to determine or judge. But I specifically include it here to show you the lengths to which an accomplished person would and should go to achieve what he has to achieve. By that, I don't mean that he needs to be okay with sneaking in a prenup (a rose by any other name smells just as sweet) but rather that he sees it as just part and parcel of doing what he needs to do.

Once they signed the document and the wedding went on as scheduled two months later, they settled in to being married after a couple of years of being engaged and almost a decade of being friends. You could say that she knew Musk really well but, at the same time, she was witnessing the metamorphosis of the man we now know as Rocket Man.

As X.com morphed into PayPal and Musk was rolling full steam ahead with it, the lifestyle that was already significantly different from the early days in San Francisco, took another leap. With that leap came direction and the choreography of how Justine was to behave. It was around this time that Alexander was born and this was probably one of the saddest times in all of Musk's existence.

He may not be there for his girlfriends or his wife, but he adores his kids and, when Nevada Alexander was born, Musk was elated and had a very specific framework of how he wanted to raise his son. He didn't have time so he passed that on to Justine, but he was bound and determined to run a tight ship when it came to the raising of his offspring.

The relationship began to show signs of strain that were there all along but were masked by the lifestyle and the excuses of a high-paced career. Justine had to relax the book writing, which had been going well until then and she had already been published. Musk was too focused on his achievements to notice that she was thirsting for her own achievements in the literary world – a world he had proclaimed to understand in word but not in deed, as it turns out.

When Nevada went to sleep one day in his tenth week, he stopped breathing and, by the time the paramedics were alerted and showed up, they were not able to resuscitate him in time to prevent brain damage, and a host of other complications came to pass. The Musks decided to pull the plug after a couple of days on life support, and Justine held baby Nevada in her arms as he slipped away peacefully.

That was traumatic for both of them on so many levels, but it was also the wedge that cracked the stone. That event showed the distinct way the Musks handled their grief. Justine needed someone to talk it through since she was balancing between her post-partum condition and the loss of her first son. But Musk grieved in a different way. He chose to not talk about it – any of it. And so they never did.

Any attempt by Justine to find reprieve was met by Musk's wrath, which was undoubtedly the consequence of his pain.

The solution, he decided, was to get pregnant again without delay so that they could divert their attention to the pregnancy, and later, to the kids that came along. Rather than leave this to chance, Musk insisted that he choreograph this phase of their life as well and they did that by attempting IVF so that the pregnancy could be better timed and better predicted. Their first attempt resulted in twins – two boys.

Prior to the wedding, when the couple was in their happy courting phase, the subject of children had revealed that both Musk and Justine were the kind of people who loved kids and wanted to have at least two or four kids. The difference being predicated on whether there was a nanny to help with the chores. As far as Justine was concerned, she had no idea of the life that Musk had laid out for himself, in the same way an army general lays out his uniform the night before reporting for duty. In his mind, of course, there were going to be nannies and helpers at home.

After the wedding, they had five helpers around the house, so the twin boys were still short of the mark. They went back in for IVF and this time they were blessed with triplets.

Justine's career as a writer came to a halt, and that is to be expected. Parents often sacrifice their dreams to provide for their kids – not just the provision of money and resources, but also the provision of time and love. Justine stepped up admirably and the days of Nevada were in the rear mirror and fading fast.

But something else was in that rear mirror as well and this was not fading, but actually racing up to Justine from behind. As time passed, and X.com became PayPal, and PayPal got purchased by eBay, Musk's wealth had suddenly jumped from the days after Zip2, and now there was some serious money involved. eBay purchased PayPal for a deal valued at $1.5 billion. Musk's take from that was a very cool $165 million. The PayPal transaction closed the week Nevada went to sleep and didn't wake up.

The sudden wealth placed a huge disparity in the marriage. In dollar terms, Justine had contributed nothing. Musk had contributed everything. But in the Calculus of modern man's minds, the contribution women place by raising the family never balances the scales where the man brings in the bacon. That's an unfortunate reality of today's dynamic. It shouldn't be, but it is. And this played out to such obvious levels in the Musk Beverly Hills household. It wasn't just in her head, in fact, he told her, point blank, that he was the Alpha in the relationship.

He handled Nevada's death and his sale of PayPal by throwing himself into the next big thing. He could not fathom why Justine wanted to talk about the past and Justine couldn't figure out why he wanted to silence it. Neither understood each other, but both had valid reasons for what they were doing and how they were feeling.

The battle between the two continued to simmer and smolder in the background – off the main stage that was meticulously choreographed. They would still attend high-dollar functions, still be seen in public, and still move in the right circles. Tesla and Space X had started up and, while things initially went well, the companies started to face trouble and that's when things got even worse at home.

Musk was being tight with cash that he no longer had, falling into debt to make payroll, and he was losing sleep and sanity. Justine had now seen the man she married come full circle. There is only one story sadder than the man who has nothing – that is the man who makes it in every way, then loses it all. Suddenly his alpha was sucked out from under him and he couldn't keep it together, and neither could Justine.

They started seeing a therapist and, after two and a half months of that, he finally couldn't take it and, in his exacting way, sought to place a deadline on the revitalization of the marriage. His deadline was that, if they couldn't make it by the end of the day, they would get divorced in the morning.

The next day, his lawyers prepared the paperwork and he presented it to her along with reference to the 'non-prenup' prenup.

Chapter 9 Life as a Man

"It's pretty hard to get to another star system. Alpha Centauri is four light years away, so if you go at 10 percent of the speed of light, it's going to take you 40 years, and that's assuming you can instantly reach that speed, which isn't going to be the case. You have to accelerate. You have to build up to 20 or 30 percent and then slow down, assuming you want to stay at Alpha Centauri and not go zipping past. It's just hard. With current lifespans, you need generational ships. You need antimatter drives because that's the most mass-efficient. It's doable, but it's super slow."

— Elon Musk

It's easy to find fault with a man's decisions. It is even easy to mock, ridicule, and reign superior in fake morality over a man and the decisions he makes. As much as a man is about the decisions he makes, those decisions do not form in a vacuum due to some magical string of character. It is all formed by the way he treads through the experiences of life. My purpose with looking into the depths of Musk's life and experiences is to learn. Not just from the things he did right, but to learn from the mistakes he made and the errors he didn't see happen. He is not perfect, and I don't expect him to be.

Within the span of eleven years, Musk went from being a high school senior, to arriving in a new country and working odd jobs, enrolling in school, transferring to a new school in a new country, and excelling in areas that he loved and accelerating in deliverable accomplishments. Within 11 years of leaving South Africa and within eight years of coming to America he made his first million (twenty million, actually). What does that say about the art of achievement? What does that say about the path one needs to walk to succeed?

It has been widely reported that Musk has no interest in taking his kids back to Pretoria and have them meet his dad. That's a significant issue for anyone and not one that we should discard in our effort to understand the man that has been hailed as this generation's Edison.

People do certain things because it gives them pleasure, either in the act itself or in the execution of the habit that encompasses it. People typically stay away from things either because they know, at a cerebral level, that the consequences of the act will not be acceptable to the refrain from acts due to a visceral response to the pain that the act causes just by thinking of it.

I have an aversion to alcohol, not because I have some sort of moral guideline, but because at some point the aftereffects of a drink, no matter how small, became intolerably unpleasant. It turns out my constitution couldn't handle it and my body promptly rejected it and, in the process of doing so, made me feel horrible. After repeated experiences of the after effects, my response to anything alcohol was subconsciously dictated by the unpleasantness. I didn't consciously think of it; I just reacted with grimace. My response was not calculated; it was automatic, visceral and visible. What wasn't visible was the memory of the pain that caused the response. All our actions can be measured in similar frameworks. We do everything based on a quantifiable reason even if we don't really know what that is or how it came about.

The point is that sometimes we react to things because of the accumulated unpleasantness that we are subjected to. It is the same way with Musk. The abuse (psychological) was just unbearable to the point that, when the fuse blew, there was no going back. But that sort of thing is not something to judge. The abuse was physical in school and psychological at home. That was just the beginning – then there was the emotional abuse that was a function of the divorce. As the oldest child in the family, there is always a sense of blame that they place on themselves. Whichever way you cut it, the burden that Musk, in his youth, carried was tremendous, and it had a bearing on the man he became.

Fortunately, for us, we can learn from that. The key is to understand who we are and how to keep it together. The thought that Musk is trying to keep it together can be seen in many of the things he says and does. At the end of a conversation with one of his biographers, Musk asks him if he sounds crazy. And that is not the only time; it happens quite a bit. There is the sense of insecurity that pulls on the stings of Musk's frame of mind.

Within a couple of weeks of the divorce from Justine, Musk was back in the saddle again and dating.

Musk has a vision in his head, and that is the point of this chapter and the other chapters that cover his personal life with partners. He has a vision that he is in a race to perfect and make real. He sees in his head that he needs to have a family, a number of kids, a sports car, a certain caliber of friends, a specific type of plane, and certain kinds of names for himself. He has all this in his head, and the way it works is that he just starts gunning for it at a clip that is not typically known to regular people. It may make him seem cold and calculating, but it really isn't. Justine was just another piece of that puzzle that he had to assemble and, when it fell through, he put it in his mental calendar that he needed to fill that void in the overall picture. It was not an emotional investment that most of us make; it was a puncture that most of us don't see.

Is this a good or a bad thing? It's neither. It's just the way he does things. But there is a lesson to be learned. When you go after success, there is no emotional and visceral fantasy – there is just the inspiration to do it and then the march to get it done. It is the surest way to get to where you are going.

Think about marching from New York to Los Angeles. If you were to ever contemplate such a feat, all you would need to do is plan the trip and follow the plan meticulously, without giving up in the event that something outside your plan happened. You would spend as little time as possible correcting your course in the event of a deviation and then get back to it. Plugging away till you get to where you are going.

Most people can't do that. They get distracted. They get blinded. Something else happens that gives them a new goal to shoot for. All sorts of things happen and, in the end, you realize that you are about to retire and none – absolutely none of your dreams have materialized. People like Musk don't have that problem. They coldly calculate where they are going and they march toward its accomplishment relentlessly. Sometimes people around them get hurt, but that, in the minds of people like Musk, is just acceptable collateral damage.

Life as a man is hard enough as it is. And that statement is not about gender equality but about the resources that are backed into us and the way we are raised with expectations. We are like wine, how we are raised – the soil beneath us, the humidity around us, the sun above us, all determine the unique flavor that we begin to mature with. If we change that soil, alter the humidity, or shade the vines from the light, then the taste of the wine thirty years down the road is something very different.

The events that unfolded over the course of Musk's life may not be palpable to some, or may not seem significant to others, but either way, he should not be judged. Musk is neither the Technological Edison of our time nor is he a monster in disguise. He is who he is, and his actions, his mistakes, and his accomplishments have much to teach us. And that is the point of a biography.

There are two things that I have personally learned from Musk's life story as I spent the better part of a year researching the stories and understanding the background. The first is that dream and inspirations, whether they come from within us or from within the pages of a comic, can eventually come true if we put our minds to them. Musk and I share the same generation – that means we share the same comics, the same cartoons, and the same science fiction. We also share the same collective imagination where cartoons like Flash Gordon, Carl Sagan's Cosmos, The Apollo Landing, The Jetsons, Logan's Run and all those TV programs, books, and stories inundated us with ideas of what the future could be. Whether we like it or hate, it, whether we realize it or are oblivious to it, it soaked into our roots, nourished us, and illuminated our minds. Musk grew up to embody that inspiration and you can see it in the projects that he takes – space travel, vacuum tube transportation, electric self-driving vehicles, brain-controlled computers. All the projects he has undertaken are strangely familiar to those of us who share the generational space with Musk. It's what we watched on TV. He just set himself on a path to make it come true.

When it came to relationships, however, there were a few elements at play. The perfect woman had to be in the image of his perfect mother. She was a huge influence in his life and also a source of guilt when he had to move to his father's home because he wanted a man's guiding hand. The South African chauvinist tendencies were not lost on young Musk – and they are still not lost today. Justine thinks that the Alpha in him, which he reminded her of so often, was because he made more than she did, but the truth is that it's not about that entirely, it was also about the fact that the bully-macho South African strain was so deeply rooted in him.

The second was that Musk grew up in a world that was isolated. Whether he was being lectured at by his father in terms that were harsh, or he was hiding from getting beaten in school, or the fact that he hardly had friends of the opposite sex in high school, it caused him to withdraw into his own mental space. Compound that with the fact that he had a unique mental framework that would be able to focus deeply on just about anything he was able to extricate himself from the world around him. It made him a genius, but it also resulted in a very lonely life. That feeling of being lonely was unpleasant and disturbing to him, so he placed that on a list that he was to remedy when he unshackled himself of the chains of his formative years. He cannot stand to be alone and, now that he has the wherewithal, he makes it a point that being alone is not an option.

That is a powerful admission from a man who seems to be able to accomplish anything, and it is one that more of us need to be able to admit to when we feel the need. Most men, and to a large extent women, do not like the idea of being alone but we never get down to realizing it or admitting it to ourselves. Being alone is a scary thought, and it is one that drives us to do a lot of good things, but it is also one that drives us to do a lot of crazy things.

Not wanting to be alone and the fear of sleeping alone at night or not hearing another person's breathing sounds next to you is something that makes absolute sense for a man, and Musk was quickly in the arms of another person as soon as Justine had moved out.

Dating Tallulah Riley happened quick and happened fast, and it seemed like Musk was just heartless. It's not that, and it's not that he didn't love or have real feelings for Justine. It's more that he never wanted to be alone. Even when he split from Riley, he jumped into the arms of someone else and just kept looking for that perfect partner.

It is not that he is a bad person, it is that he is driven by fear and it shows in many of the things he says and does. We are all the same way, but we can learn to be stronger by learning from the people that we read about. But just because Musk has certain weaknesses doesn't mean that the lessons he can teach us to achieve amazing things should be discarded.

Musk is a man of tremendous talent and work ethic. He does not take his gifts for granted, and he does not waste them. He may be someone that lacks original ideas, but he is a man that takes ideas that are on the shelf and makes them work.

Chapter 10 The Future According to Musk

"No, I don't ever give up. I'd have to be dead or completely incapacitated."

– Elon Musk

We've spent much of the book looking at the shadow of the man's mind to be able to get an idea of the share of his real being. That's the best way to go about understanding a person and his motivations. Everything we do has a wave that ripples away from that and, if we can't see the event hidden underwater, we can certainly observe the tsunami it creates on the surface.

That's what this biography has been repeatedly doing.

Looking at his words and deeds gives us a credible way of piecing together his motivations and the projection of his thoughts.

If there is one thing that you cannot disagree with, it is that Musk has a vivid imagination. Even if this was fired up by all the comics he read and TV he watched. Don't mock it because some of the greatest ideas and inventions came from fiction writers like Isaac Asimov. As an integrated society coming ever closer to each other with the prevalence of technology, Musk sits at the juxtaposition of two worlds. A world where his imagination was stirred by the greatest dreamers of our time when we were kids, and he brings that along and converts it into our reality. I for one am grateful that all the things I saw as a kid on TV are getting built in reality in my generation. And we have Musk to thank for that.

The other side of the equation is that Musk's own imagination is now poised to field the imagination of the generation that is sitting in front of their TV (or iPhone) watching the launch of the Falcon Heavy and, as those rockets ignite, so do the minds of millions of kids around the world. Hats off to someone like Musk for doing that. We would not have been able to if there wasn't someone like Musk who could take whatever had happened in his life and then keep moving. We needed someone to not be distracted by the everyday distractions that cross our path every hour, every minute and, sometimes every second.

He started young and at the age of 12 wrote and sold his first computer game for $500. I am not going to try to put that into perspective but, just to say that, if you remove the quantum of the payoff and the fact that he was twelve, you are left with the fact that Musk was in this game when computers were just starting to make it into the mainstream. It was 1984 and not everybody knew what computers did or how to use them, and this person got over all that and made some money accomplishing something in a new industry. That's an accomplishment for anyone at any age.

Then he went on to run a number of small businesses in the dorms by making and upgrading computers and game boxes – not much of a big deal there but still, most of the kids I knew in college just went to school and spent their time hanging out.

Then came the time that he was making money on campus at Penn by doing parties and charging a five-buck cover. He and his partner made enough in one night to cover rent for a month. Calling it enterprising doesn't seem to cover it.

Then came the big ideas. He came out and did Zip2 while he was at Stamford – which he left after a short while then roped his brother into the software ideas he was working on. If you haven't Googled it already, Zip2 is a kind of a directory that visualizes the advertiser on a map. It is something like what Google Maps does. It's just that this was a year ahead of Google. Google started their search business in 1998 and didn't bring on their Google Maps till much later. But the idea of Google Maps was pretty much something that resembled Zip2.

His next idea was X.com, and we know that became PayPal, and we know how that ended and then that gave rise to Space X and Tesla. These companies, as much as they are a hit today, had their share of teething pains when they first started. The headaches that they caused were no small matter. It affected Musk at a deep and psychological level, and he just couldn't bring himself to accept defeat. But before that, he had already started investing in other endeavors. While he was at the tail end of PayPal, he invested in a company that was founded by his childhood buddy and cousin, Lyndon Rive. That company, Everdream Corp, sold to Dell and Musk made some profit from that sale.

In the same fashion, he invested in a satellite company while he was in the midst of building Space X. The synergy was obvious and he wanted to make sure that he also had a client in the area that would one day be able to use Space X's services. He was made a director of the company, which he eventually left to focus on his other more urgent businesses.

He then invested and promoted Solar X, which is still ongoing and looks to revolutionize the way we harvest and distribute energy. He has changed not just the infrastructure and the source of energy, but the architecture of the distributions and consumption of it. This is a holistic reinvention of the way we see and use power.

But his investments and his smaller involvements that we know about splashed on newspapers and online are not the extent of his entrepreneurial endeavors. There are more to come and, with the well-known endeavors as a backdrop and the new endeavors as a guide; you start to see where he wants to take the world.

Space X itself is seen as a rocket company. But don't get confused with the blast offs and the launch of the Roadster into space. I admit my experience with the live telecast distracted me away from the true jewel that this is. While most of the hardware is off the shelf, and the additional hardware that went on top of it was purpose-built, the software coordinating the whole thing and the software running the individual systems was built from scratch.

He has, of course, mooted the Hyperloop and he has taken positions with PayPal's competitor, Stripe. He has also made a number of investments in AI companies and, according to him, the investment is not for profit sake but rather to keep an eye on the progress of AI. There is something about AI that really spooks Musk, and he has been warning everyone around him that AI is the doom of the world. That is not unexpected really because, if you've been paying attention, the way it has developed has been on the back of TV programs and movies. When you look at the way movies have viewed AI and the takeover of the world, you can imagine what's fueling his imagination.

That brings me to the bulk of his drive and passion.

The future according to Musk, is really the future that luminaries like Carl Sagan and Isaac Asimov have imagined. This avid reader has taken the imagination of those men and made something of it. So, let's give credit where credit is due.

While Musk is not the visionary that everyone thinks he is, he certainly has the drive to make things happen. We need all kinds in this world. Think about the atom bomb, for instance. It was based on Einstein's equation – the idea and the theory – but the bomb itself was built by a different group of people. Think about Apple. The computer itself was built by Woz, but Jobs was the one that pushed it to success. There are many kinds of success and, if we really want to find the string that vibrates in each, then we have to speak the truth of what it is that makes them succeed. If you are a fan of Musk, but you are looking for that original idea, then you are in the wrong shoes.

The best thing that you can take from Musk's experience depends on two things. The first depends on your own personal situation, and the second is the way you choose to see the accomplishments Musk has made in the course of the last twenty years, and beyond.

Musk is undoubtedly a complex character. And I urge you to not fault his weakness but to spend your energy understanding them so that you can sidestep those same mistakes.

Soon after his payday from the Zip2 deal, aside from the F1 that he purchased, he also bought a single-engine aircraft, no doubt prompted by the ghosts of his memories and imagination kindled by the stories of Grandpa Haldeman.

It took him close to six months to get the license, and that's not because getting a single-engine Airplane Private Pilot's license is the hardest thing in the world, but because he had to spend time doing so many things in the wake of the Zip2 transaction.

But his enthusiasm to fly is not one that is in passing. He does see himself being able to pilot the vehicle to Mars one day and he does see himself dying on Mars sometime in the future – just not at the same time.

The vision for Mars that he has is one that is not only deeply-seated, but one that comes naturally to him. There are certain things that you come across in life that you just know you will do or accomplish. There are certain things I know with such certainty in my life that I don't worry about whether it is going to happen; I just get impatient that today was not the day that it happened. Musk is the same way

– we are all for a different number of things. For Bill Clinton, he knew on the day he shook JFK's hand that he would one day be President. For Einstein, he knew one day he would build a life around a world deciphering the secrets of the Universe, unlike his father's direction to be an engineer and to make a living. For Edison, he knew that the light bulb, and so many other inventions, were just a matter of time. In the same way, Musk knows with certainty that walking on Mars is in his future and, because of that, we can also know with confidence that our species landing on Mars is in our future as well.

That is the real value of Musk in our society; he raises all up to a point that we can only imagine. His dreams are the dreams of a nation, of a planet, and of this species. I know, sitting and watching the launch of Falcon Heavy, that it dawned on me that I had been waiting for this moment for such a long time – in fact, I had given up on it because no one was doing it. Sure, there was talk of it from Branson's Virgin Galactic. Sure, there was talk from Bezos's Blue Origin, but that was all talk, conjecture, and trials. This was real.

Watching Falcon Heavy blast into space with such apparent ease, experiencing the exhilaration of the people on the ground as the mighty rocket lifted effortlessly into space and released its payload was just a childish sense of excitement that I have not felt since my dad took us to the screening of the first Star Wars installment.

Musk made all that come to life. And for that I am grateful.

There is much we can learn for the life that Musk has led. There is much that we can observe in the decisions and in the mistakes he has made. The one that is most obvious is that anybody can be whatever they dream of as long as they are willing to never give up.

Conclusion

"I would like to die on Mars. Just not on impact."

– Elon Musk

There is a long list of men and women who have risen to the surface of the world's collective consciousness and appreciation. In the generation before mine, it was people like JP Morgan, Thomas Edison, Marie Curie, and Albert Einstein. In this generation, the pinnacle is populated by the likes of Bill Gates, Steve Jobs, Stephen Hawking, and Elon Musk.

I find tremendous inspiration looking at the men in this generation that have moved mountains aside and brought planets closer. I have looked at the lives and accomplishments of men like Sir Richard Branson, Steve Jobs, Bill Gates, and a number of others and find that all these men have similar DNA when it comes to key areas. The most common of all is that these men are unrelenting in their pursuit and unyielding in the realization of their dream.

Musk is at the top of that list. He came to North American shores with a dream and a couple of hundred dollars, with no one that he could rely on and no one he could spend the night with. He pushed his way out of a repressive society under a racist regime and focused on the area that best suited what he wanted to do, then did not give up. How many of us can say they pursued their dreams across the horizon? How many of us can say that we never took no for an answer?

To the common eye, Musk is obsessive in his pursuit. For anyone to be successful, that is a prerequisite. Jobs was the same way. Musk, however, has labored to portray his life in a manner that is choreographed and precise. It follows from a choreography that started with his relationships, his aspirations, the resulting achievements, and the lifestyle. All of it is highly planned and executed, and the ones that don't fit in are altered or enhanced. Like Justine's and Tallulah's hair color.

You wouldn't think it, but Musk is indeed a master of illusions. He is a genius at making things happen, but then there are the details of his imagination that, when they do not appear, causes him to go through the trouble of airbrushing when he can. But I have to give him a lot of credit for that because this is a man that sees an image in his head and is relentless at seeing it get done. He's like Arnold Schwarzenegger in that way. Schwarzenegger had a vision of what his body should look like back in the day when he was a bodybuilder and he would relentlessly pursue it regardless of how much it hurt or whatever the pain entailed.

Musk did the same thing. He didn't just get into that furnace – in what must have felt like the depths of hell – and work at it, but he had a vision that he was working toward and he pulled it off.

The loyalty to the image you have in your head is what makes a man accomplish what he needs to accomplish. That is the first rule, ahead of all rules. Anything less renders the vision as a fantasy and nothing more.

Musk took a huge risk in moving himself from Pretoria to Canada; he took a huge risk in traveling across the country looking for relatives, and he took huge risks in investing in space and automobile technologies.

But risk to a man in that space is not the same as the risk to a man that is not bound for success. The path to success is not carved by the knife of chance; it is paved by the lessons of mistakes.

Most of you see risk as something to mitigate. By looking at risk as inevitable, you see the inevitability of failure. For those who succeed, be it Jobs or Musk, Gates or Jack Ma, success is inevitable. The risk they take is not the risk you fathom. To them, it is just a path that can be overcome with relentless effort and a keen mind for observation. You don't need to be extra smart or have an IQ of 180. You must be willing to learn and willing to make mistakes and pull yourself back up.

Musk is not someone who has had success after success and not tasted failure. That is furthest from the truth. There have been times that he has made mistakes and there are times that he failed. Take the company that he invested in and was quite gung-ho about. It was a company that was trying to perfect human genome sequencing. It was a company where you'd walk up to them, give them a sample of your blood, wait ten minutes and they would give you a detailed readout of your genetic sequence. Sounds simple enough but Musk couldn't make it work and, with the times he knows that it is not about the effort, he knows when to fold.

'To thine own self be true,' says the master of literature, William Shakespeare. I find that whatever his characteristics and whatever his flaws the one thing that Musk has always been clear about, regardless of what words he uses to express it, is that he has always been true to himself. He understands his needs, his dreams, and he understands the resources that he has within him to make the leap from not having something to make it materialize.

All his decisions were made along these principles and he knew how to be true to himself. It's just one less distraction to deal with when you know that you want to see your rocket take flight, but you don't have the design to do it. Instead of forcing something to work that doesn't, he found the path to making it a reality by besting the old designs. Putting together the Falcon and Dragon designs based on existing hardware but cutting down on areas that were unnecessary and supplementing it with software, made the rockets lift more into space for less, in terms of resources and propellant. It may be a large carbon footprint, but his computations and design ideas made that footprint 70% less than what it would have been for the same payload.

Musk isn't this generation's Edison, just as Einstein wasn't the last generation's Newton. They were two different men thrust into two different times, with two different environments who accomplished two very different accomplishments. We have proven that we couldn't do without Edison's creations, just as history will prove in a few hundred years that we wouldn't have made it without Musk's current efforts. His fear that we are running out of time in terms of the environmental degradation will work to humanity's eventual benefit. If it wasn't for his fears that the rest of us seem so oblivious to, we might just be faced with not having the necessary lifeline that gives our species a way to extend our existence without perishing under the burden of a rapidly changing environment. His notion to terraform Mars and to create a viable means to transport society there will be the lifeline we need in times to come.

I wish him Godspeed!

Steve Jobs: The Man Behind the Bitten Apple

Steve Jobs: The Man Behind the Bitten Apple

Insight into the Thoughts and Actions of Apple's Founder

JR MacGregor

Steve Jobs: The Man Behind the Bitten Apple

Insight into the Thoughts and Actions of Apple's Founder

Published by CAC Publishing LLC.

ISBN 978-1-948489-84-3 paperback

ISBN 978-1-948489-83-6 eBook

This book is dedicated to those of us who use Apple products daily and who have been impacted by the technological genius that was Steve Jobs.

Preface

We read biographies to learn about ourselves, not to pay homage to the subject. We study how others have tackled this world we live in so that we can make some sense of the curve balls thrown at us and of the failures of our own ambitions to take off. At other times, we reach out to biographies for inspiration and direction. The reasons we seek out the illumination of a soul that has passed before us are as varied as the lives we lead. What matters is not the reason we come to the table, but that we come at all.

If there is only one person you read about in your life, it should be this man, Steven Paul Jobs. If you haven't yet read anything about him, this book will serve as a good place to start; if you have already read about him, then this book will guide you toward a deeper insight.

This book is not about the who, the where, and the why. It's not about the how Steve Jobs was born, what school he went to, or the particularities of his life. A lot of that information is freely available on the Internet.

Instead, this book is about the leadership skills that Steve Jobs had, and the game he played and showed the rest of us how to play. This book should give you insights you can take away from looking at what made Steve Jobs unique, insights that will help you to blow up your own corner of the world.

Introduction

"I want to put a ding in the universe."

Steve Jobs

Think of Steve Jobs and the ubiquitous bitten apple comes to mind. Think of the Apple Computer, the iPhone, or the iPad, and the larger-than-life Steve Jobs comes to mind. They are indeed inseparable in the collective mind of this generation.

This book cuts through the hyperbole and anecdotes to find the true spirit of a man who captured the imagination of a nation through the vision he left behind, and who redefined the world in a variety of ways for different people. For the man on the street, Jobs redefined expectations of consumer electronics by bringing superior designs and intuitive user interface standards to the market and making those the norm. As a business professional, he demonstrated the unique ability to see things from both the macro perspective and the micro perspective.

There are a lot of misunderstandings about the way that Jobs did things, and many expectations directed toward him because of the myth that rose up around him. Steve Jobs may have looked and acted like a regular guy who sometimes walked bare foot in the conference room or bare foot on the grass outside, but to judge him by the standards of a regular guy would be a mistake. On a closer look, Steve Jobs was anything but a 'regular guy.' While he may have been humble and reverent, he was an exceptional man.

Studying the great men of history, you find that no two are alike in their achievement, but all of them have one thing in common – their inspiration is more than what the brain can ordinarily conjure. Their inspiration is almost divine, from Einstein's black holes, to Alexander the Great's ability to battle and bring communities together, from Newton's understanding of gravity, to Ford's assembly line that revolutionized personal transport.

To understand the workings of Steve Jobs' mind, you need to look at each individual aspect of his actions and trace the threads as they manifest through who he was, weaving together to form the person of Steve Jobs. I've tried to condense the observations I've made about this man's life, the movements he sparked, and the ideas he spread, and attempted to prioritize them in a way that will not only help you, the reader but will also pay homage to the man we are seeking to understand better.

To start with, Jobs had the ability to achieve such a deep focus that nothing else going on around him could penetrate the wall around his mind and attention. It wasn't until he finished what he was doing mentally that he would emerge to give his time to whomever or whatever demanded his attention in the outside world. He wasn't being arrogant when he stood silent as someone tried to engage him, he was just not present while he worked things out inside his own mind.

Steve Jobs is a giant among men not just because he created the world's most valuable company (by market capitalization), but also because he raised the standards of what we expected things to be and changed the way we did things. If you think of Steve Jobs just as a man who built computers, you'd be wrong. If you think commercialized computers, you'd be right, but you still wouldn't have encapsulated his contribution to this world. It isn't until you realize that Steve Jobs' contribution spanned across technology, entertainment, design, functionality, publishing, music, and hardware that you will begin to gain an insight into the expansive way his mind operated.

Because of Steve Jobs' influence, there is more to Apple than a computer, or a tablet, or a phone.

Apple is about the way we, as humans, interact with technology, and how the standards Jobs established help us to conquer that technology to do things for us – without the frustration and intimidation that lesser products often produce.

Steve Jobs wasn't just an innovator. He was also an inspiration for those who want to break out of the mold of mediocrity. Some would argue that Steve Jobs' effect on those around him was the consequence and natural unfolding of his perfectionism. But it's never just one thing that drives a person. There is always a balance of forces that makes the actions of a man speak only of him for that moment in time. Once that moment passes, the man himself changes, and becomes a new man in a new moment.

The final analysis of a man should not be one that points to the aggregate of his actions to arrive at a mathematical average of his contribution. How could that be fair or accurate? Instead, the true measure of the man, a measure that excludes bias and envy, should be formed on the trajectory and intention demonstrated over the course of his life, giving weight to the areas of his life that touched the life of others. When you look at Steve from that perspective, what you find is a man who did not start off as someone who wanted to change the world, but as someone who wanted to have an impact in whatever way he knew how.

For those who think of Steve Jobs as a hardware genius, I hate to tell you this, he wasn't. For those of you who think that he was a software genius, I hate to tell you as well – he wasn't. He didn't invent the Internet like Sir Tim, he didn't create an operating system, and he didn't create anything physically tangible.

What he did do was to rethink the way we did things, how we saw things, and the standards we use to experience things. Steve Jobs took the computer from something that was, until then, a big, clunky machine for office and professional use, and had Woz redesign it for personal use. It was Woz that was the technical brains behind Steve Jobs. iTunes was born in response to Apple being left out of the music revolution when music was still just the ability to play a CD on a personal computer. Rather than falling behind and screaming "Me Too," Jobs didn't just install a CD player/burner on the Mac. Instead, he created iTunes so that all the music you wanted could be shared between devices, and there would be no need to burn the disk and play it on something else. It was an elegant solution to a growing problem.

When Jobs saw the invention of the mouse and the ability to use a GUI (Graphical User Interface) to operate a computer, he latched on to it to make the computer more user friendly. He took existing ideas and made them better and cheaper so that the man on the street could use those advances in technology. Jobs didn't invent any of these things – he just made them so that we could use them. He made it so that you and I, not just scientists in lab coats, could use them, and we didn't need to sell the farm to get one.

Steve Jobs made things relatable; he made things so that they would make sense to us. So, in a way, he may as well have been the inventor behind many of the things that have changed our lives, because he was able to look at those things and simplify them to make them relatable.

Jobs' idea of simplicity was not about dumbing things down. He didn't have a disparaging view of society; he had an appreciation - the kind an artist has while still seeking to elevate what the audience experiences. For Jobs, simplicity was not about shunning things that were not simple, it was about conquering complexity. To master complexity, you have to face it and tame it. The lion tamer doesn't exchange his whip and chair for a gun to destroy the lion, nor does he trade his lion for a cat to avoid the challenge. Instead, the lion tamer learns how to master the lion, just as Steve Jobs mastered the complexity of existing technologies for us.

Jobs' idea of simplicity didn't arise from being a simple man. Quite the contrary, Jobs was a complex individual, with complex thought processes, who was able to simplify the complex.

Chapter 1 Focus

"We don't get a chance to do that many things, and everyone should be really excellent. Because this is our life. Life is brief, and then you die, you know? So this is what we've chosen to do with our life."

Steve Jobs

Steve Jobs began a life not much different than most of us are presented with when we first gain a conscious appreciation of the world around us. Steve Jobs considered his adoptive parents, Clara and Paul Jobs, to be his only parents. He hardly acknowledged his biological parents who conceived him out of wedlock. They had given him up for adoption at birth due to the strict catholic views of his maternal grandparents.

Steve Jobs' rise to greatness can be attributed to his ability to focus and weed out distractions. During his early years, Jobs faced challenges with controlling his thoughts. To understand the level of focus that Jobs was ultimately able to achieve, you need to look toward his background in meditation and the lengths he went to in order to develop his ability to focus.

Many who are creative and driven tend to have a multitude of voices in their heads, pulling them in many different directions, making them want to do many things at the same time. These are the folks that have some of the best abilities to multi-task, but that ability is an illusion. Multi-tasking can seem superhuman in the beginning, but over time it wears you down and it causes you to be less than effective.

Steve Jobs was so filled with ideas and thoughts of his 'destiny' and mark on the world that his mind was a noisy place. To combat this, Jobs sought out ways to help him bring these thoughts under control. Jobs was not crazy, though some people equate having thoughts running in different directions as craziness. Nor, on the other extreme, was he superhuman, although he eventually became capable of an intense level of focus that almost seems superhuman.

Like Jobs, most people who are highly successful seem able to focus to the point of not being mentally present in the space they occupy physically. The ability to focus on one matter at a time and to be inspired by what is at hand is something that escapes most of us because we are not, consciously or subconsciously, able to be comfortable in the moment we occupy. There is always some form of distraction that becomes the excuse to move away from what we have otherwise deemed important.

There are two main things that cause distractions in our mind, and Jobs certainly battled at least one of these, although which one is not totally clear. The first are the competing thoughts that distract from other thoughts. This is common to many intelligent and creative people. There are many instances that seem to provide evidence that this was Jobs' issue. From his early days, he had so many competing thoughts that he struggled to find the path he so desperately needed.

This type of distraction usually occurs when you have an inspiration concerning something you are working on, and, as that thought develops, you become immersed in it and start to expand on it. That all works great until you get another great thought, and then you have two thoughts competing for your attention. This eventually becomes an avalanche of distraction. This type of distraction can typically be straightened out by the power of meditation. The key is to know that it is a distraction.

California in the seventies had a growing counter culture with a lot of talk about meditation and experimenting with drugs that took the mind to different states of consciousness. The era influenced several great thinkers, including Richard Alpert, who experimented with LSD and the power of meditation and transcendence. Richard Alpert, later known as Ram Dass, wrote *Be Here Now* about his travels in India and his discovery of life, meditation, and the inspiration of the soul. The book would become a beacon and guiding light for the young Steve Jobs who was looking to make sense of his divergent and competing thoughts.

When Steve Jobs was 19, he travelled to India, on a quest to meet with a Hindu guru named Maharaji, the same guru who had inspired and taught Ram Dass, the author of *Be Here Now*. The meeting never took place, but it was during that trip that Jobs would find the spark that eventually grew into a flame, becoming the source of his wisdom, the inspiration of his genius, and the foundation of his art.

Jobs ultimately embraced Buddhism more than Hinduism. In fact, Steve Jobs and his wife were married in a Buddhist ceremony, and his practice of meditation and Zen were more based on Buddhist principles and teachings.

In a sense, it is possible to see, in the way Jobs approached the tangible things of life, an integration of the power of that mindfulness and meditation into everyday high technology. This does not come from mere tinkering, only from being truly inspired. His designs, be it the iPhone or the iPad, were works of absolute sophistication.

Most importantly, meditation and mindfulness helped Jobs achieve a level of focus unlike any he had previously experienced in his life, and formed the basis for his ability to focus in on his thoughts and cut out the noise. He continued to develop this further as he got older and practiced it increasingly.

Ultimately, one of Steve Jobs' core skills was his ability to focus on exactly what was necessary, chiseling away and discarding everything else. I once heard him speak shortly after returning to lead Apple. The company was still in the mess it had found itself in during Jobs' absence, and people were regularly asking Jobs why Apple had stopped doing particular products and why they were not moving forward with certain areas of the business. The simple answer from Jobs was that focus is about saying no. Hearing that changed something deep within me.

"Focus is the ability to say no." Now think about that for a minute. Jobs was absolutely right. Our minds are built in such a way that we get random inspiration from every direction, by association, by triggers, by seeing something. Ideas pop into your head from everywhere, all the time.

And it's not just the thoughts that pop into your head, there are a myriad of other distractions that present themselves to us, especially today, with tweets, updates, and Instagram photos. Everything is beeping and buzzing away at your hand-held device or your tablet. Messages and phone calls come in, and there are ever more distractions at all hours of the day, at work, at home, even while you sleep. The only way to actually get something done is to say no.

Jobs developed the ability to look at things in strategic way and consider whether "the total was less than the sum of the parts." That was one of his engines of focus. When he looked at something and the yield was less than the vision, he would drop it. Many of the ideas pursued by the capable engineers at Apple, in the early days or during Jobs' absence from the company, were quickly axed when they didn't pass this test because of the quality of focus Jobs had developed over time.

Steve Jobs was a man who understood the difference between what is important and what seems urgent. Whether it's a distraction or an opportunity, if your plate is already full, the ability to say no is the foundation of your ability to focus.

Chapter 2 Taking Responsibility

"And no, we don't know where it will lead. We just know there's something much bigger than any of us here."

Steve Jobs

Steve Jobs possessed a unique characteristic above and beyond many in the same category, whether in Silicon Valley or among entrepreneurs generally, in wanting to take responsibility for more than what people were asking of him. When he looked at the interaction between his consumer and his product, he saw something that most designers or CEOs still don't fully appreciate. He saw the user experience in an atypical way from other industrial engineers. Rather than just simplifying something, he wanted the result to be a seamless integration. That kind of mindset set the stage for products that rolled out almost seamlessly and performed better than anyone ever expected.

Jobs believed that there shouldn't be a distinguishing demarcation between where the user's hand ended and the Apple product began. He knew that to be able to make everything simple, every single product they offered needed to integrate forward, backward, and sideways, in every way possible that so a user could pick up any one of his Apple products, put it down, and then pick-up another without changing one speck of his life. This is one of the reasons why your Mac can be your base station while your iPod plays your music. When they developed iTunes, the whole idea was to have these hardware devices be on the go. That idea revolutionized the way we saw hardware, and it created a new demand on the way we stored our content. It changed the face of functionality.

For this approach to work, and for the hardware to integrate seamlessly, Steve Jobs had to take end-to-end responsibility. Which he did. Not only did he take on all of the design and aesthetics, he went in deeper to understand how he could bring all the hardware elements together and tie them up, so that, at the touch of a button, everything was laid out for the user to experience. Due to Steve Jobs' vision, I can now whip out my iPhone and continue watching the movie I left off yesterday on my Apple TV. Because of his ideas, I can upload my documents from my iPhone, and then go onto my MacBook and retrieve them. The seamless integration of the different pieces of hardware was the direct result of Steve Jobs' refusal to accept less when he took on the responsibility for what he designed.

Steve Jobs wasn't looking at what he did from the perspective of profit. Profits were not his guiding motivation. Instead, he took end-to-end responsibility for the user's experience, and that would eventually make Apple one of the most profitable, wealthiest and largest companies on the face of this planet. Steve Jobs was playing the infinite game.

In the analysis of finite and infinite games, there are two kinds of leaders. One leader goes from quarter to quarter, jumping on every technological advance their competitors make. The other takes his company, regardless of what everyone else is doing, and moves forward. From only one perspective does the infinite player move - and that is the quest for an unprecedented standard of perfection. In the case of Steve Jobs, his focus was on the consumer and how to make lives better. In the infinite game Steve Jobs played, he did not follow the rules others played by when they followed the profits from quarter to quarter. When Jobs saw a technology that he didn't have, he didn't simply copy what others already had. Instead, he went the one step further.

When the Mac came out, it didn't come with a CD drive. So, when everyone else had CD drives, the Mac was left out of that game. Jobs was completely baffled that he had not seen it. But he didn't just decide that the next version of the Mac would come with a CD-ROM so that people could burn music and take it with them. Instead, he decided to give them the seamless integration that would eventually become iTunes. With that, he put Apple back out in front again, and, in so doing, he revolutionized the industry. No longer did you need to burn a CD or copy your music to a portable media player to take your music with you. All you needed was a strong and stable Internet connection to be able to automatically synchronize all your devices.

That was how Steve Jobs responded to a situation where he felt left behind. He didn't just jump in line and copy others. It would have been the easiest thing in the world to go to his vendors and ask them to design a CD-ROM to fit the Mac platform. Instead, he revolutionized the music and movie industry by taking responsibility from end-to-end for the user experience. That reveals a man who viewed his space in this world differently than the way an average person views theirs.

Ultimately, Jobs strove to take responsibility in all aspects and at all stages of everything he touched, from start to finish. He didn't just want to come in in the middle, do a small part, and take the credit. One of the things Jobs was very proud of was that Apple controlled both the hardware and the software. Neither was licensed out to intermediate vendors to do with as they wanted around the software; people could not just pick the hardware and install any software or operating system they wanted. Jobs provided an end-to-end solution and stood as a guarantee to say, "*this will work, and if it doesn't I will fix it.*"

There would be no passing of the buck when a problem arose. Hardware vendors didn't have the opportunity to blame it on a software problem, and the software guys could not pass it off as a hardware problem. When you take responsibility, the only promise is that it works, no excuses.

When I try to look at my own life through the lens of how Steve Jobs looked at his, I don't find myself wanting to copy his life and what he did. I don't want to go out and make the next iPad or build the next Apple. What his example does make me want to do is to take stock of the way I do things in my own corner of the world. His example causes me to reflect on the way that I see and analyze things and what I prioritize. Do I tie my goals together in a harmonious way? Or do I prioritize my goals just to get a higher quarterly result?

This is a man that took over the responsibility of being able to provide the simplicity and the functionality of the products that he saw lacking. He decided early on that if he could do this, the profits would follow, but if he chased after the profits, all this would sink. He was right. Once while Steve Jobs was out of Apple for a time and the company was run like any other Fortune 500 company, chasing the bottom line from one quarter to the next, Apple fell. It took the return of Steve Jobs to the company he founded to turn it around, back to his original vision. Now, Apple continues to follow that vision, years after Jobs has passed on.

Chapter 3 Simplify

"I'm an optimist in the sense that I believe humans are noble and honorable, and some of them are really smart. I have a very optimistic view of individuals."

Steve Jobs

If focus was Steve Jobs' blueprint, then simplicity was his path. His brand of simplicity is unlike anything I've encountered in the other great men I've studied. Everything around Jobs was analyzed down to its most effective components, whittled down to the point where functionality and effectiveness increases substantially.

Most people misunderstand simplicity, particularly Apple's brand of it, as a lack of complexity. There may be some truth in that, but, for Steve Jobs, simplicity was not the avoidance of all things complex. Instead, it was in the conquering of what was complex in his daily life and in the products that he eventually engineered with intuition and emotional sensitivity that you find the ability to create products that intuitively transcended the inherent complexity of technical matters.

If you look at other technology companies, whether it's Dell, Microsoft or Compaq, in each, there is an air of unfamiliarity and unnecessary complexity. It almost represents a foreboding corporate structure that denies the pleasure of simplicity. It really puts the word 'hard' in hardware. With Apple, you don't find that. You see a device that is user-friendly. And because of that, Apple and Steve have been able to transcend, from computers to communication, to smartphones, to movies, to tablets and music.

When my son was three years old, he stood in front of an iPad at the Apple store and looked at it for the first time. He instinctively knew how to tap the home button to activate the device, and soon maneuvered his way around the main menu. It is both a testament to how smart children are these days and to how something as complex as a high-tech device can be designed to overcome unnecessary complexity. That is Steve Jobs' lasting legacy. That is what Apple has grown to embody. And that is what Apple's brand promise has continued to signify.

The common thread that runs through all the things Steve touched is not computers, but rather consumer goods and services enhanced through the use of technology. The intersection of tech and services empowered people to take their efficiencies to the next level. It empowered the consumer to go about their daily lives and to do it in style. People buy iMacs for two reasons: iMacs are powerful enough to sit at home as their base station to play games, download music, and enjoy movies on their stunning screens, and iMacs are attractive because they are aesthetically pleasing. On one hand, Steve Jobs empowered the consumer, while on the other, he put them at ease.

There is a story that makes its rounds on the Apple campus. It seems that when the Macintosh was being designed, one of the designers had included a handle for the top of the computer. Keep in mind that this was a solid piece of desktop machinery. Production engineers cried out at the added manufacturing expense, arguing that it was not worth the price because the handle wouldn't do anything for the computer since the Macintosh was designed to sit on top of a desk and stay there. And, truly, during the time I owned my own Macintosh, it sat on my desk, and I never once moved it until I replaced it. Yet, when Jobs saw that handle, he instantly insisted that the handle remain. He instructed the engineers to do whatever they had to do to make it possible.

What Steve Jobs recognized in that handle was the ability to change the mindset of consumers who, at that time in 1984, looked at computers as something forbidding. Computers, back then, were designed to sit in rooms, like the minicomputers and the supercomputers that had required large dedicated spaces. The mere idea of a computer intimidated people. Adding that handle empowered a person psychologically by communicating that he would be able to lift that computer up and walk away with it. That gave the ordinary person power over the computer.

On the screen and inside the computer, many other changes had also taken place. The computer now had a graphical user interface that allowed regular people to sit down and intuitively click on what they needed. You didn't need a manual to tell you what to do. You could look at it, move the mouse around, and figure out how to get on your way. You could click on it the same way my three-year-old was able to maneuver his way around the iPad the first time he laid eyes on it.

Simplicity is a curious thing. Einstein once said that things should be made as simple as possible, but not simpler. Steve Jobs personified this idea in his life and in his vision.

Simplicity is not about shying away from matters that are complex. It's about conquering complexity. Jobs' practice of simplicity was to tear down anything that didn't make sense or didn't need to be there until he reached the point where it wouldn't benefit from being simplified any further.

We can all find out how to master complexity, but Steve Jobs did it for us by designing products that, while enormously complex in the background, don't seem complex to us at the point of use. You don't need to know how the operating system runs a computer in the background for you to be able to effectively use the computer. When you click to open an app, you don't need to know the list of subroutines that causes the computer to activate, or how the microprocessors bring about other actions. You just need to know that when you click something, it opens, and it's ready for you to use. And this happens seamlessly and intuitively.

During the design process for the iPod, Steve Jobs was in a meeting where they were working on the design of the user interface and the way users would get their music to come up. Already months into it, they had a comparatively complex process where the user had to enter the menu and look for an answer, searching slowly, making his way down through different directories. Despite all the work that had already gone into the development of the iPod, Steve Jobs decided that it wasn't elegant and decided to tear down anything and everything that did not sit well with him. His benchmark was simple – he wanted users to be able to get to the music they wanted to listen to in three steps from wherever they were on the iPod. That was an extremely tall order. But eventually the design process stopped and everyone realized that it was the right thing to aim for.

Jobs even looked at the power button and questioned its existence in his effort to make the iPod more intelligent. The designers were stunned but came to realize that he was right. The on/off button was indeed obsolete, and they designed the iPod without the need to have an on/off button.

I remember my own first iPod and the first time I realized there was no power button. I was flabbergasted because I had been frustrated from all the times I had to turn things on to use them. Eventually, as old habits wore off, I realized how simple life became when you didn't have to turn a device off and it just came back on whenever you picked it up.

Apple has continued to follow that legacy of simplicity in their introduction of new products, especially the new iPhone X. The technology behind the product is of no concern to the consumer. What matters is how it works for them. Apple continues to create products that follow the essence of Steve Jobs' genius of simplifying things for us.

Chapter 4 Drive

"Woz is living his own life now. He hasn't been around Apple for about five years. But what he did will go down in history."

Steve Jobs

No matter what the person's ability to inspire the imagination or their ability to think of solutions, without the drive to lift a finger, none of that intangible thought is going to matter. In Steve Jobs' case, he had the passion and the drive to push things beyond human limits. Steve Jobs certainly wasn't superhuman, but he does show us that the ability to drive one's self is within us all. It just depends how far we are willing to take it. Jobs sought to take it as far as possible.

Each successful person has a different way to energize their own march toward success. Some are driven by profits, some by fame, and some by the simple and pure satisfaction of accomplishment. There are others who just get to work doing what they feel to be their best at that moment, and once they have achieved their best for that goal, they move on to something else. They get up and build a computer. Then they get up to build a phone, and when that phone is done, they move on to build an iPad. When that iPad is done well, they just keep building more things to elevate the human experience. And that was the sort of man that Steve Jobs was.

But what really drove him? What was the force that kept driving him whether in the face of defeat or illness? What was it that drove him toward his goals, and to have one goal after another? How did he fire up his focus or his ability to bend reality?

Steve Jobs, and probably other thought leaders and industry titans, seems to have had an ability to bend the reality of those around them – and thereby bending physical reality for all of us. Jobs was able to shift the sense and perception of reality of his colleagues and business partners by driving them purely on the energy flowing from his words. Jobs screamed at, tormented, and pushed his workers and colleagues even to the point of exhaustion. His colleagues called it the "Reality Distortion Field."

It was widely known on the Apple campus that Jobs could literally warp the reality around him. The phrase "Reality Distortion Field" used to describe Jobs' ability to alter average reality was taken from the Sci-Fi show Star Trek. (All the engineers and people who work at Apple, including Steve Jobs, are, to a certain extent, geeks.) This reality distortion field was pretty much an ongoing thing that altered the way you would see things. It could be argued that Jobs had the same effect on the rest of the world too. Before, there were no sleek lines; there were no iPads. Jobs changed our reality. He distorted it, and, now, because of him, we demand a different kind of product instead of the old boxes. And we demand integrated solutions that complete our lives seamlessly.

There is a well-known story from the period when Steve Jobs was still with Atari, according to which his boss told him that if he could redesign one of the Atari products and simplify it using fewer parts so that it would cost less to make, Jobs would get a bonus. Jobs accepted the challenge and went to Steve Wozniak – the one with the technical brains behind the operation – and told Wozniak that if he could do this task there would be a bonus for the both of them. Jobs didn't mention the actual value of the bonus and told Wozniak that it was only a four-day deadline. Wozniak was certain he could never comply. In Wozniak's mind, the task would take a month, at the least, if not more. But Jobs jumped into his reality distortion mode and got Wozniak to sit down and focus. Low and behold, in just four days, Wozniak had managed to create a simpler version of Atari's hardware. Jobs had cut 26 days from Wozniak's original belief of how long it would take. That's some serious reality distortion and it is something that really works.

Steve Jobs' ability to change reality was a function of his enthusiasm, his sense of purpose, and his believability. Combined, they formed a formidable triumvirate of credibility that caused others to believe what they once could not. That kind of ability only comes when you have the belief yourself.

That ability to bend reality was something that Jobs applied to all situations, and often at Apple. Did he know a different reality, or did he deliberately distort the sense of reality to get others to follow? I'm convinced that it wasn't that he was deliberately distorting others' reality, it was that his own mental experience of reality was actually different.

I notice this same ability in the minds of other movers and shakers. I see it in the minds of up and coming entrepreneurs. I see it in thought leaders and product innovators. And it is different than what we see in the general population who are more followers than innovators. The thought leaders who can alter reality become the people we rely on to make our lives better and improve our tomorrows. These are the people that stand out as the finest examples of what humanity has to offer.

Steve Jobs was different from everybody else. If it weren't for his ability to bend reality and his ability to drive his staff, he would have been just another regular guy. But every single person who stood in the shadow of the Apple campus – everyone that had been in some way pushed and prodded and yelled at, even ones who left under less than perfect circumstances – would stand up to say that they were better off because of him, that they were able to produce a better quality product because of him.

As I look at Steve Jobs' life, I find myself asking, "What drives me?" The answers I come up with suggest that my life is as mediocre as the next person's because I keep doing what everybody else is doing. And yet my days are filled. To step out of a mundane existence of achieving small goals in small-minded ways requires a decision – a decision to change one's perspective on one's own life. To change what you can accomplish, to change what you want to accomplish is always based on a decision.

Steve Jobs decided early in his career that he was going to touch the lives of others by improving it in any way he knew how. That thought predated his viewing of Steve Wozniak's microcomputer – the circuit board that launched everything. Jobs already knew that he wanted to do something. He just didn't know what it was going to be. That's the reason he could jump from personal computer to cell phone, from hardware to software, from communication to entertainment. None of these, before Steve Jobs, had anything in common.

It wasn't until Apple that everybody realized the possibility of integrating hardware and software. Even Microsoft was purely an operating systems company before it went on to other software. Steve Jobs was criticized for not allowing the OS (Operating System) to be licensed on any other device built by third parties in the way Windows was. Although Windows is in 90% of the world's machines, Microsoft doesn’t make 90% of the world's machines. Instead, Microsoft focused only on the operating system and licensed it out to whoever wanted it.

Microsoft was not in it for the experience; they were in it to expand their bottom line. They didn't look at the consumer as a person; they saw the consumer as a contributor to their bottom line. Steve Jobs looked at his consumer as a person who would have an experience with his product, and he wanted to take end-to-end responsibility for that. To do that, Jobs had to alter and reshape everyone else's reality through the sheer force of his drive.

Chapter 5 To Hell with Profits

"What we want to do is make a leapfrog product that is way smarter than any mobile device has ever been, and super-easy to use. This is what iPhone is. OK? So, we're going to reinvent the phone."

Steve Jobs

Steve Jobs' drive to focus on the product and make it work for the consumer meant that profits were not his first motive. Profits would come to Apple if they kept to his vision.

During the period that Steve Jobs left Apple, Apple tried the usual way of doing things, running Apple the way Fortune 500 companies are run, based on quarterly profits and annual targets, using the benchmarks used by every Fortune 500 company. Since they all used them, it had to be right. Right? But that didn't work for Apple.

Apple proved that it didn't work that way, and it began to fail. Steve Jobs had to come back to help his company grow again. And he did. He turned it around by bringing back his brand of focus, his brand of taking responsibility, and by simplifying matters. He drove his people to achieve perfection, and he said, "To hell with profits."

Whether at Apple or Pixar or anywhere else, the effect Steve Jobs had on those who worked with him or took direction from him can only be described as frustration. Regardless of the location, Steve was never known to be the easy on the people that worked on his products. It wasn't just the constant demands on their time or on their mental strength, it was also the fact that every time a project they were working on had advanced to the stated goal, Jobs would step in and take everything back to the drawing board. Jobs would feel that something had gone askew somewhere along the line, and he would not be able to accept it. That was just what he was like. It happened at Pixar during the making of Toy Story, it happened while designing the iPad, and it happened with the iPhone.

Every product that came out of Job's involvement faced this point of inflection. This was what would push him – his quest for perfection. Job's standards of perfection were beyond what anyone else could dream of coming close to.

One of these moments came during the development of the iPhone. The idea for the tablet had come first, and Steve Jobs' team had already begun developing the iPad when the idea to push the iPhone took priority. So, they put the iPad back on the shelf and redirected their resources toward developing the iPhone.

The iPhone was to be a game changer. It was designed to transform the way we interact with our cell phones, change how we see the entire experience, and change the relationship we have with our cellphones. The vision that Jobs had for the iPhone was extremely ambitious.

The iPhone was to change how we communicate by voice and text as well as how we interact with the Internet, and so the physical object - the tangibles – needed to symbolize the intangible. It was the herald of a new age, and so it was not going to be cast in plastic. It was set in an aluminum case and covered with glass.

One morning, during the late stages of design, Jobs put a stop to the process. He hadn't been able to sleep the night before because the design suddenly wasn't sitting well with him. There was too much aluminum case and too little glass. Instead of showcasing the phone, they were showcasing the case. Jobs wanted to turn that whole thing around. So, the designers of the iPhone and Jobs came together and rethought the concept and the aesthetics. It felt impossible because they were already running close to the deadlines to get production underway, but they still went back to the drawing board.

They needed to reduce the masculinity of the phone which had more case and less glass. They needed to get to that tipping point where the masculinity balanced the femininity, so the product would comfortably appeal across the board. As it stood, the aluminum overpowered any sophistication the phone might have had. It looked like an expensive brick, but a brick nonetheless. And so the perfectionist in Steve Jobs, fueled by the desire to connect technology to the human experience, took over and redesigned the phone so that you could look into a window of glass.

It became clear that everyone would need to stay weekends and nights to get the iPhone project back on track. And they did. As much as people complained about how much Steve Jobs demanded of them, they never sat back and declined his call to action. For Steve Jobs, it was one of his proudest moments not only because the product was brought to life, but also because he saw the people who worked at Apple come together as one seamless organization focused on one idea with one inspiration.

When Apple went back and resurrected the concept of the tablet to continue its development,

Steve Jobs repeated the process, demanding perfection when he started to feel less than satisfied with what they had already come up with.

When the iPad came out and I purchased my first one, the thing my little boy noticed was how inviting it was to just grab it. I hadn't noticed that because I, too, would just grab it. One of the reasons why I chose the iPad over anything else was simply because it did not feel overbearing. Instead of using square edges on the iPad, Apple had tapered it. That tapering allows you to slide your fingers and grab it as you go. That made a big difference in the product's acceptability and in how it is used. It wasn't just something you could replace your laptop with. It created a new class of product.

Steve Jobs' genius was to make products that did more than their job; he made products that integrated with human psychology. He wasn't driven to make profits; he was driven to create perfection, and this made our experience better. If we want to emulate Steve Jobs, and change the world the way he did, we need to strive for that sort of perfection, not profits.

Chapter 6 Balance

"This revolution, the information revolution, is a revolution of free energy as well, but of another kind: free intellectual energy. It's very crude today, yet our Macintosh computer takes less power than a 100-watt bulb to run it and it can save you hours a day. What will it be able to do ten or 20 years from now, or 50 years from now?"

Steve Jobs

To many, Steve Jobs would not be considered an embodiment of balance, and, yet, I believe he had the concept of balance mastered, and that he was highly effective because of that. Just because someone is highly focused and excels at what they do doesn't necessarily mean they are out of balance in any way. In fact, I have argued to colleagues and friends for years now that the more balanced you are, the more you can do. Steve Jobs was the embodiment of this very concept - the ability to excel comes from the ability to balance. There are a couple of ways that we can look at this concept of balance.

First, balance is about centering, and focus is all about centering. We have already talked about Jobs' extraordinary ability to focus. To focus, you have to bring all your energies into balance so that you can occupy that single, central focal point that unites everything else. Too much of one thing throws your balance off, putting you too far from something else. Balance is a delicate state requiring the mental fortitude to hold disparate things together. Steve Jobs saw this balance in everything he did.

Jobs knew early on that there was more to this existence of ours than our intellect. He understood the value of meditation and mindfulness. He knew there was more to advancing our existence than achievement over a quarter or over a financial year. There was more to product engineering than refining something that already existed. There would always be a higher plateau to reach and a new horizon to move towards.

The most intriguing aspect of understanding Steve Jobs in terms of balance was his capacity to stand at the juncture of divergent areas, and remain comfortable with opposites and extremes. He could occupy the intersections of science and art, of creativity and engineering, and of humanity and technology. He became the nexus bridging the human experience with the technological revolution. Steve Jobs was our interpreter, and the only way you can be an interpreter is when you understand both sides of the story. You can't interpret something if you don't know half of it. Jobs was able to translate technology into the human experience. His creativity was not limited by science, nor was his scientific understanding limited by his ability to humanize it. This special ability to balance opposite ends of the spectrum elevated Steve Jobs above the pantheon of other successful men.

Although Jobs was at the forefront of technological innovation, he had the balanced perspective to understand that technology could not replace direct human contact, and that two souls collaborating could not be emulated online. Even though he was the creator of and inspiration behind high-tech electronic communication tools like the iPhone and the iPad, with their apps like iChat, Steve Jobs hardly used them himself if he had the option to stand directly in front of the person he needed to speak with. The creator of one of the most ubiquitous communication devices on the planet for this generation preferred to meet someone in person rather than chat or text.

Likewise, when Jobs created workspaces for his employees, he designed them to promote one-on-one meetings and impromptu discussions. When Pixar's new building was designed, Jobs made sure it was designed to promote direct person-to-person collaboration. When he wanted to get Corning to develop the glass screens for the iPhone, he went to talk with the Corning people in person. When he wanted to understand meditation and spirituality, he boarded a plane and travelled to India in person.

The second type of balance Steve Jobs exemplified was the ability to see both the forest and the trees. Most people see either the details or the big picture, but not usually both in a balanced way. Jobs was consistently able to see and balance the big picture with the minutest of details. To understand how rare a talent this is, consider what happens when two people, one who sees the big picture and the other who sees the details, try to collaborate. There are usually huge variations in perspective and objectivity, and often the conversation breaks down. That is the reason CEOs have difficulty speaking to bean counters, and why mid-level managers can't seem to get along with those who work the lines. It is always this breakdown not in communication but in perspective.

When you look at the human experience, we occupy the extremes of the spectrum, micro and macro. Steve Jobs was able to balance and function at both ends, and appreciate both. His balance was the result of repeated practice and an innate desire to look at things from the larger perspectives, to see the broad strokes, while drilling down to the smallest details to understand what he was doing. It is rare to find the capacity to balance both perspectives in one person. Jobs had the broader vision that great kings have but also had the ability to look at the immediate details that great soldiers have.

To conquer the world of business and make it big, we've been advised to see things from a holistic perspective, and we have gone on to think that 'holistic' means 'macro,' to see all things within one large frame. But that sort of overarching, wide-angle perspective tends to hide the details and obscure intricacies in a way that results in problems down the road.

Steve Jobs could develop an iTunes because he saw the transformation of an entire industry from a macro scale perspective. While his urgency may have been fired up by the Mac being left behind with the introduction of CD-ROMs, Steve Jobs' balanced perspective produced a solution that was elegant and shifted the ground under the entire industry and consumers alike. He was able to direct the development of the iPhone, seeing in its intricate features how those would relate to a tactile human experience, and seeing the details that would ensure the overall smoothness of its operation.

***

Chapter 7 The Game Steve Played

"There's no other company that could make a MacBook Air and the reason is that not only do we control the hardware, but we control the operating system. And it is the intimate interaction between the operating system and the hardware that allows us to do that. There is no intimate interaction between Windows and a Dell notebook."

Steve Jobs

As a student of the psychology of success, I frequently analyze the nature of men's actions on their routes to significant achievement and lasting legacy. Sometimes, I begin my analysis during a person's teenage years, as I did with Elon Musk and his rise from middle-class roots in South Africa. In some cases, I look at the beginning of a man's career. I've also looked at the life of someone like

Jeff Bezos beginning when he first got to New York after completing his education at Princeton. I use a variety of different frameworks to try and comprehend the complex actions and the even more complex thought that may have been going on in the minds of my subjects. They may not be completely accurate frameworks, but they come close to placing each person in a context where we can identify their unique ability so that we may cultivate it, and the world can be a better place for it.

In the case of Steve Jobs, the framework I have found most useful to understand my subject is game theory. I don't mean the game theory developed to help us identify optimal situations. I'm talking about the game theory designed to look at men according to the games they play in the work they do – the finite game and the infinite game. If you have read some of my other books, you may have encountered this type of analysis done on other subjects I have observed. For those who aren't familiar with this framework, let me briefly take you through it.

There are only two kinds of games in anything you do. One is the finite game and the other is the infinite game. In a finite game, you play to get to a finish line that is determined in the short term. The only objective is to win – the only object is to vanquish the opponent. The time horizon is short, and it's like playing a game of chess. The whole point of the match is to vanquish the opponent and to do it within the time it takes to complete a certain objective or to run down the clock.

The infinite game is nothing like a finite game because the objective of the infinite game is the exact opposite of the finite. While the finite game is designed with the purpose of winning a limited game, the purpose of the infinite game has nothing to do with winning or losing. The goal of the infinite game is to keep the game going.

For those familiar with the eighty's movie 'War Games,' you may remember that the computer decided to play tic tac toe and to use the same logic in a simulated thermonuclear war. The computer, Joshua, gamed out each scenario according to the strategies available to it, and considered the range of its opponent's possible responses. When you play only one game and the objective is to win, but there is the chance of losing, it is okay to go all out and expend all of your artillery, use all of your strategies, and exhaust all of your supplies in pursuit of that ultimate win. Once you have won or lost, the objective of the game has been reached.

But what happens when the game is not designed to be won, but to continue indefinitely? That is when you have the infinite game.

Finite games are played by finite players. Infinite games are played by infinite players. If only more understood the type of neural wiring they have – whether they are more suited to finite games or to infinite games – you would see more people who are extremely successful because success is not defined by whether you play the finite or the infinite game, but by whether or not you play the game you were built to play.

If a finite player plays an infinite game, he will lose. You can see why. A finite player will be trying to win for that quarter or that year, and if he uses finite strategies to win a game designed to be played over and over, he will exhaust his resources and have nothing to show for it. On the other hand, if he is an infinite player but playing a finite game, each game will render him a loser, and he will eventually exhaust his psychological frame.

On the other hand, when a finite player plays a finite game, his true opponent isn't another finite player, his opponent is success at large. The same applies to the infinite player; when the infinite player plays an infinite game, his opponent is not another infinite player, it is also success at large. When a finite player tunes his resources and plays that finite game, he triumphs. When an infinite player plays an infinite game, he also emerges victorious, given the right set of circumstances.

With this cursory understanding of the finite in the infinite game framework, we can look at Steve Jobs according to this context. Considering Jobs in both scenarios to identify whether he is a finite or an infinite player, I find that he is well adapted and well suited with his skills to be an extremely formidable infinite player. And that is what you see – not only in the person of Steve Jobs but also in the company he founded.

Apple, whether they realize it or not, is still playing the infinite game. Apple builds products that transcend today's fads and temporary trends. They build products that are not designed to compete with its closest competitors but to completely conquer that technology, breaking out of the confines of short term competition.

For example, the latest release of an Apple product is the iPhone X. And the biggest, newest feature of the iPhone X is its facial recognition technology. The day after Apple's launch of the iPhone X, there was a lot of excitement on the internet from those in attendance at the launch. That excitement soon gave way to mockery in the forums and blogosphere as supporters of other manufacturers started to weigh in on the product. By the day after Apple made the announcement, many Monday morning quarterbacks were saying that Apple hadn't come up with anything new, arguing that facial recognition technology had already been in Android devices for a couple of years now. And this was true.

However, Apple's release of facial recognition technology hadn’t been intended to compete with Android. Apple could have easily purchased or merged with a company that provided facial recognition technology during the same season that Samsung released its version. Emulating another company would have been easy, especially in this industry, but Apple didn't do that either in the same season or even during the following season. Instead of competing over short-term profits, Apple chose to go into research to develop the technology much further than what already existed in the marketplace.

You see, Samsung had been playing the finite game: this quarter, this result, they asked, "What can we put on the shelf that beats everything else, NOW!" It didn't matter that Samsung’s facial recognition technology could be duped by a static image. You could use a photograph or even a 3D sculpture of the person's face, and the phone would unlock, spilling its information.

But you couldn’t do that with the new facial recognition technology Apple developed because they had gone a few steps further in being able to map the face with special heat recognition technology. If you were to put a sculpture or a photograph in front of it, the phone wouldn't sense any heat from the sculpture, especially not the heat map of an individual's face, and it would not find the three-dimensional points that mapped the face using bifocal cameras. Instead of competing on what already existed, Apple redefined the game, breaking right out of its finite limits.

The point here is that one company, Samsung, plays a finite game, and does very well at it, while the other company, Apple, plays the infinite game, and does very well at it. Comparing the two would not be fair to either. You can't take Apple, following Steve Jobs' philosophy, and compare it against Samsung, with Samsung's philosophy, because each does well in their own type of game.

In the same way, you can't take two different leaders and compare them if they are wired to be two different kinds of players. Jobs, and those who follow his example, are infinite players because they play not to win in the short-term quarter but to make lasting change. When they achieve that lasting change, others come along to build upon it, developing it further – benefiting Apple as it sits on top of the redefined industry. Apple has no problem in playing that infinite game, because the company has mirrored the Steve Jobs legacy and personality extremely well.

Chapter 8 A Faster Horse?

"We're going to be able to ask our computers to monitor things for us, and when certain conditions happen, are triggered, the computers will take certain actions and inform us after the fact."

Steve Jobs

There are two kinds of leaders. The first type subjects his decision-making process to focus groups, public opinion, the opinion of the masses, and to the whims and fancies of fads. He seeks to see the trend in the fads, and he rides the leading edge of those trends to satisfy the popular view. This is the populist leader. In many cases, the populist leader is a finite game player.

The second type of leader is one who does not look toward the opinions of his customers or the masses but creates what is best for them. He is almost like a father creating what's best for his children. If children were allowed to choose their dinner, it'd most certainly be M&M's and Skittles, but if the father chooses dinner, he chooses what is best for them in the long run. This is the infinite player.

Steve Jobs was famous for his refusal to be limited by what focus groups had to say about a product. He did, however, design products based on how the product would impact the life of the consumer. He was of the opinion that people don't really know what they want. This is much like the story often told of Henry Ford. When Ford was asked about how people would look at his product, his straight and resoundingly resolute answer was that, if he had left it up to the people, they would have asked for a faster horse. Instead of a faster horse, Ford gave the people an automobile – and changed the course of history. That's exactly how Steve Jobs approached things. He didn't seek the opinion of a consumer who wants a faster horse; he sought to define the consumer's opinion and make the consumer's life easier.

Previously, we talked about Jobs' ability to find a balance in looking at science and technology set against humanity, and to bridge these apparent opposites. But, in fact, Zen-like, Jobs did not actually see them as opposites. He saw with his intuition an all-encompassing ideal that takes everything as it is.

The universe is not built out of chemistry, physics and biology, cosmology, and astronomy. The universe is one big amalgamation of everything. In its Zen and Zen-like purposes, we find everything is what it is. There is no discipline that is separate from the rest. It is only broken down into digestible parts because our mortal minds can't find a way to absorb all of it at once. But there is a big picture, and there are some who can see it. In our generation, there are a few people with that ability, and one of them was Steve Jobs.

Jobs had the ability to see the big picture, as well as drill down to the details. He could appreciate the whole picture, and see where the small reacts with the small to create the big and see how the big interacts with each other to create the whole. That is what it's like to be inside the mind of an infinite player.

That is what it's like to be a leader. A leader who is an infinite player is a person who plays the long game, a person who looks to change things, not to keep up or keep ahead of trends. That is the kind of person we can trust to lead us. The other type of leader is not a person to lead us – that's just a person who satisfies our penchant for a quick fix.

A scene in a recent movie portraying Steve Jobs illustrates a quality that made me reevaluate my own way of doing things. In the scene, they were in Jobs' parents' garage trying to build the first Mac. Jobs looked inside the box at all the chips on the circuit board, and saw that all the chips were not properly arranged, so he mentioned it to his colleagues, including Wozniak, saying that he wanted those chips aligned and nicely arranged. Jobs' colleagues argued that no one was going to look inside the box. In the movie, Steve Jobs' answer was "They may not know, but I will."

Steve Jobs was more concerned with how he, himself, saw something than what others would think. When he took the responsibility to create something, he took full responsibility for it. Consequently, even if someone wouldn't see what was going on in the back end, he wanted to make it elegant. Apparently, he had learned this from his father, who was very good with his hands, with carpentry, mechanical work, and doing stuff around the house. Jobs' father had taught the young Steve that even when no one gets to see the back side of something, or the rear end of the fence, he would still know. His father told him that it didn't matter what other people got to see, what matters is what you get to see. That work ethic, that pride in what he did, and that knowledge of what went on behind the scenes was very important to the way the mature Jobs did things.

When you see everything, you see the big picture, you see the aesthetics of the lines on the outside, and you see what the chips are doing on the inside. That was quintessentially what Steve Jobs was all about. He didn't need focus groups to tell him what was good. He didn't need engineers to tell him that putting a handle on the top of a Macintosh was a waste of money. He didn't need bean counters to tell him that it wasn't how it should be done. It was by staying true to his own vision that he built a company from scratch to the point that it redefined how the rest of the world operates. His competitors run their businesses with the sole purpose of competing with the legacy Jobs left behind. They go to work every morning to try and beat Apple at the game Steve Jobs created. Jobs not only sparked a revolution, he was the revolution.

Conclusion

"Innovation distinguishes between a leader and a follower."

Steve Jobs

My entire motivation for reading about, studying, and observing men of significant success, and for talking to people who have left a formidable mark on this world, is to learn the lessons they can teach us. There are many reasons to inquire into the life of a man who has touched our experience in so many ways. From the way Steve Jobs could inspire us through his simplifications to the way he conquered complexity, we discover that we are capable of far more than what we witness and perform in our daily lives.

I have laid out this book very differently from other books I have written about men of great accomplishment. Over the past eight chapters, the goal has been to take one characteristic at a time and break it down to how and where it applied in Steve Jobs' life, and how or what resulted from it. To understand Steve Jobs, I broke down his way of doing things into eight categories, across those eight chapters, so that we could find inspiration and apply his way of doing things in our corner of the world.

We started by looking at one of the bedrock abilities of this man, his ability to focus on exactly what was necessary, chiseling away and discarding everything else. Jobs said, "Focus is the ability to say no." When there are so many distractions and opportunities clamoring for attention, the only way to actually get something done is to say no.

Second, we looked at the power of taking responsibility. When you take responsibility, whether it's for a mistake, or it's for a product you create, whatever you take responsibility for can flourish. Steve Jobs took responsibility for all aspects and stages of everything he touched, from start to finish. He made sure Apple retained control of both their hardware and their software, so that Apple provided an end-to-end solution with the promise that it would work, or they would fix it. No excuses.

Taking responsibility can convert even a mediocre act into a great legacy, and Steve Jobs took responsibility for everything, end-to-end, without any qualms whatsoever. Not only does Apple have control over the hardware it builds, and the software it writes, but it now also has control over the content that it distributes. How is that for end-to-end responsibility?

Third, we talked about simplification. How to simplify everything so that users don't have to be rocket scientists to operate the devices.

Look at any Apple product and you will find that there is significant technology behind those sleek lines and polished surfaces. Everything Jobs created stood at the intersection of high technology and practical usability for the average person. When you pick up your iPod, you don't need to worry if it's going to play, or if the touch sensor has enough tactile pressure to activate it, or if it even turns on. You know, after years of use, that whatever happens, it will work. That takes complex engineering behind the scenes and even higher standards of taking responsibility than you can imagine. When you pick up your iPad, the capacity for that iPad to function as you expect it to requires flawless engineering, foresight, and a strict adherence to standards.

Apple products remain as evidence of the man who created them. Whatever you think of Apple products, they reveal the handiwork of one man, and the integrity of his standards, and clarity of vision he had for simplifying complex processes. Everything from the Apple T.V. to the iPhone has been marked with Steve Jobs' signature vision, and by his care, patience, and determination to conquer the complexity of the technology and simplify the human interface with it to make devices easy to operate. You don't need to be able to understand programming to operate some of the most complex hardware in existence because of the standards that Steve Jobs stood for.

The fourth chapter talked about Jobs' ability to be driven. We looked at the factors that drove Steve Jobs and how he drove himself, taking ideas and incorporating them into the things he believed would make people's lives better. We also looked at how and why Jobs drove others relentlessly to succeed, but they loved him for it because he brought out the best in them.

We also looked at what he focused on in the product. He believed that the pursuit of profits was a worthwhile endeavor, but it was not the core of what he should focus on. Jobs believed if he focused on the product and made it work for the consumer, the profits would follow. He was right. As long as Jobs ran Apple according to his vision, it flourished to become as gargantuan it is today. Taking end-to-end responsibility, Steve Jobs drove his people to achieve perfection and simplicity, and said, "To hell with profits."

Next, we looked at Steve Jobs' ability to balance. To balance is to focus. Through his ability to find the balance in everything, he created a bridge between humanity and science, between artistry and technology.

In today's world, every company uses focus groups. They test the market, and try to learn what the consumer wants, but, in the end, they can't seem to beat what Jobs did without focus groups. You can't always hope to lead a market while you are being led by that market. That's what politicians do. There's a saying in real estate, "Know where everyone is going and get there first." The rationale is that when the others get there, you will already own the property, and you will make your money from that. That's what focus groups do – they let you in on the trend that people are creating and making.

Steve Jobs wasn't the kind of leader to follow the trends. He didn't really care about focus groups. So how did he look at products? How did he determine what products to take on? What products to refine? What features to incorporate?

Instead, Steve Jobs was the kind of leader we follow. He was the kind of leader Henry Ford spoke about when he talked about innovators. He was the kind of leader who shows us what is possible before we can even think of it. We did not anticipate the existence of the iPod until Jobs came up with it. We did not anticipate iTunes. Imagine if a focus group had been asked, "What do you want next, the

CDROM or iTunes?" Many would have chosen the CDROM because the concept of an iTunes would have gone right over their heads. Now, iTunes is a major revenue earner for Apple.

Much of the work that Steve Jobs did while he was alive continues to reverberate through the lives of people around the world, whether consumer or competitor, whether Apple supporter or Apple detractor, or something between. Steve Jobs followed the dictates of his own vision, and played an infinite game that allowed Apple to break out of the limits of what was already available in the market to become the leader in human-friendly technologies.

Bill Gates:
The Man Behind Microsoft

Bill Gates:

The Man Behind Microsoft

A Look at the Man

Who Changed the World We Live In

JR MacGregor

Bill Gates: The Man Behind Microsoft

A Look at the Man Who Changed the World We Live In

Published by CAC Publishing LLC.

ISBN 978-1-948489-86-7 paperback

ISBN 978-1-948489-85-0 eBook

This book is dedicated to those who want to study and learn from one of the greatest visionaries that has ever walked this planet.

Preface

"Money has no utility to me beyond a certain point. Its utility is entirely in building an organization and getting the resources out to the poorest in the world."

Bill Gates

It is challenging to write about a man who is recognized the world over. The challenge is not in finding data and narrative, but is in finding something that has not already been said or something that has not already become part of the reading public's collective consciousness. Ultimately, the real challenge is not in finding something to write about Bill Gates, but in telling the truth of the man amid the rumors, bias, confusion, and exaggeration.

We tend to emulate our heroes in one thing or another. That is the underlying reason we look at biographies of great or prominent men. Some will look at Bill Gates primarily because of his ranking at the apex of the Forbes list for 24 years in a row. But this book is not about the fact that Bill Gates has sat on the top of a variety of Forbes' lists. The success we are looking at here is not about the wealth that he has amassed. Any discussion of the quantity of wealth or the price of MSFT's stock price tends to minimize the real benefit of the lessons we can take away from Bill Gates' story.

So, let's set fortunes aside, and boil down our discussion of Bill Gates to just two things we can focus our attention on. The first are his strengths and weaknesses in mind and body. The other is what inspires him and his overarching views about life and his place in it.

This narrative has two parallel objectives. One is simply to satisfy our curiosity about the success of one man whose vision has touched billions of lives in this generation and will continue to touch countless more in coming generations. The second is to strip away the noise that skews the description of the effort and energy that went into accomplishing what Bill Gates has done.

For Bill Gates, the effort was not about the rewards and riches. After all, once you get to a certain point, rewards do get boring. If you stood at the banks of a pristine lake, how much of it could you really drink in this lifetime? Ultimately, it is not about the rewards or their accumulation. It isn't about the status, or whatever power that brings with it. The real glory is in seeing how much you have used your time here on this earth to make a difference.

If you make enough of a difference, then the reward lies within what you have accomplished. The key to understand those who have truly accomplished their vision is that the rewards are not their primary motivation. They don't start out with fantasies of golden towers and luxurious lifestyles.

Ones who are truly inspired don't need to be showered with lavish ornaments. Those who do need that are often the ones who don't really contribute anything in return for the rewards they gain (or sometimes steal). Emperor Nero is a famous example.

In my book on Jack Ma, founder of the Chinese business giant Alibaba, I describe how, when he first ventured out on his own to start a translation business, he had to work a second job selling odds and ends at a market outside his city just to keep the lights on at his fledgling business. His translation business finally turned the corner after three years. If it had been only about the money, Ma would have quit long before then.

In the same way, Bill Gates quit Harvard (with its rewards) so that he could devote all his attention to his passion. Harvard would have been the wiser choice—from a conventional perspective. Most would see admission into Harvard as a one-way ticket to an easy life at a lucrative job at an investment bank or at some other cushy job. Instead of slogging his way through the first three years of Harvard College, Bill Gates took the inspired step to focus full time on his start up.

In leaving Harvard, Gates wasn't making a decision that some imagined pursuit of fame and glory outweighed the value of a strong education. Instead, he calculated his options, and, for him, his decision to pursue his dream was a logical one. Bill Gates was not the type to take risks. When he left Harvard, he had a little over year to graduate and didn't yet have the IBM contract in hand, but he did have a clear vision of what he wanted to do. (I can just imagine the conversation my parents would have had at the kitchen table that night, if I had called to say I was quitting Harvard to pursue what had been, until that point, only a hobby.) But Gates was a very straightforward person with no theatrics prior to a decision—and no regrets after it.

At first, we might look into a person's biography out of curiosity, but that curiosity really comes from a deeper desire to find similarities between that person's life and our own. When we are young, we look for heroes to emulate; when we get a little older, the flavor of those heroes evolves along with our age and maturity. Our heroes change, and the aspect of their lives that we want to emulate also changes.

When I was a kid, I wanted to be Steve Austin—the original Six Million Dollar Man. I wanted to be the astronaut who went down in a blaze of glory and was rebuilt with superhuman strength and power. In time, that changed, and my heroes went from the fantastical, like Steve Austin, to the commercial giants, like Mike Milken and Gordon Gecko.

A person's heroes reveal who they are built to be, not that our lives are preordained, but that we have the tools that makes one path easier to navigate than another. Take, for instance, Mark Zuckerberg, the founder of Facebook—as a kid, his hero was Bill Gates. And look at the path Zuckerberg was to excel at.

To really fulfill and wake up the giant within you, you need to get beyond the motivations of reward and look for motivation in contribution and achievement. Most men of great accomplishment do this, and it pays off in the end. Bill Gates did this from the beginning. He had no utility for money or wealth in the way we normally fantasize about. What we really hope for is the freedom to do whatever we want, with the imagined liberation that wealth brings.

Eventually, abundance of wealth and accomplishment come to those who aren't focusing on the reward but are totally and absolutely focused on their contribution. That is the mark of a person who has truly earned every penny.

Most of the men I study and write about—Steve Jobs, Jeff Bezos, Richard Branson, Jack Ma, and others—have this one thing in common: they were not mentally spending their money before they have worked for their achievement with their hands. Each of them has followed the path laid out in the books I have written in the success series.

Introduction

Bill Gates was born William Henry Gates on October 28, 1955 in Seattle, Washington to William Henry Gates, Sr. and Mary Maxwell Gates.

To understand Bill Gates and the nature of his accomplishments, we must look to the environment he was a part of—his father, mother, siblings, grandparents, and the kinds of friends and extended family he was exposed to. The success story of Bill Gates did not happen in a vacuum; his background, the powerful parents he had, the time he was born into, and the town he grew up in, each played their parts.

Both of Bill Gates' parents, Senior and Mary, had prominent roles in the modern development of Seattle and Washington, and were, in their own rights, respected names in the state.

Bill Gates' father, William Henry Gates, Sr. (originally named William Henry Gates III), was an attorney and shifted his primary focus to philanthropy upon retirement. Not just "father of the co-founder of Microsoft," Gates Senior has been one of the most accomplished Americans alive today—in his own right.

Bill Gates, Sr. was born in 1927 in Bremerton, Washington, a town just west of Seattle across Puget Sound. He grew up in Bremerton in a simple and loving home. His father owned and operated a furniture store that he later sold. After the store was sold, Senior's father continued to work in the furniture industry. It was a time and place where honor, respect, and accomplishment were part of one's lifestyle. Senior was raised in a loving home that was firm and focused on an honest day's work for an honest day's wage. A deep sense of nationalism, pride in one's country and their own northwest culture pervaded the community.

The town of Bremerton was the home to the Puget Sound Naval Shipyard. In World War II, the shipyard played an important role in America's naval efforts. It was the key location in the Pacific for the maintenance and repair of battle-damaged ships for the entire US Pacific fleet, and everyone growing up there had a very personal experience of World War II. After the Pearl Harbor attack, it became conceivable that the US west coast could be a target too, and there were nightly blackouts.

While most of the United States was at an arm's length from the war, Bremerton, and other towns like it in the Pacific Northwest, faced the war in a very real way.

Bill Gates, Sr. attended Bremerton High which he graduated from in 1943. A year later, he was ordered to enlist for active duty. He joined the US Army and went through officer's training. Shortly after, he was shipped out to Japan where he spent time in Tokyo and war-torn Hokkaido. After, Senior returned to Puget Sound and attended the University of Washington where he earned his undergraduate degree in 1949 and his law degree in 1950.

Bill Gates, Sr. returned to Bremerton to take up the position of assistant city attorney. As his distinguished law career unfolded, it moved toward the corporate world, and, in particular, the world of technology.

Nearby Seattle was the original natural incubator for new ideas and new technology. Bill Gates, Sr. and his law firm worked with the cutting-edge technologies that were sprouting up in the prosperous days following WWII. Senior found himself at the intersection of technology, commerce, and law, which gave him a front row seat overlooking the areas of ascendency that would lead the United States into decades of prosperity. For instance, the barcodes we still take for granted at the grocery store checkout were a technological revolution brought out by a Washington company that was a client of the firm Senior worked at. To this day, one can find Senior's fingerprints on a number of successful ventures in the Washington-Pacific Northwest area and across the United States. Over the years, his law firm evolved and is now known as K&L Gates.

Meanwhile, on the home front, Bill Gates, Sr. had met and was dating Mary Maxwell, also a UW student, two years his junior, before Senior left for Japan. They were married in 1951, after he returned.

Mary Maxwell came from the upper echelons of Washington society. Her father, James Willard Maxwell, Jr., was a prominent banker in the Pacific Northwest. Her grandfather, James Willard Maxwell, was also a respected banker in the west, and served on the board of the American Automobile Association and on the Seattle Chamber of Commerce.

Mary Maxwell Gates, herself, served on the Board of Regents for the University of Washington for 18 years before passing from breast cancer in 1994. She also sat on the boards of United Way and the First Interstate BancSystem.

Bill Gates, Sr. and Mary Gates had three children, Bill Gates and his two sisters, Kristianne (Kristi) and Elizabeth (Libby). Kristi Gates, the oldest of the three siblings, born in 1954, graduated from the University of Washington and is now a CPA. She also sits on the Board of Regents for the University of Washington. Libby Gates, the youngest, was born in in 1964. She is currently a social activist living in Seattle. She graduated from Pomona College with a degree in Economics.

Chapter 1 Childhood

"Many of our deepest motives come, not from an adult logic of how things work in the world, but out of something that is frozen from childhood."

Kazuo Ishiguro

Bill Gates has retained most of the qualities he had as a child into his adulthood. Looking at his childhood provides insight into how Bill Gates developed and into the two forces that have played a major roles in his life, family and humanitarianism.

Let us start with how his family influenced Bill Gates' childhood. Looking at my own childhood, or the childhoods of most people I know, I would not be able to find one story that remotely resembles the childhood that Bill Gates had.

First, from early on, Bill was remarkably mature for his age. His maturity had everything to do with having a very stable thought process. Bill never had any of the problems in how or when he spoke that most kids have (most kids have the innate ability to put their feet into their mouths).

Second, even for young Bill Gates, fairness came in explicit form. The more formal the statement of terms and benefits, the more fair and equitable it was. If it was not reduced to paper, and, if it was not equitable, all bets were off. To ensure this, he used to sign agreements with his siblings for various promises.

Third, Bill Gates observed his father's actions and motivations intently. Senior was all about the oneness of humanity. While Bill Gates, Sr. had been posted to Japan after the war, he had seen, first-hand, the devastation that lay in the wake of a war. For most Americans, the war had been an ocean away, whether east or west, but, for Gates Senior, his experience of the effects of the war, and the condition it leaves humanity in, resonated so powerfully and loudly throughout his life that it spilled over and touched his son.

Gates Senior projected an imprint onto young Bill in three areas that were to feature prominently in Bill Gates' own life: Senior's empathy, affinity for technology, and definition of equitability.

The other force that steered Bill Gates' childhood was his mother, Mary. Bill's relationship with his mother was close and complex. Young Gates learned as much from his mother as he did from his father.

There was a sense of ambition and competition that he learnt from his mother and his maternal grandfather. He learned from the stories about James Willard Maxwell, Jr. that Mary Gates and her mother told Bill. Overall, he could see the forces of his banker grandfather manifested in his mother and he absorbed a lot of their instincts and powers.

Bill's mother, Mary Gates, was well known in King's County for her ability to organize and socialize. Those skills didn't necessarily come naturally to Bill Gates, but later he found that shortcoming (if you can call it that) nicely compensated for by Melinda, his wife. In many areas where Bill comes up short, Melinda has been the one to carry it across the finish line.

Gam, Bill's maternal grandmother, was also a major influence in his life, as the Gates children were often left in her care. She was a hard-driving woman who pushed them to excel and fostered a strong sense of competitiveness in her grandchildren with games and athletic contests.

Bill Gates was not at all what you might imagine he would have been as a kid. He was not the quiet "geeky" type who was too meek to get out into the real world, far from it. He was more than well-adjusted. He simply happened to like programming and was good at it.As a child, he had a lot of spunk, and was quite the mischievous sort, a lot like Mark Twain's Tom Sawyer.

Even as a child, Bill Gates had a way about him that many misunderstand, mistaking it for arrogance. For example, when he was ten years old, and in an apparent bout of exasperation with his mother, he asked her if she was ever able to think things through. At the time he said it, he meant it literally the way he said it, but to anyone overhearing, it would have seemed extremely rude and impolite. But that was Bill—he had no time for niceties and polite discourse. He has always needed to get to the point and make sure the other person was on board right away.

Bill Gates was certainly academically advanced, but that didn't mean he didn't get into his share of trouble in his youth. Even in childhood, Bill failed to see the world the way the rest of us are inculcated into seeing it. Along with ambition and freedom to think came a lack of adherence to rules. Not so much a lack of respect for authority, it had more to do with not being able to see the point of the rule in question. As a child, he did not think that the rules applied to people like him.

As a kid, Bill was quite the hacker. He had the smarts to do it, he learned the tools to execute it, and he was fearless to pull it off. He hacked numerous computers as a kid—and those are just the ones he has talked about. While hacking, generally, may be frowned upon, there are many kinds of hacking. The one thing all hackers needed, especially back when the tools for hacking were not as prevalent as they are today, was the intelligence to do it. And Bill Gates has that genius.

Later, even though Gates understood that there was a law that set limits on driving speed, he wouldn't keep to speed limits. To him, there are two aspects to that law. First, the law existed to protect the public from people who were not so smart and did not really know how to drive or didn't have the skill to be safe at higher speeds. In his mind, he was obviously not in that group. However, his speeding was not without accidents. He once took a friend's Porsche and severely damaged it, just pennies below the definition of "totaled." Ultimately, his lack of respect for authority got him a ton of speeding tickets, so many he ended up in court and had to engage a lawyer to sort it out.

Even once he was at Harvard College, he was known to spend nights playing poker. His poker days, when he lost thousands at a time, were not exactly within campus rules. They played across the halls, but on the quiet. Yet, as he spent nights playing poker, Bill Gates was learning two things more effectively than any classroom could ever teach him.

First, playing poker, Gates learned how to assess risk. It is one thing to understand probability, statistics, and risk. It is a completely different thing to develop a knack for it and the understanding to overcome it. His hands at poker on Harvard Yard brought him up-close and personal with the realities of risk. He came to understand that to make anything of himself, he needed to embark on endeavors where he could control and mitigate risk. He never let go of a sure footing until he knew he had something to cling on to. This intimate understanding of risk prepared him for the way he would go out into the world and conduct business.

Gates had learned about risk in an up-close and personal way and had paid for that lesson time and time again. Later, in his dealings with IBM, he would demonstrate the lessons he had learned in how to handle business in a risk-averse manner. He showed IBM the operating system but did not buy it from the original developers until he knew the deal was a sure thing. Gates had hedged his bets.

The second thing Gates learned from playing poker during those nights at Harvard was the skill of bluffing. Bluffing is what poker is all about. If you don't know how to bluff, there are two things you should never do. First, you should never play poker. Second, you should not go into business for yourself. Bluffing allows you to control the dynamics and information flow in a negotiation.

Some may consider bluffing to be the cousin of lying and cheating. No. It is not. Is it lying and cheating to tell your mom that her bland pot roast tastes delicious? Is it lying and cheating to tell your wife that her new hairdo is fantastic? Or is it lying and cheating to tell your significant other you have a headache? Those are all bluffs done in the pursuit of bridging the gap. On the other hand, if you steal someone's technology and resell it without paying for it, that would be cheating and lying.

Bill Gates' childhood is peppered with incidents that reveal his ability to think independently and behave outside the norms of society. But even though he marched to the beat of his own drum, he was not into harming others intentionally. He was simply so sure of himself that he believed in all earnestness that the norms and laws of common people didn't apply to him.

Remember—one of the ways to succeed in life is to break a few rules, redefine your reality, and engineer your chances. Bill Gates knows this concept very well.

While he was in high school, he was hired by the faculty to do some programming for the administration. He did what was asked, but he also hacked the system to put himself into a class where he was the only guy—the rest were all girls. If you were to ask a teacher, an administrator, or a headmaster if that was the wrong thing to do, they are likely to say it was—but it didn't do any harm. However, the episode reveals a lot about Bill Gates' relationship with risk and reward. He understood keenly that, by reducing his competition, he tipped the chances in his favor. Most of us have probably thought of doing similar things, but we didn't because either we didn't have the skill to pull it off or we didn't have the guts to put our skill to use.

Bill Gates was a tough boy and strong-headed in many ways, but he had his fears. Unlike most kids, his fears didn't revolve around stories of monsters and bugs; Bill Gates' fears were about not winning. He was the kind of person that needed to win everything and be at the top. For him, winning was his paramount purpose in life, and, whatever he did, wherever he went, the thing that was on his mind was how he would win the day.

In the Gates household, everything was about ambition and hard work. It all boiled down to competition. The notion of competition in the Gates family was somewhat different than it would be in most families. It was the norm in the Gates family to compete for everything. Senior and Mary made it a point to instill a competitive spirit in their children because they believed that competition, above all else, was the mother of success. Often, competition was more important than the outcome, but the winner was always rewarded, and the loser was always made to compensate the loss.

That competitive nature was a universal for young Bill. He applied competition to everything, to every program he wrote, to every race he entered. In every shadow in his mind, there was competition.

His nights of poker in college were also about competition. Sure, it was about money, but not as much as it was about winning the challenge and emerging victorious in the moment. Poker evolved into a competition of wits. The smarter person, the person better able to bluff, became the winner. To win this affirmation, no amount of money was too much.

Consider, for example, Gates' contempt for sleep. It was well-known among his friends that Bill was a night owl. That was when he would do his work and get things done. Even after Microsoft was founded, he would go days without sleep, then crash on the office floor for a nap before getting up and getting back to whatever had been fully occupying his consciousness.

He was always on a mission to get the task or the job done; Gates was competing against time which was always against him. That was the way he knew to do things so that he could win the competition being played out in his mind. His contempt for sleep was more about winning that competition than about anything else.

Gates' contempt for sleep, and for anything else that would distract him from what he was trying to accomplish, was the result of his uncommonly singular focus. His ability to get into a program and pull it to pieces before putting it together again was not without challenges. The only thing that got him through those times, as they do today, was his ability to do just one thing at one time.

He would not allow anything to shake his focus or distract him from accomplishing whatever he had set out to do. That was the only reason that he was able to go without sleep. That was also the reason it was so difficult to tear him away, even to meet someone important for dinner. Bill Gates simply chooses to apply his time differently than the rest of us.

What would it be like to have the kind of focus and strength to continue focusing on something as you grow increasingly tired? Most people can only keep their attention on something for 5-6 minutes, and then they are done. Their focus wanes and they get distracted. It is a fact of life. It is almost superhuman to be able to focus on things for extended periods of time, yet, that is something that came easily to Bill Gates.

***

Chapter 2 Mother's Influence

"There is no influence so powerful as that of the mother"

Sarah Joseph Hale

There are many ways Mary Maxwell Gates contributed to her son's personal development and life, but she was also behind some decisive moments in Bill Gates' history. Many people don't realize that it was Mary Gates who was responsible for introducing Bill Gates to Warren Buffet—whom Bill had referred to, at the time, as someone of no value and as a person who sold pieces of paper having no value. She was also instrumental in helping Bill get the meeting with IBM that turned the table for his start-up company, Microsoft.

Bill Gates' mother was a force to be reckoned with in her own right. As prominent as Gates Senior,

Mary Gates stood right alongside Senior doing her own thing and powering through the community under her own steam. She was a well-respected philanthropist and socialite, and a member on several prominent boards. Just before she passed away, she was scheduled to receive the Citizen of the Year Award for her contribution to the local community in Kings County. Her activities in the county and the state had by then spanned more than two decades.

Mary's social calendar blended with her philanthropy, and Bill Gates had a front row seat to observe the way she did things. She was as objective-oriented as her husband, Gates Senior, and she was just as forceful in getting things done. It is no wonder that Bill Gates became as tenacious as she had been throughout her life.

At first, a quality that did not pass down to Bill Gates was Mary Gates' ability to socialize. Bill found it a waste of time. The first time Mary Gates invited Warren Buffet to their home in Seattle and asked Bill to join them, Bill refused. Eventually, however, she persuaded him to come, extracting his promise to spend two hours before heading back to the office. Bill ended up spending the entire evening and late into the night.

Because of her social skill and penchant for organizing community events, Mary Gates rose to the top of the United Way Board in Kings County, eventually leading it. That gave her a stepping stone to get onto the board of United Way at the national level, and she eventually became the first woman to head it. That was to prove extremely well-timed and fortuitous for Bill.

Just around the time Mary was President of the United Way, Bill Gates was pulling his startup together. Microsoft was coming together, but not as fast as he would have liked. He was working hard, and there was a lot of good he was doing, but it was nowhere close to enough. During one of her United Way board meetings in 1980, Mary Gates spoke with a fellow board member, John Opel, the Chairman of IBM, and mentioned her son, Bill—and Microsoft.

John Opel took that back to the other executives at IBM. They called Bill Gates in about the operating system he had pitched to them sometime earlier. Not long after, Microsoft was awarded the contract to write the DOS program for all the IBM personal computers. That was Microsoft's big break.

Until then, Bill Gates and Paul Allen were just another small software programming company without a long term major client. They did have some large clients before that, but nothing on this scale. IBM's decision to award the operating system contract to Microsoft is what catapulted the company to where it is today.

Earlier, when Bill had decided to make the pitch, he didn't have any operating system (OS) to offer IBM, but he did know of someone who did. So, he took that software and offered it to IBM for evaluation.

IBM tested the OS and found that it worked as they intended, requiring only a few tweaks. So, they agreed to have Microsoft to do it. Microsoft then went to the original owners and purchased the rights to the operating system. The company pulled together all it could and paid the original developers the agreed price. Once the purchase of the software was secured and paid for, Bill Gates signed that pivotal contract licensing the software to IBM. The rest, as they say, is history.

Mary Gates also had a hand in setting up her son to meet the man who was to become one of Bill's best friends—and an important ally in his later philanthropic efforts. Bill Gates and Warren Buffet remain the best of friends to this day, chit-chatting, and going to McDonalds for burgers. It would be fascinating to watch and eavesdrop on the conversation of these two titans of the business and philanthropic world.

***

Chapter 3 Father's Guidance

"My dad expanded his horizons way beyond what he grew up with"

Bill Gates

Whoever else a man has a relationship with, be it sibling, best friend, mother, wife, or child, what has a larger bearing on who the man becomes, for good or bad, is the relationship he has with his father and the kind of man his father is. This influence is more than evident in the relationship between Bill Gates, Sr. and Bill Gates.

Most of the lessons Bill Gates learned from his father were not ones that Senior needed to sit Bill down to drill into him. Instead, Bill's lessons in life were provided by example. In a home dominated by women, Bill's focus and attention on how to become a man was trained squarely on his father. Senior was a silent and powerful force in the development of his son. Gates Senior was a man who thought before he spoke, evaluated before he acted, and made his position known in as few words as possible. His moral authority spoke for him. And Senior's empathy for humanity and all things was the path that young Bill Gates followed.

There is no doubt his lawyer father had a strong influence on Bill Gates. At an age when most kids were playing sticks and stones and taking their sibling's things without permission, young Bill (or Trey, as he was called at home) was drafting contracts for the use and borrowing of his things or his sisters' belongings. He'd write up a contract and have his sister, or whoever he was dealing with at the time, sign it, and he would work off the contract. He never deviated from the terms of the legal paper.

You have no desire to go off the rails when you are always in the shadow of a man who does the right thing—not one who simply professes to do the right thing or claims to be the best, but one who quietly does the right thing—and that becomes apparent for the world to see. Bill Gates experienced this first hand and was molded by it.

Bill Gates Senior was a powerful presence, towering over everyone at six feet seven inches, but his intellectual honesty and moral authority tower much higher.

When you come face to face with someone like Gates Senior, you are instantly subjected to a moral authority that is uncommon these days. His air, his words, his presence all just make you want to do the right thing without hesitation. There is a moral authority that comes when a person is on the right side of events and on the proper side of choices. It creates an unmistakable sense of authority that resonates.

We have already mentioned Bill Gates Senior's connection to barcode technology. There are many other similar stories about Senior's role in iconic American institutions. One of them—about what may be your favorite coffee place (certainly, it is mine)—illustrates the Senior Gates' powerful presence and his influence on events and people—something the younger Gates grew up observing.

In 1982, a man named Howard Schultz stepped into a local Starbucks, at a time when there were only six stores anywhere. He loved it so much that he pursued a meeting with the owners to persuade them to give him a job. They hired him a year later. He had a good time, but eventually outgrew the then-small Starbucks and found an Italian brand on one of his trips. Schultz brought that brand back to the United States and set up Il Giornale.

In 1987, Jerry Baldwin, the founder of Starbucks, decided to sell the six stores for a total of $3.8 million, and the first person he thought of was Howard Schultz. Baldwin called Schultz to give him a 90 day exclusive to raise the money for the purchase. Schultz agreed.

Two months into the process, Schultz got a call informing him that one of the investors of Il Giornale had made an all-cash offer topping out at $4 million. It was to be a straight forward no-due-diligence deal that would put money into Baldwin's pockets right away. The offer was too good to refuse.

Schultz was devastated and disclosed the matter to a friend who was a lawyer. That friend told Schultz to come in and meet his senior partner who might be able to help. Howard Schultz was about to meet Gates Senior.

Senior listened intently to the whole story, and, at the end, got up and signaled, as he got his coat, for Schultz to follow him. They walked across downtown Seattle to the office of the man who had made the offer.

When Gates Senior and Howard Schultz got to the office of the competing buyer, Senior spoke to the buyer directly and without hesitation, telling him to back off the attempted purchase. There was no threats, no condescension, and no hostility. All

Senior had in his arsenal was the will and power to make things happen. Senior was a force in that way.

Howard Schultz went on to buy Starbucks, consisting of those first six stores, and grew it to over 20,000 stores worldwide serving millions of customers speaking dozens of languages. It is safe to say that the iconic coffee chain would not be what it is today were it not for the ability of Bill Gates, Sr. to move mountains.

Senior had a way about him that could make anything happen—and that was one of the many characteristics he passed on to become part of the younger Bill Gates. While Senior was a force that you could feel naturally, Bill Gates had to work at emulating the qualities and traits of his father. And he did.

When Apple Computer CEO and founder, Steve Jobs, hired Microsoft to build the software that Apple needed for its new line, Bill Gates saw the work that Steve Jobs was doing and advised him to acquire the code behind the point-and-click-based operating system. Jobs declined because he was focusing on the hardware, not the software.

So, when Gates returned to Seattle in November 1983, he announced that Microsoft would introduce a "Windows" based system. Two years later, Windows was released. It became global phenomenon, extending Microsoft's winning streak far beyond the success of the MS-DOS operating system. Gates had seized an open opportunity, working off a project that had no copyright issues. He didn't cheat anyone out of anything—he just stuck to the contract.

The older Gates also had a sense of social responsibility that was to become an even greater part of how his son, Bill Gates, does things today.

Bill Gates, Sr. took an active role in his local community. He had once been advised by a gathering of up and coming leaders that the most fulfilling and satisfying thing anyone could do was to take part in community development. He knew one thing to be true, and it was that we are all here to actively develop our shared space and time. But he did not have to beat the drum about it. There was no air of superiority about him over his philanthropic activities, only humility. Knowing that he and his family were drivers of social development did not make him feel anything but honored to have the opportunity.

His ardent belief that every life is of equal value has been one of the driving forces of Senior's life, and that legacy has been carried forward into the life of Bill Gates as well. The Bill and Melinda Gates Foundation, which Bill co-founded with his wife, does philanthropic work around the world. Bill and Melinda have personally donated more than $28 billion to its efforts. Of that, more than $8 billion has been primarily for health infrastructure.

A clearer example could not exist of the continuity between the way Senior sees things and the way Bill does things. His civic mindedness dictated acts beyond charity. Senior was a powerful advocate and force in the philanthropic community. Senior championed everything from the United Way to Planned Parenthood and state tax initiatives.

Bill Gates has been no different, as evidenced by the depth of involvement their Foundation has had in communities around the world. In total, the Foundation is responsible for over $48 billion dollars, and has offices in Asia, East Asia, Africa, and the Americas. It is a well-structured and highly serious organization that oversees the health and welfare of those left behind by the imperfect organization of societies. Bill and Melinda are driven by the same principal, when it comes to their foundation, as Senior has been—that everyone's life is of equal value.

On top of that, the younger Bill Gates did not just happen to stumble upon programming and technology. He didn't start to look at programming, computers, and technology in a vacuum. Technology was such an important part of Gates Senior's professional life that Senior can be found at the point of genesis for many of the tech and biotech industries that we see today. Senior and a handful of people clearly understood the utility that technology would have in the development and advancement of everyone. Bill Gates got to know the world of technological innovation through watching his father. Then, as children sometimes do, Bill picked up on it and took it further, but the original spark came from Senior.

Two divergent narratives about Bill Gates have made their way around blogs and the internet. Both the ones that demonize Gates by talking about how undeserving Gates is and the ones that exalt him as a boy from a simple family who grew up to dominate the world of software are wrong. Bill Gates needs to be seen as the product of his childhood, as a man who developed under the example and guidance of a towering figure in Washington state's history, his father.

***

Chapter 4 A Character to Emulate

"I believe that if you show people the problems and you show them the solutions they will be moved to act."

Bill Gates

It is unrealistic and even dangerous to imitate the ways and means of a single person in everything. As accomplished as Bill Gates is, as much as he and Melinda have achieved with their Foundation, and as much as he has succeeded over the course of his life, winning too many awards and honors to list, there is no chance I would follow everything Gates has done, trying to directly transpose it onto my life. I like my life the way it is, and I have dreams of my own that are nothing like the dreams of any other accomplished person.

On the other hand, analyzing a person's successes, the actions they took, and the responses those actions brought about is a useful way to get a holistic perspective of what one should do and what one should stay away from. There is no need for me to imitate everything to the last detail. You should not either.

Instead, look to the individual characteristics that appeal to you across a multitude of people and discover why those things appeal to you. A number of things appeal to me about Bill Gates. Many things also appeal to me about Steve Jobs, Jack Ma, Bill Clinton, Barack Obama, and, yes, even Donald Trump. (Not everything about someone is bad.) Bill Gates has some qualities that I would emulate, but not all.

One thing that has impressed me and made me consider how I do things myself is the way that Bill Gates prioritizes a task at hand and does whatever it takes to get it done. That is one of the characteristics I have started to see in many people who are highly successful. Whether or not they are comfortable admitting what could be seen as unflattering, people who are successful will do anything they have to in order to get what they want.

There is one thing I would most like to emulate about Bill Gates, more than anything else. What comes naturally to Bill Gates is his empathy for the world in general. Gates' successes are innately linked to it. I am not much into software or building companies, but, for me, the idea of caring for others and looking out for others makes all the difference in the world. When you combine that with the intelligence to do something about it, the result can be explosive.

Putting aside whatever people may think about Bill Gates and Microsoft, something that anyone can appreciate is the way the company revolutionized the world. And in Gates' mind, he was the one to do it. I tend to agree with that.

Certain people can just make specific things happen. There were things Bill Gates was able to do with the launch of the IBM PC that, I believe, no one else could. Only Gates could have done what he did with the operating system that he bought from the original developers. Only he could have made Windows happen. Were it not for Gates' tenacity in getting the products to market, who knows where we would be today in terms of personal computing. Similarly, it is because of the specific talents and legacy of Steve Jobs that Apple sits at the apex of company value. And were it not for Howard Schultz, it's not likely that Starbucks would be around every corner around the world.

When you know that you are the one to make something happen, you owe it to the universe to do everything in your power to get it done. Bill Gates does that, day in and day out, even after leaving the day-to-day operations of the largest software company in the world.

Imagine if you fought tooth and nail to do everything that you set out to do. Imagine the successes all of you, each and everyone one of you, could become.

That is what success is all about. If you have a vision of yourself changing the world, get moving on that vision and don't stop no matter what. Don't be worried about the speed limit. Don't worry about chaffing up against someone. don't worry about dumpster diving to find what you are looking for. It is all about how passionate you are. Just go out and do it. One of the things that I admire about Bill Gates is that he never stops—not even to meet Warren Buffet.

When young Bill Gates first started using computers heavily, he was allowed to access the computers at his school. They had a deal with a local computer company where the kids could use a certain amount of the server time that the company wasn't using. Few kids thought that was much fun, so they didn't take up the opportunity. Bill, on the other hand, jumped at it, and started using the server time to do as much as he could. In fact, he overused the server time and the company started to bill him for it. To access it for free and avoid having to pay for the server time, Bill tried to find a way into the accounting system at the office to get the Admin password. Paul Allen, his high school friend and later co-founder of Microsoft, helped in the effort. Together they managed to get into the accounts and got the password. Before long, the company discovered what they had done and booted them both out of the system. It is just another case of Bill doing whatever it took to do what he needed to do.

Hesitation is a luxury the successful have no time for. When you have something within your grasp, you need to jump on it and worry about the possible consequences later. When you have risk, you should mitigate it to the best of your abilities before you get going, but don't let the risk stop you from moving forward.

Bill Gates worked hard at the things he wanted to do, and didn't allow the time he had to slip by. In fact, the reason he left Harvard the way he did to set up Microsoft wasn't because he imagined there were millions waiting to be made—it was that he knew the best way forward was to get started.

***

Chapter 5 Clarity

"As we look ahead into the next century, leaders will be those who empower others."

Bill Gates

The first comment Bill Gates made after meeting Warren Buffet, and having a long conversation that lasted into the wee hours, was that Buffet had an unusual sense of clarity. Buffet could see how the world works. Bill Gates has the same gift, and that is the real reason the two of them became fast friends, and that is the reason each has dominated in his respective field. It was with that same clarity that he recognized a kindred spirit in Warren Buffet.

Gates' clarity is the reason he is able to do things most only dream of. His intense focus gives him that clarity, without which he wouldn't have the certainty about what he does. If you ask how Gates could quit school so close to graduation, considering how risk-averse he is, and how much he hates failure, the answer is that he was extremely clear about what he intended to accomplish, and he was extremely clear on what he needed to do to accomplish it.

Without that clarity, nothing comes. If you have been working all your life but you find it difficult to move beyond your current life, then I would bet my bottom dollar that you have a problem with clarity.

Clarity is a critical element for Bill Gates and Warren Buffet, and for others like Elon Musk and Bill Clinton—all legendary for what they have accomplished. They are all known even more for the things they have been able to do even in the middle of seemingly debilitating distractions. For them, those distractions become invisible. For Bill Gates, anything that gets in the way of his accomplishing the tasks at hand becomes virtually invisible.

Clarity is both a physiological condition and a psychological one. Many people who spend their time thinking, as Bill did as a kid, are the ones who get to understand and practice clarity. It's not enough to understand what clarity is; it is essential that you practice it.

In my other books on meditation and mindfulness, we talk at length about all the Zen-like qualities and mindfulness, but, in essence, all that mindfulness and meditation is designed to do and to implant is the clarity of who you are, where you are, and what you are doing. That is the essence of all mindfulness training. Deep down, every one of us knows what we need to do, but most of us are so distracted that we need to clear away the distractions to find clarity.

But, for someone like Bill Gates, clarity is even more than just clearing away distractions. It's about not even noticing the distractions in the first place because he is so tuned in and drilled into the point he has focused on. Building the world's largest software company from scratch isn't something that happens by luck or accident. You must relentlessly pursue and painstakingly nurture it. You can only do that when you have both clarity and focus, flip sides of the same coin.

***

Chapter 6 A Strong Mind

"Success is a lousy teacher. It seduces smart people into thinking they can't lose."

Bill Gates

Those who achieve a lot in life typically do so with the aid of a strong mind. It is a prerequisite to being able to handle the challenges presented on the path to success. Without a strong mind, the effort needed becomes relatively insurmountable. A strong mind is more than one attribute; it exists on multiple planes. Whether an Elon Musk or Jack Ma, an Ivy League grad or someone who has barely passed their entrance exams, the measure of their mind is more than academic test scores and institutional certifications.

From childhood, Bill Gates showed signs of superior mental faculties. On one occasion when he was 11, his Sunday School assignment was to memorize the Book of Matthew—that's about 2000 words. The teacher gave that assignment every year to the confirming class. The incentive was a trip to the Space Needle for dinner. When the time came, with lots of starts-and-stops, misquotes, and jumbled passages, all the students did their best to recite the 2,000 word gospel. Then, it was Bill's turn. To everyone's surprise, he belted out the full 2,000 words without a single error, hesitation or reservation.

Consider for a moment, the power of Bill's mind to be able to memorize those passages. And consider that at age eight he had already breezed through the entire World Encyclopedia. I had one of those when I was eight too, but it took me more than two years to get through it—and that was with the not-so-gentle-prompting of my father.

The ability to memorize is not reserved for a few people. If you try it, and are willing to put in the effort, you will find that, in time, you will be able to memorize as well. Learning to memorize is not going to make you successful, but it will sharpen your mind. The ability to memorize not only expands your mind's abilities, but also develops your will power to focus your mind on one thing at a time without having to ward off distractions.

Gates got through his years at Harvard because he could flawlessly remember everything he read, something that helped him to bridge the gap when it came time for exams. Harvard was just not the challenge he needed. He didn't have to make an effort to get through his classes—memory came naturally to him. On the other hand, programming became a passion for him because it required solving and it provided instant results. He could see the code he needed and manipulate it to do what he wanted.

Bill Gates was always able to apply a singular focus to anything he was doing—whether it was programming or memorizing his Sunday School homework. His mind was powerful but also crystal clear. Combining those two traits produces a person who can see things at a whole different level than those who haven't trained their minds.

It wasn't just about memorizing or doing homework—when Gates set his sights on something, he was persistent and never backed off till it was done—even if it meant diving into dumpsters. When Bill Gates was still in school, he and Paul Allen decided they needed more information on a computer company and wanted to see what the company was working on, so they went to the company's office complex one night. There, Paul boosted Bill (who was much smaller and lighter) into the dumpster. They did this repeatedly, finding all sorts of little treasures, including the source code to the operating system that ran the DEC computer.

Gates relentlessly pursued what he wanted—and that was the way he did things every day. That is characteristic of a man who would go to the ends of the earth to get anything that he wants.

Bill Gates pursued his future wife, Melinda, with the same persistence. The first time he asked her out, she said no. The way he asked reveals a lot about who he was, brimming with confidence. When he bumped into her, he did a mental check of his calendar and knew he had a slot open two weeks from that day, and so he asked her out for two weeks later. She said no, stating that she had no idea what she'd be doing at that time. That was probably an excuse as her real feelings were that she didn't want to be dating the boss. It was uncomfortable, but she did think he was a funny guy and not too bad to be around. After she turned down the invitation, and they had each returned to their respective offices, he called her on the phone and, this time, told her that he was free that night and asked her out again. She agreed.

Bill does not know how to stop, does not know how to quit, and can't take no for an answer. He always gets what he wants. There is no such thing as hesitating for Bill Gates. He doesn't even consider that something's impossible or that it might be a struggle.

That's a quality that I would like to emulate, but I am the kind of person that will think an idea to death before moving on it, by which point it's usually too late. Bill Gates, on the other hand, never hesitated and never slowed down. That, I have come to realize, is a person with a strong mind/ It takes a strong mind to have that kind of confidence in the outcome of their endeavors.

When you combine this mental strength with fearlessness, what you find is someone who will not stop until they have achieved what they have set out to do. When was the last time you went after something—and were relentless until you got it? And I mean something substantial. I don't know about you, but it's been quite a while for me.

***

Chapter 7 Fearless

"Fear is only as deep as the mind allows."

Ralph Waldo Emerson

Right after the clarity that comes from having a strong mind, the characteristic that most defines Bill Gates is the ability to move forward without fear. Don't get me wrong, he has his fears—but it's not about doing or going after the next goal. Gates' fears are about going backwards or not moving forward. His fears are Stoic in nature.

The Stoics have an interesting approach to being successful. Among the values they subscribe to, one is the practice of looking at what's behind you and keeping a healthy sense of fear so that you keep moving forward. The way they do that is by looking at where they are and being thankful for what they have and the opportunities that provides, and then reminding themselves that it can all be gone in a second. Bill Gates has a healthy sense of the notion that it could all be gone in a second. It is also the driving force of every success story I have seen, from Cesar Augustus to Cesar Marcus to Warren Buffet.

The idea is to be fearless going forward and fearful of staying stagnant. The idea is to be fearless in trying and failing, and to be totally afraid of not having the guts to try. You, too, can be fearless—fearless in the same way Bill Gates was when he pitched the operating system owned by another company to IBM and sealed the deal.

Bill Gates was also physically unafraid. Water-skiing is his favorite thing in the world, and he broke his leg doing it. When he got back home in a cast that evening, he didn't make a big deal of it. He was under strict orders to keep the cast on for a specific amount of time, but he didn't listen. His singular focus was to get back on the skis, so he yanked off the cast—with his legs still black and blue—and he got back to it. He wasn't afraid of the pain or the consequences.

Truly successful people aren't afraid because they know that, when the time comes to face a challenge, they have the resources to do it. Jack Ma (Alibaba) was the same way, as was Steve Jobs (Apple), and

Elon Musk (Tesla). Elon Musk's trek from South Africa to the United States via Canada is a story of fearlessness you really should read about.

To be clear, I don't suggest you completely abolish all sense of fear. I don't even think it is possible, but if you could, don't. Instead, look at the fearlessness of achievers. They are fearless because they calculate each move in real time. They are not stuck in indecision as they try an idea or an inspiration. They are fearless not because they do not understand the risk but because they know how to handle and mitigate that risk.

It was the same when Bill left Harvard, and the same when Elon left South Africa. It may have seemed like they were blindly pursuing a hair-brained scheme or a Hail Mary, but that wouldn't be how they saw it. They saw an inspired vision of what the future is—not some fantastical pie in the sky, but an idea that had true merit and a desire that was spot on. They were not fantasizing about golden towers in the sky and sail boats in the Mediterranean. They were planning a rigorous path that would allow them to cultivate and sow the seeds of success.

When you have clarity, you can be fearless because you can see where you are going. You are never afraid of what you can see, you are only petrified of what you can't see.

You may see at the tech industry as something alien, but Bill Gates didn't—he was immersed in it. It was his natural element. He knew it best—he was an expert at it and a genius to boot. He could see what was coming. In fact, he was not just able to see what was going to happen, he was part of the reason some of those things happened.

At that level, it becomes a different game. Don't wait to get there to play the game. Start playing the game now—so that you can get there.

***

Chapter 8 Philanthropy

"To me, global poverty is a humanitarian issue. People are dying, and we can save them – and that ought to be enough."

William Henry Gates Sr

There is a difference between a donation, charity, and philanthropy. Most of us make donations on a fairly regular basis. Giving to a charity based on its focus and reach is also something many of us do. But being a philanthropist is not something most of us are able to do or have even thought about doing.

While there is still a lot of little Bill left in this sixty-something-year-old, a lot has changed since the events you have read about in this book, but much has stayed the same. For instance, his perspective of risk remains different than the way most of us perceive it, while his reflections on failure have become more Stoic than they were when he resigned himself to losing at poker in college.

Bill Gates, and many super-contributors like him, find satisfaction in knowing they have touched the lives of many in a positive and constructive way. The more you contribute, the happier you become because that is the most fundamental circuitry of the human purpose.

It's not about making deals and getting the better of the other person. It's not about ravaging the earth and profiting from it. Bill Gates has been about mutual benefit and growth. He moved to enable an entire generation, and that generation serves as the foundation for generations to come. He may not have thought about it in those terms, but that is what his efforts have produced.

When we are inspired to do something, and we combine our talents and interests to do it, we never really know how far it will take us, or where it might take the rest of humanity for that matter. What clouds that is talk of money. Considering the profit you plan to make is fine if you are looking to stay in business, but you shouldn't stop at that.

***

Chapter 9 To Infinity and Beyond

"The Internet is becoming the town square for the global village of tomorrow."

Bill Gates

The books I write about thinkers, leaders, and achievers are based on significant research and analysis. I use a matrix to qualitatively and quantitatively reduce the person I am studying into bite-sized chunks, and use the 80/20 rule—well, it is really more like 90/10—because I have observed that 10% of the man accounts for about 90% of his success.

One of the metrics I use to distill the person to their critical 10% is the finite-infinite matrix in which I consider the way the person views his place in the grand scheme of things. If you haven't read any of my other books, let me quickly describe this matrix and what it does.

The finite-infinite matrix is about matching your internal clock to your actions. There are two kinds of people. One type is the person who is more attuned to the finite measure, and the other is the person who is more tuned to the infinite measure.

It's not whether you are finite or infinite that determines how successful you become, but rather it is how closely you match your own internal rhythm. If you are a finite character, you need to take finite actions and behave in the way that works in the finite world. If you are an infinite person, and you take steps that mirror your infinite nature, you will be successful. The problem arises when you are a finite person but you take steps of an infinite nature. Likewise, if you are an infinite person, you should not do things appropriate for the finite person.

Success is typically determined by how well you do the things that are part of this dimension of your nature. When you see and do things according to your finite-infinite profile, then you will undoubtedly become a success.

This world, however, throws a twist at us. It is designed and made for those who are finite in their personality.

So, just what is a finite personality?

A finite personality is a person who looks at things according to a measurable scale. They look at weekly reviews, quarterly projections, annual revenue, and income, all the benchmarks that can be expressed in finite terms. Even customer service can be expressed in finite terms according to a measurable scale. All these scales and goals are designed to feed the finite personality.

On the other hand, the infinite personality is a person who cannot and will not comprehend the finite numbers, instead looking toward the long term impact of doing something. For instance, if you were to give an infinite person the numbers on why it is okay to burn fossil fuel, they would turn around and look at the issue in a way that cannot be measured and tell you that it does not make sense.

Finite personalities are typically IQ-driven (intelligence quotient), while infinites are typically EQ-driven (emotional quotient). Steve Jobs, for instance, had an infinite personality, and it can be seen in the way he went about designing and looking for the perfect refinements in his product.

A real indicator of a person's personality type is whether they can see the value in the unseen and indefinable elements as easily as they see the value of the parts that can be seen or measured.

When Steve Jobs first got together with Steve Wozniac to create the first Apple computer, Jobs told the guys putting the boards together to arrange them neatly in an organized way. They were confused because the "box" was to be sealed up. No one would see the arrangement of the chips, but Jobs said that he would know. He even made each engineer put their name on the board.

Bill Gates, on the other hand, is a finite person, as revealed in the way he managed his companies and manages his foundation.

Finite and infinite refer to more than just the horizon of one's thinking. It's about the elements a person instinctively prioritizes. When you remain consistent with your priorities, you find that success becomes inevitable.

For instance, the infinite person who is looking to build a long-term engagement with the customer is going to have the habit of fixing things and making them look aesthetically pleasing even under the hood. If that kind of person is asked to slap things together, they will eventually feel drained and unproductive and will lose motivation. On the other hand, the finite person who is looking to make this quarter's numbers is going to overlook whatever does not contribute to that goal and move on to what does.

Have you heard of the 80/20 rule? (The 80/20 rule or the Pareto Principal states that 80% of the results are generated by 20% of the inputs.) However, the rule is only half true because the 80/20 rule applies only to the finite personality. If you are an infinite person, following the 80/20 rule will not work for you; in fact, it will bring you down. The reason a creator of a rule like this believes it works, and will swear by it, is that it works for them. When it works for them, they logically think it will work for everyone. What is overlooked by the creators of such rules is the underlying personality of the person. For some people, rules like the 80/20 just will not work.

You just need to understand who you are. Many people instinctively follow their gut and do what is best for themselves. Parents can make the mistake of forcing their kids to conform to the standards set by schools and the whole academic infrastructure. That ends up forcing the kid to take on a finite personality even though they are wired differently. This is the reason for having so many drop outs and failures—or at least one of the reasons.

Jack Ma (Alibaba) is a classic case of an infinite person in a finite world. This mismatch is the reason he was rejected from schools and couldn't even get a job at KFC. Now he is China's second richest person, with a company that holds the record for the largest IPO day stock value. He found his groove—he started living an infinite life in his own infinite world.

On the other hand, Bill Gates is a finite person who does everything in the now and here. His need for speed, his need for instant results, his need for numbers and trials are all strong indications that he is a person who performs best in the finite world. The Gates manage their foundation by the numbers, and they are very good at it. Remember, one personality type is no better or worse than the other. Finite personalities are great and so are infinites. You just need be loyal to your profile. Bill Gates is.

To understand your own personality, you can read about these successful men, and you will begin to get a practical understanding of the finite-infinite matrix. You can look at men like Steve Jobs, Jack Ma, Richard Branson, and Elon Musk, and start to see their traits and where they fall into the personality groups. As soon as each man found his groove according to his infinite or finite nature, things started to work for him.

Conclusion

"Life is not fair; get used to it."

Bill Gates

If you were expecting a chronological order of events in the life of William Henry Gates, this was not the book for you. This book has been about a man and the events that shaped him and the people who were responsible for how he reacted to those events.

Of course, the number one influence on Bill Gates was Bill Gates, Sr., his dad. Bill Gates was influenced by all the things his father did and the way his father did them—from the technology that his father was so interested in to the philanthropy that Senior knew to be the best source of lasting satisfaction.

Bill Gates' ambition, intelligence, empathy, immense focus, ability to ferret out essentials, and his ability to negotiate and design documents that reflected that agreement were all already part of him as a child and remained part of him as he grew up to become the successful man we see today.

My first exposure to Bill Gates left me a little uncomfortable. The combination of my youth, and the righteousness that inevitably comes with it, combined with a lack of information, left me unimpressed with the man that stood behind the operating system that, for the past quarter century, has been on a majority of the world's computers. Truth be told, I am not a fan of Windows, but I respect what it has done and how far it has gone.

Since then, I've realized that Bill Gates was not in it for the money. Bill Gates may have had his moment of going overboard for a while, splashing his money around, but that passed quickly. Most of his money now goes to the foundation where he has also pledged even more in his succession documents. Warren Buffet, who is arguably Bill Gates' closest friend, also donated his fortunes to the Bill and Melinda Foundation. Together, the two men have gone around trying to convince the world's wealthy to follow their example and give up their wealth for charity.

Bill and Warren have both left instructions that around 90% of their wealth will go to charities doing research to help develop the nations that are in such dire straits we cannot even begin to imagine it. From agricultural genetics to reproductive health in some of the poorest third world countries, Bill and Melinda have personally been involved in determining how the research is funded and how the solutions are structured.

Ultimately, Bill Gates is proof that we live in a world where we are all connected, and we are responsible for the way we develop and the path we choose. Bill chose to follow a focused path that resulted in a tremendous contribution to the world we all live in. Whether you agree with his methods or not, or monopolistic tendencies, the net result, in the end, was one that was good for all.

He has given as much as he earned, and it was evident from day one that it was never about the money. It was about the accomplishment. A person who is in it for the money will not only cheat and swindle if things do not go his way, he will also subconsciously find ways to lavishly tell the world how rich he is (which is usually an exaggeration). In Bill's case, his philanthropic efforts and the life he lives reveals that it has never been about the fame and fortune so much as it has been about seeing the objective in his head come to fruition.

Bill Gates has a unique intelligence, with knowledge that goes beyond a nerd's understanding of technology and programming.

Not only could he memorize and program, but he could also weigh everything and understand things at their most fundamental level. He could also understand the movements of business and society. While Gates is a highly cerebral and immensely logical person, not interested in niceties, he is concerned with practical needs of community and humanity.

Bill Gates is indeed a unique person, as you and I are. We are all unique.

***

I hope you have taken away some interesting insights from this book. I hope that somewhere in its lines you find the note that resonates with you and awakens your spirit to gain the clarity you need to accomplish all the things you have thought about. I hope that it brings you happiness and that you find the path that lights up your soul and animates your existence.

May you find all that you want in life. Compare yourself to no one, but just move forward improving on your yesterday's self.

***

Jack Ma:

A Lesson in Trust, Honor, and Shared Prosperity

Jack Ma:
A Lesson in Trust, Honor, and Shared Prosperity

Reinventing the Motivations of Commerce - Insight and Analysis into the Life of Asia's Richest Man

JR MacGregor

Jack Ma: A Lesson in Trust, Honor, and Shared Prosperity

Reinventing the Motivations of Commerce – Insight and Analysis into the Life of Asia's Richest Man

Published by CAC Publishing LLC.

ISBN 978-1-948489-90-4 paperback

ISBN 978-1-948489-89-8 eBook

This book is dedicated to those who study great men in hopes of one day joining their ranks. Remember, studying and finding what works is only half the battle, it's up to you to implement what you learn and take massive action, so that, one day, you may be studied yourself.

Foreword

What is it about men who scale great heights and reach the summit? Why are we enticed by such success? Why do we yearn to know their secret sauce?

I think it is because we are looking for the spark that will ignite our own giant within. I think it is because we know deep down that we are meant for greatness and achievement, but we are at a loss as to how to go about getting it.

It turns out that the best way for us to find our own spark is to observe the way others have found theirs, but, because no two people get their spark in an identical fashion, we can't find all the pieces to our own puzzle in one place. Instinctively, we have a curiosity that becomes insatiable until we find our own groove.

During my own pursuit to understand success and achievement, I have found a number of recurring themes that apply regardless of what stage of my life I happen to be at. There are three of these truths.

The first, most relevant, truth presents itself as an irony. It is the fact that we are all different, yet we are all the same. Each of us has more dimensions than our one-track mind can initially fathom. The reason so many of the things that work seem so bizarre and nonsensical is that we are all different yet the same. There are areas of our life that can seem completely different on the surface, but on closer inspection we find more similarity than difference.

The second truth is that we typically repel those who are most like us. If you find that you hate something in a person, the chances are very high that you actually have something in common with them. You can use this to your benefit. Observe and take note of the feelings you have about someone, but refrain from criticism. Keep criticism to a minimum, or to none at all, because today's criticism becomes tomorrow's barrier to advancement. In your pursuit of success, everyone has something to contribute.

The third and final truth is that success is not just about mastering one single aspect of action. It is not about having great vision like Jack Ma when he, in the early days, recognized what the internet could represent. It is not just about the attention to detail that Steve Jobs showed us. It is not just about empathy like Elon Musk and Richard Branson display.

Each individual ingredient is complex in depth and shade, with more complexity than the words used to describe them can convey. To be successful, we need to have each these single filaments of success and weave them together to form our own cloak of invincibility. Since no word can capture the true meaning of each individual characteristic needed to be successful, we are left to the next best thing, and that is to personify these individual characteristics of success in men who have come to embody them.

It helps that our species is a curious bunch and we want knowledge—we want to know what it is, how to make, and how to use it. Likewise, when it comes to success, we want to know what its characteristics are, how to emulate those characteristics, and how to apply that knowledge to our own corner of the world. And, so, we want to know how successful men become successful.

On our path to develop our own personal suite of characteristics, we constantly try new things to see how they fit. It is like trying on a new shoe. We try it, see if it fits. If it suits us, and if it works, we hang on to it. If it does not, we put it back, and try something else. That is, in essence, what making mistakes and experiencing failure is all about. It is improbable that every new thing you try is going to work every time. It is good to be curious about everything.

Studying Jack Ma provides a wealth of material for understanding the human condition and spirit. Unlike the many other accomplished men I have studied, Ma was raised in a very different culture. Jack Ma is a beacon embodying pure intention and desire winning against forces of circumstance. His story demonstrates that it is possible to make something out of nothing, and to advance positively through a sea of negativity. Culture, geolocation, initial surroundings, and circumstances have only a small part to play in how one's life unfolds.

If there is such a thing as fate, it is not determined by where you are born. That is liberating to understand, wherever you come from. So often, in today's world, we are brought face to face with the diversity of our origins. Forces to exclude those of diverse origins try to rise against the voices that champion the desire to include. While I can understand the fear of displacement, I find inclusion to be a wholly better endeavor, something that Jack Ma exemplifies.

I hope you find as much insight from this book as I did while writing it. I hope you come closer to your own truth and find your own wings to fly. May success be your guide and achievement your goal.

***

Introduction

"The very important thing you should have is patience."

Jack Ma

Hangzhou is a city located southwest of Shanghai. It sits by Hangzhou Bay which connects to the East China Sea. It is a vibrant city in today's China, dominated by commerce and industry. Today, the mention of China evokes images of large factories and vibrant commerce, large populations, and delectable food. It was not so in 1965. 1965's China was a very different story, and Hangzhou a very different place.

Jack Ma, China's richest man until recently, was born in Hangzhou, on October 15, 1965, to working parents and a modest lifestyle. He was born Ma Yun, the middle of the three siblings, with an older brother and younger sister. He was seven years old before he realized there was a world beyond the land speaking his native tongue.

Richard Nixon had entered the White House and begun to make strides in opening a path to Beijing. In 1972, Nixon's historical trip to Beijing included a visit to Hangzhou, which put the town on the map and marked it as a destination for throngs of tourists. With Nixon's arrival, Ma learned that a whole new world existed somewhere out there, and his mind was lit. That new revelation combined with the opportunity to meet people from the new world redrew Ma's path and changed the trajectory of his life.

By any measure, Jack Ma was an average kid. There was nothing spectacular or outstanding about this scrawny kid. He was small for his age, and that attracted the bullies like bees to honey. The way he responded to being picked on constantly at school shaped the way he has behaved the rest of his life. Ma found a part of himself that could stand up to bullies. Like all of us presented with adversity, we face choices. We can choose to run or fight. When young Jack was faced with this choice, he stood his ground and fought. At first, there was not a lot of winning. He did get knocked around a bit, but he learned, and he fought back, not because he was the belligerent sort, but because he was staking his claim to the spot where he was standing.

Being the scrawny kid can be a challenging affair. You need to be twice as brave to make up for your slight presence, and you have to be fast. Jack was naturally fast—both in agility and in thinking. This helped get him out of trouble and ahead of the game even as a kid.

Jack Ma spent much of his childhood entertaining himself in a city that was fairly cultural and ethnic. Remember, China in the sixties was changing in a staggering way. Infrastructure change was accompanied by changes in outlook, fashion, values, and lifestyle. Back then, rising to the top of the pile was a lot more difficult, especially if you are not one connected to the corridors of power. To make it in China as an outsider was unheard off. And Jack Ma was the quintessential outsider, as you will see through the unfolding of his life.

Ma was a typical kid, curious about everything, from language to crickets. He was also observant. One of his favorite hobbies was collecting crickets on the outskirts of Hangzhou and pitting them in battles against each other. He went to great lengths to understand those crickets so that he'd have the best ones he could find and would be able to win the next matchup. He became so good at it that he could identify the best crickets with great accuracy simply by listening to the sounds they made. He could pick the winners just by watching them for a few minutes.

Later, in a speech, Jack Ma was to say, *"The very important thing you should have is patience."* The patience Ma describes is not about letting the chips fall where they may, but is a very deliberate and powerful sort of patience, uncommon among successful men. It is the patience of the waters of the Colorado River imperceptibly chiseling through the rock to form the Grand Canyon.

Throughout his life, Jack Ma's work has been a blend of hurry and patience. It has been like powerfully and relentlessly turning the wheel of a grinding stone but giving the stone the time it needs to sharpen the blade, rather than stopping it every few minutes to see if the work is done. This is the same kind of patience the Stoics were about.

There are three direct consequences of developing patience. The first is that you get to enter the nature of things and understand your actions in a way that is deep and thorough. This allows you to go further than others would, and that, in turn, allows you to succeed when others fail.

The second consequence of developing patience is that it staves off frustration and allows you to do what is necessary when it is called for, without wasting mental and physical resources by worrying and fretting over outcomes.

Third, having patience allows the universe to do its part. You can only do half the work when you want to bake a cake. After the batter is done, you need to let the oven do its thing. If you keep opening the oven door and letting the air out, you are going to have a poorly baked cake. When I compare myself to Jack Ma, I realize that patience is something I could have used a lot more of in my life. Do you have enough patience?

***

Chapter 1 Jack

"People think, 'Jack, you do too much'."

Jack Ma

It was 1972 and Richard Nixon had just made his historic visit to China to normalize Sino-US relations. While he was there, Nixon met with Mao Zedong and Zhou Enlai, visiting three cities, Beijing, Shanghai, and Jack Ma's birthplace of Hangzhou. That visit had a direct impact on six year old Ma Yun.

With the thawing Sino-American relationships, tourists and businesses from the United States flocked to the newly opened China. One of the places they flocked to was Hangzhou. The tourism industry was one of the first areas of commerce to see a boom in the wake of Nixon's efforts. The little, free-spirited Ma Yun was exposed to an entirely new culture from across the waters of the East

China Sea while the hotel and tourism industry started to boom in Hangzhou.

In his teenage years, Ma Yun's fascination with the new cultures and new languages prompted him to learn English, but, since he could not afford to take English lessons and they weren't taught in school, he decided to do the next best thing. He began to barter for it. In return for tours of the city, he would ask American tourists to teach him how to speak English. It was an effective and creative way to learn English.

As Ma Yun spent time with the tourists, showing them around town and learning their language, he realized that life did not have to be limited to the way the Chinese did things, or to the way the Ma household did things. He realized that the world out there was large, larger than what he could possibly imagine, and he was determined to make something of it.

He gained one more thing from his endeavors that remains with him to this day. Aside from learning English from these tourists, he also acquired the name Jack. So, one day out of the blue, he left home as Ma Yun, and came back as Jack Ma.

***

Chapter 2 Academic Life

"China is still the fastest growing economy in the world, but we need to learn how to use money in a better way, and it's about quality, not quantity."

Jack Ma

We are often fooled into thinking that, without the proper educational background or name-brand college certificate, we are destined to follow a less desirable path, but that is not always the case, especially today. However, like many before, Jack Ma decided that the first thing he needed to do if he wanted to get ahead was get an education.

The educational system in China is not as liberal as in the United States; you cannot just walk into a school, and say, "Here I am." In China, you must sit for rigorous tests at the National level, and your scores determine which college or university you can go to. The tests are not optional like the SATs or the APs in the USA. In China, if you take the tests and fail, you are not going anywhere. And Jack failed twice.

Taking standardized tests in China is nothing like taking the college entrance exams in the USA. The Chinese tests are tough. If I were to bet, I would wager that more than two-thirds of US college graduates wouldn't be able to get through China's college entrance exams. They are designed to be tough and separate the wheat from the chaff.

Sometimes you don't get what you want on the first couple of tries. When Ma went back for the third time, he was better prepared. He had resolved to do whatever he needed to, and he hit the books hard. Jack Ma passed the exams and was able to attend teacher's college, eventually graduating as an English teacher. His barters from two decades before had paid off—but not as much as they eventually would.

Jack Ma was an average student, not because he was lazy or slow on the pick-up, but because he was focused on different things than the typical student. He was diligent, no doubt, but his heart was elsewhere. He knew there was more to life than he could get from sitting in a one-size-fits-all classroom.

Yet, while Ma was all about celebrating his own unique perspective and his unique pursuits, he also knew one thing we all need to realize sometime in our lives. Even successful men like Andrew Carnegie and Jeff Bezos have known that we all need to do what is necessary for today's living while we prepare for tomorrow's success. So, when Jack Ma graduated teacher's training college, he taught English for $12 a month.

***

Chapter 3 The Internet

"I know nothing about technology."

Jack Ma

We live in a unique time with a new phenomenon called the internet. For the first time ever, we now have an adult population that has known the internet since their birth. The Millennials, as this cohort is called, is the generation born between the 80s and the mid-90s. This generation has always been fully immersed in the internet.

The older Generation X crowd occupies another unique position, starting life when there was still no internet, watching its birth, and seeing, with amazement, how far the internet has come during their lifetime. That is the generation of Jack Ma.

When he first saw the internet up close, Jack Ma was electrified, with the same instincts emerging as he felt when he saw the first batch of foreigners in Hangzhou as a kid. The internet fueled some of his wildest imaginings, and he instinctively knew that an opportunity like no other right was before his eyes.

When we see the internet as a normal state of daily life and events, we can become blind to it in a way that Jack Ma was not. We see the internet as a source of goods, services, content, and connection. Jack saw the internet as an open portal to reach out the world. Even though he had no coding or programming experience, he knew the internet was a frontier he needed to explore.

Jack Ma still knows nothing about technology other than what he absorbs through the daily operation of his company. But therein lies the essence of what it means to be successful. You do not need to know the nuts and bolts of something to make it big. You do not need to be an inventor to make it big. We don't all need to be a Thomas Edison or an Alexander Graham Bell. Henry Ford did not need to redesign the wheel to multiply the market for automobiles. Steve Jobs did not need to know how to solder a motherboard, and Richard Branson did not need to know how to read a balance sheet. Yet, each one understood the value they could contribute to the value chain.

Jack Ma today still does not know how to code, but he knows how to create value in a global trading and payment system that is one of the largest in the world. When Alibaba debuted on the NYSE, it was the largest IPO the market had ever seen—$168 billion. When they ended their first day of trading on the NYSE, Jack Ma said, "What we raised today is not money, it is trust." That statement reveals that Jack Ma sees Alibaba as an extension of himself, one that is part of the value he offers the world, and that the value he offers is the trust of the participants in the market he created.

There is no success to be had unless it is based on value. Your contribution is not complete until you add that value. Success is when your contribution adds so much value for others that the only way they can pay you for it is by rewarding you. But that reward isn't what you go after in your pursuit of success—you go after achieving a level of contribution that no one else can offer.

Jack Ma saw the opportunity to add value to a marketplace that was missing one essential component. There was a problem with trust in the online marketplace. What Ma brought to that market was the ability to instill confidence in the buyer. When he earned that trust, he was able to catapult the company to stratospheric heights. On Singles Day, China's answer to Valentines Day, Alibaba had a sale that totaled more than $18 billion in sales. That would not have been possible were it not for the trust that Ma had structured into every transaction made through Alibaba.

Jack Ma's contribution was to touch buyers and sellers alike and reach out to them across vast seas and across borders. Ma's version of success has been based on trust and structuring that trust into every transaction. Have you ever tried to buy anything from Alibaba? They have options to choose shipping with or without tracking numbers. Whenever I place an order, I take free shipping without the tracking number, and, yet, not once in the many times I have made a purchase have I not received what I ordered. Think about that for a minute. How do you institutionalize that sort of efficiency and trust?

That was the value Jack Ma created and executed; trust was the lynchpin in creating a robust and efficient market. It isn't just the seller who has benefited, it is the buyer as well. Buyers go on to add their own value, reselling their products to other customers. Without Alibaba and Alipay, there would be a huge hit to global trade—and to the capacity for wealth creation that has been made available to the smaller guy.

The day Alibaba hit a market share of $168 billion was a testament to the trust Jack Ma has been passionate about creating in the marketplace. It was the value that he added—and he was rewarded with a $25 billion personal payday.

***

Chapter 4 Question Everything

"Before I left China, I was educated that China was the richest, happiest country in the world. So, when I arrived in Australia, I thought, 'Oh my God, everything is different from what I was told.' Since then, I started to think differently."

Jack Ma

As a kid growing up, whether in China or just about anywhere else, you are not aware of the politics and take for granted the biases. All you may hear is that you are from the best country—until you actually meet someone from another country.

It wasn't until Jack Ma got outside China and began to travel the world that he realized that there is a difference between the hype and the reality. He realized that many conventional truths weren't really truths at all, and that, if he wanted to get the real story, he needed to question everything.

In 1995, Ma traveled to the United States on behalf of a client who was looking for a solution to an accounts receivable issue. At the time, Jack had an English-Chinese translation business, often helping clients with more than translation. During that trip, Jack Ma was introduced to the internet and shown how to find anything using a search engine. To his dismay, when he tried to find Chinese beer, his search came up empty. He wasn't even able to find any Chinese websites on the internet, so he decided to do something about that.

When he got back to China, he set up an internet company focused on building websites for Chinese businesses. (This was not Alibaba yet.) Ma was interested in accomplishing three things. First, he wanted to create a platform for his countrymen to get out onto the world stage. Second, he wanted the rest of the world to know China, how far it had come, and what it had to offer. Finally, he wanted to take advantage of the opportunity that he saw so plainly.

So, Jack Ma set up China Pages. At its heart, China Pages was a cross border effort in international trade, introducing the new China to the rest of the world. That was 1995, and China had been building up its capacity for some time and was well on its way to becoming a manufacturing powerhouse.

This large industrial complex had created numerous small and medium enterprises (SMEs) that were open to international business but didn't yet know or understand how to get that international business. Ma's idea was to give them a leg up on the international scene by having China Pages act as a portal into China.

To expand the scope of the business, Ma teamed up with a few friends, and brought in a government entity as a partner. The idea was to expand China Pages with an infusion of resources and to have the government agency open doors in the right places. It did not turn out as he had planned. Instead, Ma found the bureaucracy stifling. There wasn't much Jack Ma could do, so rather than fighting an uphill battle, he quit and moved on.

Ma went on to get a job at the Ministry of Foreign Trade and Economic Cooperation. This wasn't what he really wanted to do, but the opportunity proved beneficial in the long run. He made strong connections through the job, one of which was with Jerry Yang, the founder of Yahoo.

Upon leaving the ministry a short time later, Jack Ma spent some time soul searching. He had an inner drive, and a lot of built-up frustration and pent up energy. Even now, anyone who meets him instantly recognizes the wound-up energy that pervades his presence. It is not frustration or anger—it is simply unbridled energy that comes from battling with whatever hand life deals you. It is the same energy that kept him going as he got rejected time and again, for everything from a job at KFC to admissions at Harvard. (At KFC he was the only person to be rejected out of 24 applicants. He applied to Harvard and was rejected ten times.)

That kind of raw energy is not sustainable without a purpose and vision to direct it. Jack was intent on going somewhere. He may have not consciously been aware of where that might be, but he discovered the direction that would consume him when he was at the keys of a computer in the United States, unable to find a single Chinese company when he searched for Chinese beer.

Jack Ma has moved from nationalistic motivations to altruistic motivations over the years as he increasingly sees the whole world as a common humanity, not as geography with political lines drawn across them. His original idea of the need for jobs for all Chinese has grown into the desire to spread jobs and prosperity to all people regardless of their street address.

Ma has said that SMEs are the instruments of wealth creation, and he wants to see every SME become larger than Amazon. He sees himself as the enabler that would facilitate this revolution. He has looked into the future, saying,

"Every revolution takes about fifty years."

Jack Ma

Chapter 5
Championing Shared Prosperity

"As a business person, I want the world to share the prosperity together."

Jack Ma

Jack Ma is motivated by many of the same things that typical Fortune 500 companies are, but one thing that is front and center in his mind, which rarely occurs to the others, is shared prosperity, or prosperity for all.

Ma wants to raise China and its millions of workers to a level of prosperity yet unseen in that country. But his desire to elevate the man on the street does not stop at China's borders but reaches around the world. That was one reason he recently pledged to the American President that he would create a million jobs in the United States.

Ma believes that shared prosperity comes from shared contribution. That means that everyone must have a job; everyone needs to be employed and contributing to each other's success, thereby creating a shared success and shared prosperity.

For Jack Ma, this starts at the local level. The idea behind Alibaba, and China Pages, was to advance businesses in China and launch them onto the world stage. But it doesn't stop there.

Ma understands acutely that one's prosperity is dependent upon another's. He sees global trade as crucial to joint prosperity. Ma's vision is motivated by more than money. Ma has brought his vision of pulling together the four corners of the world to the global stage. He sees that as inextricably linked to global free trade, and so he has been unhappy with the possibility of restrictive trade policies.

The key success factor necessary to institute Jack Ma's philosophy is trust. For him, trust is the foundation that needs to underpin all of his businesses and is at the heart of all that connects the world.

In 2011, an event was to test Jack Ma's core value of trust. Ma was devastated when it came to light that outright fraud taking place within Alibaba. It struck at the core of Jack's empire. A number of employees were found to have been awarding Gold Star status to undeserving vendors. It was not an innocent error, or someone not doing their job properly. It was outright fraud with the intent to cheat Alibaba's customers.

Alibaba awarded Gold Star status to vendors who had proven themselves repeatedly. When they were awarded this rating, it gave buyers on Alibaba a sense of trust in the vendor and its products. This was one of the ways Alibaba bridged the trust gap in the electronic marketplace. It was an obvious and important part of their reputation management system.

Unfortunately, some unscrupulous employees had colluded with outsiders to set up shops selling all kinds of electronic goods. There were more than a couple of hundred involved, taking orders and payments—but not delivering the products.

When the fraud was exposed, the always smiling, pint-sized Jack, flew into rage, because the scam had attacked one of the most important things he had worked so hard to build and maintain—trust. He had taken many steps to institutionalize trust and this act would diminish that. The frauds threatened a lot more than the affected customers. It threatened Jack's vision of shared prosperity.

Jack Ma had brought a firm belief in a set of principles into the culture of Alibaba and into all the companies he created. As a persona and head of the company, Ma directed the company to adhere to a specific priority of allegiance. His principles were to always champion the customer first, the employee second, and the investor third. Many times prior to the IPO, and even during the IPO, Ma said,

"If you want to invest in us, we believe customer No. 1, employee No. 2, shareholder No. 3. If they do not want to buy that, that is fine. If they regret, they can sell us."

That has been his mantra. He firmly believes that each company stands only because of the customer, and that he can only realize the goal of large scale employment for the masses if the customer patronizes his company. Without the customer, everything else falls apart.

Imagine, if you can, what it must have felt like for a man with such priorities and convictions to discover that the second most important group on his list of priorities was actively betraying the first, and, in so doing, were corrupting his values and jeopardizing his dream of mass employment. That event was the beginning of one of the hardest times in Jack Ma's life.

Ma could have taken the easy way out and swept it under the rug. Instead, he fired more than a hundred people who were directly or indirectly involved in the fraud. He even fired the CEO and the COO, because upper management is ultimately responsible for all that goes on. In the end, there was about $2 million worth of losses that he had to take responsibility for. It was a simple decision for him. Not doing so would have let down the group Ma regards as the lynchpin of shared prosperity.

Whether you call this ethics or morals doesn't matter, but these principles are lacking in much of the business world today. Many business leaders have become so myopic they have forgotten that the customer is the key to their survival.

***

Chapter 6 His Own Man

"When I am myself, I am happy and have a good result."

Jack Ma

Everyone who knew Jack Ma before his rise to fame and fortune describes him as being completely ordinary. His wife even goes one step further, and says that Ma is not the best-looking person in the world, but she was more interested in him for the way he thought and his tenacity for getting things done.

From looks to personality, from demeanor to gait, from intellect to talent, Jack Ma was in many ways unremarkable. But Zhang Ying also saw that this young man of 5'3" at teacher's college was different in his outlook and spark. What he lacked in height, looks, or presence, he made up for in spades with tenacity, energy, and ideas. Jack Ma and Zhang Ying were married right after college and stitched together a living on a teacher's salary of $12 a month.

No one, even Zhang Ying, ever thought that Jack Mas was anyone other than he seemed to be or that he was pretending to be something that he was not. There was no air of duplicity about him, nor any air of arrogance about anything that he undertook. Jack Ma has no illusions about who he is. You know how some people think they are all that when they have nothing to show for it? Jack Ma, even today, has none of that.

What Jack Ma was always true to were his own stars. He worked hard, he had ostentatious dreams, and he pulled out all the stops to make it happen.

Zhang was shocked and worried at the same time, but she went along with it when, one day, out of the blue, Jack resigned from his teaching position and announced to her that he wanted to begin his own business. This was years before their Alibaba days. On the surface, there was not one leg to stand on for this decision, but she had always felt instinctively that there was more to Jack than his physical attributes would suggest.

She was constantly unsettled as day after day went by, and Jack Ma's first business floundered. The business, Haibo Translation Agency, provided English translation services to locals. They made about $30 a month, but rent alone was about $95., so there was always a shortfall in revenue. To make up the difference and pay the bills at the translation business, Jack would go to the market at Yiwu in Guangzhou, and sell odds and ends to shoppers. It took three years, but Ma finally managed to make the translation business a success.

Just as Zhang Ying began to breathe a sigh of relief, Jack turned the tables on her again by starting China Pages. Then, he took another leap to start his ecommerce venture. Zhang Ying's growing worry and stress only increased when Jack announced that he planned to borrow 500,000 Yuan to start the website for it.

Soon, Jack Ma had put together a group of sixteen people and persuaded them to put their money in, but he gave them fair warning. He told them that they could either lose it all, or they could become richer than anything they could imagine. His investors included friends, colleagues, and students.

Jack brought Zhang Ying into the picture and told her he wanted her to be his general—his right-hand person—but for that, she had to quit her job and relinquish the only stable source of income in the family. According to Jack, the reason for having his wife quit her job and come on board Alibaba was to make everyone else feel safe that the endeavor was an all-in effort by the family and not some idle hair-brained scheme. Jack Ma was consumed by the importance of trust and the perception of it. Like Gandhi, Ma knew from a young age that being truthful alone was not enough, that it was equally important, if not more so, to be perceived as such.

With 16 people and his wife, with one son on the way, Alibaba was born. In its early stages, Alibaba sucked up a lot of the oxygen in the Ma home for Jack and the others who came there. The Ma home was the central office for all brainstorming and working ideas. They worked day in and day out. If the others were not there and Jack Ma had an inspiration, they would all be there and hard at work on the idea in 10 minutes.

As much as Zhang Ying was originally supposed to be a key member of the founding team, her duties as hostess became prioritized. As a member of a Chinese household, it was up to the mistress of the home to host and take care of all those who visited. Whatever their financial situation was, meals and refreshments needed to be provided as a matter of courtesy, and Zhang Ying executed that responsibility gracefully.

Times were tight. All the founding members took 500 Yuan from the company to sustain themselves. In the Ma household, that was used as part of the budget for feeding their guests when they were there.

This went on for more than a year. Toil, sweat, smoke, and long days rolled into longer nights. At the end of the year, when Zhang Ying asked him how much they made, Jack did not have much to report. It was a devastating conversation for both. But Jack punctuated that terse conversation with a prediction that one day they would make income enough to pay one million in taxes per day.

***

Chapter 7 Choices

"When we first started our internet company, 'China Pages,' in 1995, and we were just making home pages for a lot of Chinese companies. We went to the big owners, the big companies, and they did not want to do it. We go to state-owned companies, and they did not want to do it. Only the small and medium companies really want to do it."

Jack Ma

Sweat and toil weren't the only price Jack and Zhang Ying paid for their success at Alibaba. Beyond the usual sacrifices, there was one significant price the Mas were about to pay, and they did not know it at the time. Their son, who was born the same year Alibaba was founded, had been left to grow up virtually alone while the adults around him, from the Mas to all the founders and workers who hung out at the Ma household, worked.

The company got the lion's share of the parents' attention. Their son grew up in the same smoke-filled room as the rest of the people working on Alibaba. Young Ma was a product of that environment.

Without sufficient parental guidance from his parents, young Ma began to develop in an unwanted direction. Unsurprisingly, young Ma, having grown up surrounded by talk of the internet, ended up spending time in internet bars and online gaming centers at a young age as soon as he was given a little freedom. That is not typically a great way to spend one's youth.

At just ten years of age, the young Ma was having problems at school and was excessively disobedient with his parents. His teachers were not happy with his academics and his social skills. The causes of young Ma's problems were finally identified as the lack of parental guidance and the loneliness he experienced from spending so much time without his parents' attention. When Zhang Ying reported these developments to Jack, Jack was in shock. They had both missed the writing on the wall. All of their success at Alibaba had been at the cost of their son's emotional and psychological development.

The Mas made a two-pronged assault on the problem.

First, Jack Ma took an unconventional approach to the problem. Jack gave his son 200 Yuan and told him to go play online games with his friends. He gave the boy permission to spend all of it and stay out for as long as he wanted. He was gone for three days. When he returned, he was hungry and exhausted, so he was fed well and put to bed. When he woke up, Jack was waiting for him, and they had a simple conversation. Jack asked his son what he had gained from all those internet games. He asked him where the money went. What had he gained from it? The approach was unusual, but it had the intended effect. It got the young Ma to wake up and recognize the outcome of his choices.

Second, Zhang Ying began to stay home to look after him. Zhang Ying stepped back from her responsibilities at Alibaba, which had, by this point, grown and was doing very well. At home, Zhang Ying stayed with their son every minute of the day. Within a short period of time, it was enough to turn the boy around, and both his grades and social demeanor started to improve.

That event had an impact on the Ma household. Internet games became a taboo subject at home. Even when Jack Ma had the opportunity to invest in them, he stayed away. It was not something he wanted to be a part of.

We all make choices and decisions. Every action is the result of a choice. Sometimes those choices have unforeseen consequences. In economics, we typically call this the *opportunity cost.* It exists for all actions. All actions have an alternative, whether you see it or not. Everything you do is a choice; everything you do has an alternative. Even sitting down and doing nothing is an alternative.

However, you cannot dwell in regret or stop taking action because the alternative you may not see or think of was actually the better choice. You need to keep moving forward. The only way you can reconcile with your choices is by not practicing the indiscipline of regret. Those who know that everything is a choice also know that once they have made their choice, there can be no regret. If you play the regret game, every choice you make will never be good enough, and your thoughts can stray to the alternative you didn't choose and the benefits that could have flowed from it.

Look at it in another way. When Jack had the opportunity to start Alibaba and his son was born at the same time, Jack Ma had a choice. What if he had decided to focus on raising his son, instead of diving into Alibaba? Certainly, Jack's son would have been well cared for and received the attention of both his parents from a young age, but, at the same time, millions of people would not have benefited from the creation of Alibaba.

We all make choices. That's part of life. It is just the way it is. Until we master quantum mechanics, and can be in multiple places at the same time, doing multiple things simultaneously, we are forced to conduct the affairs of a single path, without regrets over the path that could have been.

Choices play a fundamental role in determining the reality that unfolds for us. There are two kinds of choices. The first are the choices you make with both eyes wide open. You know all the alternatives, and you can logically prioritize and decide. The second kind of choice is the type Jack Ma faced—one where you do not see all the alternatives and their consequences as you are moving forward on a singular path with a singular vision.

***

Chapter 8 Understand Your Motivation

"I don't want to be liked. I want to be respected."

Jack Ma

Most people have a goal. However simple and uncomplicated that goal may be, they have a goal. Some want to get a job to pay the rent. Others have a goal to achieve standing in a specific profession. Still others want to have a family and a house in the suburbs. There are many kinds of goals.

Jack Ma had his goals, too. He had a goal when he sent out his college applications, and he certainly had a goal when he went around Hangzhou bartering city tours for English lessons.

But a goal can be a double-edged sword. Goals can be either cause for frustration or the impetus to make progress. It is like driving to the store. If you don't set your goal of going to the store, you will end up driving around aimlessly and burning gas for no discernable benefit.

The difference between someone like Jack Ma and the rest of us isn't whether we have or don't have goals, but is in the kinds of goals we have, the choices we make, and the motivations behind the choice of goals. In many cases, we see a goal and like the idea of it, but we fizzle out, because the motivation to get started and keep going, and the ability to get up after a failure are not there.

That is why you see success stories built on situations where the person had "no choice" but to succeed, because the failure of the endeavor would have brought about such catastrophe that they had to fight hard relentlessly to make it. Having no way out is a great motivator.

Jack Ma was highly motivated. Whether applying for a job as a teenager, or wanting to learn English, his motivation to do the things he had chosen to do was very strong. How do we know what motivation looks like? Instead of trying to describe it, imagine, if you can, the commitment it takes to keep the lights on in a business by taking on a second job. That is what Jack Ma did when he was supporting Haibo (translation company).

Studying success stories, I discovered that what I had believed important is actually less important. As MBAs (Master of Business Administration), it was drilled into us that startups need to be studied, and business plans needed to take competitor analysis, target markets, and demographics into consideration. It all had to be put into a business plan. Then you had to go out, get funded, and get started. I have tried doing it that way, and you know what always seemed to happen—someone else would beat me to the punch.

Jack Ma did not use market research or competitor analysis. His secret formula was simple—shared prosperity, an inspiration, instinct, and doing everything it took to get it done.

Jack's motivation to get things done was extraordinary. Like many super achievers, Jack was a person who could not rest until he succeeded in achieving his goal. He was relentless about it. But what was different about him from many of the people I have studied is that he did not take shortcuts.

Many could argue that Jack Ma's ideas were shortcuts in that Alibaba was created in the image of Amazon, Taobao was created in the image of eBay, and Alipay was developed in the image of PayPal. But China is a very different market, and Ma's motivations were very different. He did not just copy Amazon, eBay, and PayPal. He looked at the idea of a marketplace and a payment gateway, and he created his own version of it. Saying that he copied Amazon to make Alibaba would be like saying that Elon Musk copied Henry Ford to make a production line for Tesla. Jack Ma openly said, *"Our philosophy is, using internet technology, we can make every company become Amazon."*

It is the process of being motivated that is the key, the reason for the motivation is secondary. You can never define your motivation—it is simply a power you have inside to get done what you are inspired to do. It is like mixing the two parts of an epoxy. There is the resin, and there is the hardener. If you only have the resin, it will not harden; if you just have the hardener but not the resin, the hardened material will be too brittle to be of any use. You need both parts, mixed in precise ratio to get the right result.

Success is similar: you need the two parts of the equation filled precisely; one without the other will not get you anything. The two parts required for any success are the tangible and the intangible.

The inspiration, the intangible, for Jack Ma, was not to become rich (that's not inspiration, that's greed) but was to altruistically redefine the landscape for Chinese businesses and allow them to trek a path to buyers around the world.

In Jack Ma's case, the tangible part was the active hustle he put into everything he did. If any idea was stuck in his head, he would not rest until he was able to convert that intangible inspiration into a physical manifestation.

The secret to gargantuan success, not just minor achievement, comes from this formula. If you look at history and study the long list of positive successes that men have achieved, and if you took the time to study them intently, you would find that this tangible/intangible duality was satisfied in every single instance.

The inspiration/motivation phenomenon is one that we all understand instinctively but do not really know how to execute. It is the same thing you get when you pray. It is the same thing you get when you conduct rituals. It is even something you do when you wish on a birthday candle and blow it out. Tangible and intangible are two sides of the same coin of success.

Jack Ma instinctively handled those two sides of success by taking tangible action on his intangible inspirations. As a major component of his business, Jack Ma specifically sought after and achieved the intangible asset of trust. He paired that with the manifested physical actions of delivery and guarantee. His response to the fraudulent Gold Star sellers at Alibaba is a perfect example.

Ma's inspiration/motivation matrix is evident in everything he does and in every pairing of tangible/intangible phenomenon that he partakes in. Jack Ma has been motivated to create tangible businesses by intangible things that are literally larger than life and larger than his own needs.

***

Chapter 9 Jack's Four Failures

"Instead of learning from other people's success, learn from their mistakes. Most of the people who fail share common reasons (to fail) whereas success can be attributed to various different kinds of reasons."

Jack Ma

When you study Jack Ma's life, it becomes apparent that he was not flattered by his own strengths, but he was also undaunted by his weaknesses. Like most, Ma made his share of mistakes, but he learnt much about life from them.

Here are five mistakes that contributed to Ma's experience and ultimate success.

1. Failing in school.

Failing at school as many times as Jack Ma would have made it easy to give up. However, we are all given different natural talents and strengths for accomplishing different things.

It is conventional thinking to believe that the academic route is the best way to educate a person, but some of the greatest successes only found academic institutions to be stifling, not liberating. Bill Gates, whom I have also written about, was a school dropout. Mark Zuckerberg was also a dropout. Steve Jobs was another one without academic credentials. All these people were successes because they were revolutionaries.

To be a revolutionary, you cannot think the same old way using the same old methods, you need to reinvent the wheel whenever possible. Conventional schools are not the best way to create unconventional minds.

According to Sir Ken Robinson, education and creativity expert, the fires of creativity are not only not fanned in school, they are positively doused, and the ashes discarded into the bin of mediocrity. Likewise, Jack Ma has begun to argue for changes to education. Ma has been advocating that education should now emphasize creativity, independent thinking, innovation, and imagination, qualities where human beings will always be superior to machines and Artificial Intelligence.

2. Failing at Math.

Jack Ma specifically failed at math. On one test to determine his mathematical competency, Ma got 1 out of 120 possible points. Failure occurred at 70. While Chinese exams are specifically designed to be hard, capable of bringing even the most brilliant of students to their intellectual knees, the only thing Ma's score revealed was that he did not know any of the material covered.

3. Failing to get into Harvard 10 times.

Most people would consider this an example of Ma's tenacity, but I see it as a mistake that could not get past him. Jack Ma applied to Harvard 10 times and was rejected each time. Ma's mistake was thinking that Harvard had something to offer him that he needed.

I encounter scores of people who feel worthless because they don't have a name-brand college degree. Others doubt themselves because they have no degree at all, but that is the worst way to look at one's self. If you cannot see your own self-worth without validating it with a college degree, then you have bigger problems than not having that degree.

Look at the real successes achieved by the giants of history. Although some did go to Ivy League schools, and others went to regular state schools or community colleges, there is a large population of achievers who did not take this conventional route.

So, what was Ma's real mistake? It was trying nine more times to get into Harvard after the first rejection. That was a waste of time. However, Ma was always tenacious about going after what he had set his mind to.

It was a good thing that Harvard had not accepted him. If they had, he might only have gone to work for a billionaire instead of becoming one.

4. Failing to put the right people at the top.

Jack Ma made that known to his initial investors who put in the original $60,000 that they would not be key managers in the running of the company, because he wanted to hire those who were trained and the best in the field. Ma soon learned that was the biggest mistake, because top management who did not have skin in the game were not worth the additional intellectual contribution they brought to the table. When Alibaba was hit with the fraud scandal that shook it to its very foundation, Ma realized that founder's blood was thicker than water. A man who has a personal stake in the rise and fall of the company would do whatever it takes to keep it alive, but an employee can come and go as he or she pleases.

5. Failing to get seed money.

Jack Ma's best "failure" of all was repeatedly failing to get seed capital from Silicon Valley to fund Alibaba. He had turned to Silicon Valley to fund Alibaba during its early stages and was turned down several times. That turned out to be a good thing, although it must have been completely disheartening. His mistake was to waste time with Silicon Valley. There were two different cultures at play, the way Alibaba was run, and the way Silicon Valley expected the companies they invest in to be run. If Ma had gotten that investment, it would have stifled the prospects of the company, and it would not have become the largest IPO in NYSE history.

***

Chapter 10 See the Big Picture

"Trade is a communication of cultures and values."

Jack Ma

Jack Ma gets the big picture. Something in him has been able to see the whole nine yards since he turned 12 and wanted to speak English so badly that he went downtown and offered his services as a tour guide in return for English lessons. It would have been easy for him to offer tours for a dollar here and there, and that would have translated into quite a lot of money. Remember, 15 years later, his entire month's salary was just $12. When he offered tours, he could have made twice that, just in tips, if he had decided to take the money instead. The opportunity cost of learning English from tourists was high, but it was a stroke of genius.

Young Jack was able to see the longer term wisdom of learning English.

There was an underlying inspiration that had moved him. This sort of inspiration is actually available to everyone. Whether Jack heard the inspiration consciously or not, he was so strongly driven that he was almost charmed in the actions that he took. Ma obviously understood the bigger picture, and that the picture only grew in dimension and scope, the more successful he became.

Success is not about how rich you get—that is the reward. Success is about how efficiently you make your contribution. Once you make the best contribution you can, the rewards will flow naturally and without interruption. However, if you focus on the rewards, they will usually distract you from successfully making your contribution, and you will ultimately fall short of any achievement worthy of supernatural profits.

Most of the suffering in this world comes from chasing rewards and looking for the least contribution one can make to get the greatest return. That mindset is the best way to get stuck in a rut of mediocrity and to forgo any potential that is within you.

Thus, the question you want to ask yourself should be, "What is my contribution?" That question naturally follows from a sincere desire to make a positive contribution and requires inspiration to answer.

To see the big picture, you cannot be distracted. Most of the time, distractions come by way of rewards and material gain. Most people who chase after the riches end up empty-handed, but those who pursue achievement end up well rewarded.

So, what does it mean to see the big picture?

If you are like Jack Ma, seeing the big picture means looking out for those around you and understanding that we are all just tiles in a larger mosaic. While we are in this mosaic of existence, we are all interconnected, and the one element that connects us is mutual gain and trust.

Without trust, there is a problem with the mutual gain part of the equation. Without mutual gain, there is no equity in the relationship, and that means there is no fairness. Fairness is just another word for balance. When there is no balance, things inevitably seek to return to a state of balance. In some cultures, this is called "karma."

The big picture is all about what you give to society. Typically, the more you give, the greater the reward. It does not matter what you give. As long as it adds value, you have achieved your contribution.

Jack Ma's contribution seems obvious to most people, but, so far, we've looked at what he did in China. But what about the rest of the world? The story of Jack Ma is not only about Alibaba and the group of companies that are involved in trade. Ma is also heavily invested on both sides of the Pacific. In both China and the US, Jack Ma funds a private equity firm, Yunfeng, that invests in up-and-coming companies.

PE (private equity) firms are critical to our economy. Without PE firms, there would not be as many of the companies that are providing significant value to society. PE firms absorb the riskiest phase of a company's development, and provide their understanding of the math behind the endeavor, the quantification of risk. PE firms are experts at this, and Yunfeng has brought their own brand of risk assessment to the industry. Yunfeng assesses the risk/return balance by taking into consideration the people behind the investment, and they bring their risk mitigating strategies and the tools of the Alibaba Group to the table.

Jack Ma uses Yunfeng to advance what he started with Alibaba, which was to make every company into an Amazon and make everyone successful. In Jack Ma's big picture, we are all connected, and we can all achieve mutual benefit and success from a globally connected world.

***

Chapter 11 Saving

"People say, 'Well you know the economy's bad, so China consumption will be low. No, totally different. You Americans love to spend tomorrow's money, and other people's money maybe... We Chinese love to save money."

Jack Ma

During Jack Ma's teaching and translation days, and during the founding of Alibaba, there was a lot of hard work and money was tight for Jack and Zhang Ying. The way they managed to get by, while feeding all those Alibaba people, raising a son, and getting a dream off the ground, was by saving. The Ma household stayed prudent with their budgets and didn't go out to spend lavishly. Saving has been a natural tendency for working-class families in China. It is especially so for those building up a business to take it long term.

Saving isn't something that most North Americans know how to do. In fact, most of us are negative savers. These days, the typical household has more debt than equity and savings, which means that things can turn upside down very fast in the event of an emergency or an unplanned event.

Saving comes naturally to people who aren't looking ahead to the rewards when endeavoring to build a business and contribute. If you were looking to invest with someone, you wouldn't be comfortable investing with a person who had a spending problem. On the other end of the spectrum are those who are thrifty and not prone to high-flying habits, characteristics of those who know how to succeed and are eventually rewarded, like Warren Buffet, Steve Jobs, and Bill Gates.

Those who come from working class families typically learn how to save and conserve from a very young age. Working class families need to stretch their dollar farther. Jack Ma and his wife, also, learned it young, and have continued to apply it in their own family. Although Jack has achieved billionaire status more than three years ago, he still has not gone on a shopping spree. Jack and his wife are simple by nature. They may now be among China's wealthiest people, but that does not mean they dine on caviar and champagne.

Saving is an essential part of contribution. Saving isn't just about the accumulation of resources for later use. Saving is about not draining your resources in the present, and keeping them without the intention of future use. Saving is not about "what ifs." Saving is about putting away most of what comes in and living a life that is simple, without the fat or luxury we are accustomed to seeing some of the rich indulge in.

Saving doesn't just develop good habits. It is also a way to avoid distractions. Becoming wealthy is a function of a mindset that is focused and tuned to a single matter at hand. You cannot have any distractions from the tasks that need to be done to accomplish your end goals. Those tasks need your full attention and concentration. You also need to be aware of all the things going on and noting the effects your actions are having and be able to make real-time adjustments.

Saving, as the successful men of this generation will tell you, is key to becoming successful. You do not save your way to a billion dollars—that takes a lot of pennies—but the habit of saving turns you into someone who keeps costs low and isn't distracted by the pleasures that come from unnecessary spending. It keeps things real. Saving is not about hoarding—saving is about paying attention to the business at hand, rather than to the distractions of spending.

In the early days of Goldman Sachs, Marcus Goldman, the original founder, monitored the books every night as they closed for the day. He was notorious for being absolutely incensed if the books were out of balance even by a penny. It wasn't those pennies that have made the investment bank the titan it is today, but it was the culture and habits of attention to detail, and the laser focus on accuracy that Goldman had instilled in the organization.

Jack Ma's natural ability to live on a tight budget allowed him to focus on big dreams without fantasizing about big expenses and lavish extravagances. It helped him remain on a sure footing as his company took three years to get off the ground; he was able to use some of his own resources to support the operations of the company while it found its legs. The ability to save is not just about keeping money for a rainy day. Many years of true saving allowed the Ma family to endure the years of limited income without feeling depressed and forlorn.

Making money is not about spending it. If you become used to spending the riches you make, it is a sure sign of an impending fall. Jack Ma and his wife continue to keep their expenses in check, and understand the value of frugality and the benefits of cultivating a saving culture.

***

Chapter 12 Infinite Game

"As a business person, I want the world to share the prosperity together."

Jack Ma

In every analysis I do—and you can see this in other books I have written about the titans of the modern world, from Steve Jobs to Richard Branson and Elon Musk—I study men of wide-reaching consequence within a framework that allows me to understand their actions, motivations, and trajectories. In the same way that business analysts use business models, such as Five Force analysis, SWOT, and so on, I use a simple matrix to determine whether individuals are finite or Infinite players.

The key to distinguishing between finite or infinite players is to identify whether they are true to their inherent vibrations, or if they are pursuing goals that will ultimately cause them more distractions. You see, it does not matter whether a person is a finite or infinite player, it only matters that they are well matched to what they are doing. A finite player playing a finite game will be successful. At the same time, an infinite player playing an infinite game will also be successful. The problem arises when a finite player tries to play the infinite game or the infinite player tries to play the finite game. That's when catastrophe awaits.

Finite players are those who are aces at quarterly profits and rapid gains. They make really good CEOs, and they eventually branch out on their own doing exactly what they did for their prior bosses. Finite players hold a special place in society and are a much-needed element in the balance of how we move forward as a species. They provide continuity and they balance the equation with short-term perfection.

Infinite players, on the other hand, are completely different in outlook and vibration. They are in it for the long haul. At times, that infinite player may not appear to be moving forward, but, as in the race between the tortoise and the hare, the infinite player (who is most certainly the tortoise) eventually reaches the finish line to win in the longer term.

Jack Ma, at first glance, has all the earmarks of the finite player. His ideas and Alibaba appear as mirror images of existing companies, seeming to be a perpetuation of more of the same. It could seem that Jack Ma simply knows how to make a good copy of something, but the truth is much more than that. Not everything needs to be reinvented; not everything needs to be patented. When you take a closer look at Ma's motivations, his performance and words, it becomes apparent that Jack Ma is the quintessential infinite player.

Let's consider a comparative example to underscore the differences between finite and infinite players.

When Samsung hit the market with facial recognition software for its phones, Samsung had appeared to beat the more expensive Apple model with a significant leap in technology. Sales soared for the product and the brand. Samsung has consistently been the first to market with technologies that have buoyed their quarterly numbers. On the other hand, Apple, although the leader in the smartphone space, took its time, releasing new technology at an almost Stoic pace. When Samsung rushed out their facial recognition technology, they grew sales, but the technology was soon found to be light on security. The system could be duped using a photograph. When Apple finally released their own facial recognition technology, they had developed it further, using artificial intelligence to map the face. That mapping wasn't limited to mathematical data points on the surface of the face, but also used a thermal map of the face, plus a number of other security features that made it very difficult to overcome.

Like its founder, Steve Jobs, Apple has been an infinite player. Samsung, a finite player, has been driven by quarterlies, stock prices, market share, and whatever is on the next horizon. Apple, on the other hand, has looked beyond the next quarter. Apple waited until their face recognition technology had reached its maturity, instead of trying to be the first one on the block with a new toy. That is the essential infinite player.

Jack Ma is the infinite player. Although he did not go out to make something fresh and new and unproven, he took something that already existed but expanded its uses, enabling a large swath of people to take advantage of it. He found a new use for an existing product. The millions of people who use the site daily cannot distinguish between the person who first created the product and Jack Ma, who brought it to them. Yet, if it was not for Jack, they would not be experiencing the benefits.

Jack Ma's long term, infinite vision of building a platform that would share in prosperity is best illustrated by a true story. During the early stages of setting up Alibaba, when the company was on its way up, revenues were still low, because the benefits were still accruing more to the customer. Jack Ma was still financially strapped. Going to the noodle house for lunch, Ma would be surprised by other business men, who were profiting greatly from the existence of Alibaba, quietly paying for his meal. They would say they knew that, even though they were making money, Ma was not, and paying for his meal was the least they could do.

Infinite players are born, not made, just as finite players are born, not created. The key is being true to yourself and understanding who you are on the finite/infinite plane. If you are an infinite player, play the infinite game, and you will find prosperity. If you are a finite player, play the finite game, and you will find your niche. Do not cross over. That would be a mistake.

Consider the people you read about and whether they are finite or infinite players, and then pay close attention to the ones that most resemble you. So, if you are an infinite player, study the lessons of people like Jack Ma, Steve Jobs, and Elon Musk. If you are a finite player, look to people like Mark Zuckerberg, and Sergei Brin.

***

Conclusion

Jack Ma is an atypical billionaire who made it to the top by looking out for the prosperity of others and understanding the concept of shared prosperity. He realized that the world is not the product of a zero-sum game. Instead, the world is the resulting balance of shared prosperity.

We have seen examples of this at work before. At the end of World War II, the United States knew very well that, without the recovery of Europe, it wouldn't be long before the spiral of economic descent and repercussions from Europe's devastation would reach the United States. To prevent that, the USA adopted the Marshal Plan to help rebuild Europe. The thriving economies of Europe, such as Germany, are the result.

Shared prosperity is the natural flavor of humanity. All of nature lives in balance, and everything in nature progresses only through interaction with each other. If you have no one to sell to, there is no need to build anything. Beggar-thy-neighbor policies never work. But prosper-thy-neighbor policies always do. Jack Ma inherently understood the need to allow everyone to prosper, and that is the foundation of his success.

As a person who wasn't academically inclined or naturally book smart, a lot can be said for the natural talents of Jack Ma, but it wasn't those talents that buoyed him to the top so much as it was his ability to be true to himself. That was what drove him to start and accomplish what he has.

Of course, Ma thought about wealth and riches. The interest in profit is natural. If it were not for profit, there would be no way for him to feed himself or his family, and he would not be able to move forward. Profit is certainly a factor, but the quantity of profit is not the core concern of the typical successful billionaire. When they maintain their primary focus on the contribution they make, as Jack Ma did, their wealth and value builds to exceed all expectations.

One way to look at how to become a billionaire is to not think about being a billionaire. To become a billionaire, instead, think about what you can contribute, what value can you add to the world around you so that it can prosper. How can you enrich the rest of the world? Bill Gates made it possible to have a computer in every home. Elon Musk changed the way we think about energy. Jack Ma made it possible for small and medium businesses to prosper by reaching across oceans and transacting business in a trustworthy way. What is the contribution you can make that you can expand on until it affects the entire world? Find that and you will find your wealth.

Jack Ma is one of the most unexpected billionaires. He does not look the part. No one who knew him in his younger days would ever have expected him to amount to much. He did not have the charm or the looks. He did not have an ivory tower education. He did not have the political or business connections of a wealthy father or a politically connected uncle. He was an everyday kid, growing up in Communist China before it was the industrial powerhouse it is today. I cannot stress enough how ordinary Jack Ma was as a kid, and how ordinary he was as he grew up. He was even too ordinary for colleges and universities, and too ordinary to work at the first KFC that opened in his city.

Now, Jack Ma is the Executive Chairman of Alibaba Group—a company that still holds the NYSE IPO record. Its gross sales volume this year was almost half a trillion dollars, greater than the GDP of Thailand. On Singles Day in China, Alibaba clocked a single day's sales (gross merchandise value) of 17.8 billion dollars. In comparison, Amazon's Prime Day in July clocked in a record-breaking $1 billion over a thirty-hour period. Alibaba sold $1 billion dollars just in the first five minutes of sales on Singles Day.

All that is to show how many lives are touched by Alibaba. And all that was a direct result of Jack Ma being perplexed at being unable to find a single Chinese seller during an online search.

Jack Ma's core value and goal of shared prosperity is the reason he is where he is today. His contribution to the world was not an invention or a gadget. His contribution created real change, making a measurable difference at the kitchen tables of hundreds of thousands of families who became able to reach new customers and generate better incomes for their families. That indeed is a revolution.

Richard Branson
The Force Behind Virgin

Richard Branson: The Force Behind Virgin

Insight and Analysis into the Life and Successes of Sir Richard Branson

JR MacGregor

Richard Branson: The Force Behind Virgin

Insight and Analysis into the Life and Successes of Sir Richard Branson

Published by CAC Publishing LLC.

ISBN 978-1-948489-82-9 paperback

ISBN 978-1-948489-81-2 eBook

This book is dedicated to those who wish to do things their own way and pave their own path—those who desire successes and accomplishments that mere mortals deem impossible. Sir Richard Branson has done it. Are you next?

Preface

> "You don't learn to walk by following rules. You learn by doing and falling over."

The story of Richard Branson is not easy to tell because existing preconceptions lie in the public's consciousness that could alter the true story. This is not necessarily true for all people, and for those of you who either have no knowledge of him or his trajectory, we try to avoid repeating the common misconceptions and tired, old stories of one of the business world's geniuses.

Nevertheless, for those of you who do have some knowledge of Sir Richard Branson, keep in mind that much of what has been written about him is solid, but some people seek to apply conventional frames to an unconventional man, which results in an uncomfortable telling.

We will try to avoid both of those as we lay out the incontrovertible, project the interesting, and reveal the inner workings of a man that many incorrectly perceive, unknowingly judge, and mistakenly assume.

Take, for instance, the name of his company—Virgin. The name reflects the business experience of those who were involved in Richard's initial record business—all of them were inexperienced and barely out of school. It doesn't mean anything naughty, as many presuppose.

The idea behind this book is to peel back the layers that shroud this man and his true nature so that you can understand him better and possibly emulate areas of his life that could result in your own success.

Having said that, other books are part of this series from which we can learn much from the men featured, and not all of them are the same. The subjects for these books were chosen with intense care, and the result is a collection of books that will inspire you, perhaps give you a pointer or two, and most definitely present you with tools to change your own life.

***

Introduction

"A passionate belief in your business and personal objectives can make all the difference between success and failure. If you aren't proud of what you're doing, why should anybody else be?"

The public sees a man who is unconventional in his ways and unrepentant of his contempt for all that reflects the status quo. Beneath the facade, however, is a man that doesn't look at things differently for the sake of being different. Rather, he sees things from a perspective that is unique. From his vantage, what the rest of us see as obstacles he sees as opportunities; what we see as challenges he sees as stepping stones; and what the rest of us see as impossible he sees as a calling.

The story of Richard Charles Nicholas Branson is not one that depicts rags to riches; instead, it is a story that shows the value of uncommon perspectives.

We are all guilty of sometimes believing that there is only one way of doing something or one way of looking at something because that's how we view it or that's how we do it. How many times have we looked at the way someone did something and instantly could not help ourselves but critique that person's approach to it? It is common human nature. It is an extension of our inherent defense mechanism designed to protect us from anxiety. If we summon the courage to get past that, what we find is the ability to do things that are unique to our skill set and overlook the actions of others in a way that protects us from feeling bad about ourselves. When we remove this stumbling block and instead look at how others act and think, it gives us the empathy we need to contemplate other perspectives than our own. Having that brand of empathy requires boundless courage and intellectual strength—both of which Richard Branson certainly has to a great extent.

Richard's conviction to live life to the fullest is also uncommon in its motivation. Most of us who do try to live life to the fullest do so for no other reason than to see all we can, do all we can, and experience all we can. It is almost an intellectual endeavor to take it all in. For Richard, however, the desire to do it all and see it all is not rooted in curiosity as much as it is forged in the desire to overcome challenges. He faces challenge purely for the taste of victory when he vanquishes the obstacle.

Most of us know how Richard overcame his dyslexia and turned it around to work for him instead of against him. He is positively one of the few human beings in this world who has stopped me in my tracks and caused me to reevaluate what I had taken as foregone conclusions. I will always appreciate that part of learning about him because in knowing his ability to overcome what I thought was a typical nonstarter characteristic in the quest for greatness Richard showed me conclusively that there is no such thing.

Each time I think about the possibility that something is doomed, I remember how Richard looks at and overcomes things that come across his path. I have no delusions about the fact that things come easily for him or things are not complicated for him. That is not true, just naive.

Richard breaks the mold about how success is made and how it is expanded upon. If you look at his companies, if you look at the industries and the kinds of businesses and philanthropy he is involved in, you find that he is anything but typical, which goes back to how he sees and perceives things. More than that, however, Richard is the poster child for having fun with what you do and allowing the chips to fall where they may. It turns out that formula is pretty effective and yields results that return supernormal profits. Take Virgin Records, for instance. He established it when he was a young teenager, and he did it because he absolutely loved the business. He has even explicitly said how important it is to do what you love. If you don't feel for it, you are indeed wasting your time.

To be clear about this particular notion, each of us is capable of experiencing different emotional feelings. You can, for example, have a fleeting fancy and think that is love, but it's not. At the same time, you can love something, yet not be exhilarated by it and think "maybe this is not love." When you do things that you love, you have a teenage crush sort of feeling. You have the "do anything for her" sort of feeling.

That's the love Richard is talking about. It's the long-distance marathon of love affairs, not the 100-meter sprint sort of teenage crush that's over at the first sign of difference.

***

Chapter 1 Focusing on What's Important

"The art of delegation is one of the key skills any entrepreneur must master."

Richard comes from a long line of achievers. By long line, I really only include knowledge of his father and paternal grandfather. Both trained in the legal profession; the senior being a high court judge and member of the Privy Council. The United States does not have a position that is similar to that of the Privy Council, so a little background on the matter is in fair order.

The Privy Council is found in a number of countries around the world, especially in monarchies. Privy (meaning private) Council sits at the pleasure of the king or queen and advises them in secret on matters of the state. In the United Kingdom, this is a very important and honorable position. Richard's grandfather was knighted for his service to king and country.

Being from a family of stature and high standards, certain expectations were automatically bestowed on heirs, and the necessary schooling follows every young man of such families. That education was bestowed on Richard's father and to Richard after him. As the years passed in school, from one boarding school to the next and on to prep schools as a teenager, it became clear, however, that something was amiss with Richard. As hard as he tried, his grades were not where they should have been.

The Thing about Schools

There is a very good chance that you've been to school. There is also a good chance that you had secondary (high school) education and possibly tertiary education and beyond. So it may seem completely foreign to you even to contemplate life without the necessary academic preparation. On the other hand, some of you probably didn't attend formal school but instead were tutored and schooled by your parents or someone close, or you just didn't go to school at all. Whatever the case may be, the focus on the concept of school sometimes eclipses and obscures the importance of education. Education is not the same as academics, which is about going to school and getting an education in a certain prestructured way that caters to the lowest common denominator.

Learning on the job or in the school of "hard knocks" as they say is a lot different. Here, mistakes are your teacher; consequences are your memory aid. Learning from the school of life does not give you a safety net in case of errors. That is something you have to endure, but what life gives you for trying, failing, and then trying again is knowing absolutely how things should be done. In the end, the reward it bestows you, or in other words, your GPA is not a number on a report card. Rather, it is the balance in your bank account, which is what Richard and a number of other people have proven time and again.

Trade school is no different from regular school. You go to one to learn how to fix a car, and you go to the other to learn the rules. For someone like Richard, though, neither worked because he inherently did not want to play the game by the rules. Now mind you, I am equating rules with the law. Not playing by the rules has nothing to do with obeying the law, which is a code of conduct that you agree to by virtue of being in a shared community. If you do not want to abide by the rules, you are free to go to a land that has no society. Laws exist to keep order and to allow everyone to get along equitably. Rules, on the other hand, are merely suggestions so that the weakest among us have guide ropes to get something done . . . they do not apply to people like Richard Branson.

When we want to take life by its reins and steer it to what we want, you cannot be constrained by the rules of mere mortals. Richard has never been one to follow the rules or do what those before him have done. Look at how he built Virgin Records. Look at how he built Virgin Atlantic and the hundreds of companies that range from mobile telephony to insurance. Look at Virgin Galactic that is breaking the mold of travel and destinations. None of this would be possible if he went through the same cookie-cutter institutions the rest of us did. In many cases, if you want to build something unique, you cannot learn that which is common. It makes no sense to do otherwise.

But to be able to do that, one needs courage because the prevailing wisdom is so ingrained in the fabric of society today that the mere mention of being a dropout and the mention of homeschooling or the mention of not being academic elicits facial responses that deliver the brunt of the message that is contained in most of society's mind.

Mistakes and School Masters

When you go to school, you rely on your schoolmaster or teacher to guide you and tell you what is right or wrong based on their experience and what they think. You are not allowed to make your own mistakes and learn from your own experiences. To be sure, you have to be able to separate the basics from the advanced, and you certainly need to learn languages and have the ability to count and communicate. Beyond that, however, schools only serve to limit the full force of your experience. In essence, the school is not really trying to protect you; it is protecting everyone else from you just in case you make such a splash that it takes out those standing around you as well.

It is not their fault, and it is not that they are deliberately trying to limit you because of their ill intentions, but it is because of their desire to find the best path forward for everyone, not just you.

They are also trying not to leave anyone behind, and they are trying their best to make sure they do not make anyone feel left out, but by doing that they mess up the whole thing. In Richard's case, he was one of the lucky ones who walked out of that environment and faced the beast directly.

Before the time of Alexander the Great, Persian kings ruled the known world, and among them were different kings who imparted their wisdom on to the generations that followed. One, in particular, was Darius I. He was a conquering king and wanted his son Xerxes to learn in the best way possible. Instead of teaching him how to fight by fighting with palace guards and warriors, Darius placed young Xerxes in a locked dungeon in the dark to battle a ferocious lion.

He wasn't schooled with guards who would not allow him the full brunt of consequence; he faced a lion that left him and his senses to bear the full brunt of it, all of which made him one of the most powerful warriors who ever lived.

Schools do have a purpose, but as it stands now, most children are shielded to such a high degree that they come out useless except for being able to perform menial tasks. The real thinkers and men of accomplishment are those who were not protected by the walls of the school or the comparative safety of the schoolyard.

The Important

When we look at Richard, we need to remember that he did not leave school because he was lazy but because school was not doing for him what was in his best interest. Yes, there was the matter of his dyslexia, but dyslexia is not a debilitating illness. There is no such thing. This is what the International Dyslexia Association says about it:

> *"Dyslexia is a specific learning disability that is neurobiological in origin. It is characterized by difficulties with accurate and/or fluent word recognition and by poor spelling and decoding abilities. These difficulties typically result from a deficit in the phonological component of language that is often unexpected in relation to other cognitive abilities and the provision of effective classroom instruction. Secondary consequences may include problems in reading comprehension and reduced reading*

experience that can impede growth of vocabulary and background knowledge."

It is important to understand that we all have some form of function that does not measure up to someone else's ability. My neighbor mows the lawn better than I do, my children have better facility with the computer than I do, and my wife balances the checkbook better than I do. That does not make me an imbecile. Nevertheless, because the nature of schooling is such, they feel the need to categorize everyone, sanitize and equalize so that they can apply cookie-cutter methods to imparting the ABCs and the civics of living in society.

As Sir Richard Branson has taught us and Sir Ken Robinson still teaches us, that school kills creativity—and creativity is one of Richard's most valuable possessions.

It is then important to see Richard in this light, where he used the fire within him to find a way to absorb information through other means. He may not have been able to understand a printed document or a report, but he certainly understood talent and knew how to connect with people, which is why he was able to get a studio up and running and make breakout stars of such people as UB40, Culture Club, Paula Abdul, and many more. He did this with just his desire to make it work and surmount whatever challenges he faced.

He was sixteen when it dawned on him that he was not learning the same way as other young people. It certainly was a blow to the ego because as a teenager we sometimes tend to see ourselves the way we think others see us. For Richard, not being as quick to absorb the knowledge that was presented in books was something that initially felt uncomfortable, but he soon realized that he didn't need books to understand what was right and wrong in the broad scheme of things.

For instance, he did not know the difference between net income and gross income until he was fifty years old and had, at that point, already grown the Virgin Group to be the largest group of private companies.

Imagine if you were to tell someone from Harvard Business School that they do not need to know or understand the difference between net and gross income or for that matter even know what they are. It would be impossible for them to understand and move ahead. All that education and the sudden inability to know what a simple term is would probably throw them into a tizzy.

For Richard, however, not knowing the difference between net and gross wasn't something that one needed to bat their eyelids about. The point of running a business is not that you know what is "net" or "gross." Instead, it's knowing whether or not you are adding enough value and making a contribution to society that justifies paying you enough so that your value-add is significant to produce a net income that projects that. What a simple and honest concept!

Becoming wealthy or becoming powerful is not accomplished in isolation of the world in general. It is about contributing to the rest of the universe around you. You see the same in the Roman emperors of history. The name that survives in the collective consciousness of virtue is most likely Augustus, and the one who was the most hated of all is possibly Nero. One built Rome up and contributed to the good of the people, while the other plundered and took selfishly. One continues to be celebrated two millennia after his death; the other's palace was buried by the people, with him in it after his suicide.

Essentially then, Richard is where he is because his so-called deficiency started a chain of events that allowed him to contribute more than what he may have if he was a typical graduate. Richard's blessing was that he extricated himself from the mass market education system and in so doing let his abilities fly rather than focusing on his inabilities.

***

Chapter 2 The Early Years

"Most people would assume my business success, and the wealth that comes with it, have brought me happiness. But I know I am successful, wealthy, and connected because I am happy."

It was 1966, Simon and Garfunkel were on the radio, and Richard Branson had quit school. He started a magazine focusing on teenage pop culture, with students as his target demographic. The genius of this idea was that he used students to run the magazine that targeted students. That little bit of detail caught the attention of the advertiser, and Richard's magazine, which was called *Student*, raked in $6,000 worth of advertising for its maiden distribution of fifty thousand copies.

Within three years, Richard had enough earnings to maintain an independent lifestyle and live among the music scene in downtown London. By this point, Fleetwood Mac and The Rolling Stones were on the radio and climbing the charts. It was 1969, and Richard had started thinking about starting a mail order company. He specifically wanted to sell records through catalogs and use the proceeds to further the business of the magazine. Because they were all new to the business, they called it Virgin Records, and they were up and running in no time. Richard soon managed to make a healthy income and decided to push the business further by using the proceeds to open a record shop on Oxford Street (a major part of London).

With persistent effort, the record shop performed well and allowed him sufficient income to use the proceeds to purchase a manor in Oxfordshire wherein he had a studio built. It was 1972, and Richard was just twenty-two.

During a stage of life when most people are just overgrown kids (this was the early 1970s), you have a young man who had dropped out of high school but instead of wandering around aimlessly, he became highly successful. Amazing!

In his interview, Richard comes off as highly personable without an air of superiority. He doesn't see himself as some great genius who is God's gift to the world. Instead, he is very clear and sober about his role and what he needs to do to add value to the world around him.

His skills were just what the record industry needed, and he proved that with his new studio. Within a year of setting it up, he had signed his first artist—Mike Oldfield—who took Tubular Bells to the charts and remained there for more than two hundred weeks. That was a major success for Richard, who had entered the business without the typical record producer's experience or the track to get there. With the momentum of this success, Richard was able to sign up The Sex Pistols, The Rolling Stones, Genesis, and Culture Club. Not bad for someone who had yet to turn twenty-five, didn't finish high school, and was considered dyslexic.

Drive vs. Luck

Some people call it luck. Really? Just to provide some context—the record industry today, and even thirty to forty years ago, is extremely competitive. As charming as Richard is now and no doubt was back then as well, successful bands don't just line up to sign up with you and even more so when you are someone who has very little history. If you are trying to build your career as an artist in the music industry, you want to have a manager or a producer who is not just going to take a percentage of your sales but someone who will drive you to explode on the world stage. That is not easy in this industry even if you have years of experience, but that's magnified by the amount of time that Richard had been in this business. He had sold some records through mail order and had a record shop on

Oxford Street, but this was a different ball game altogether. It was similar to the owner of a car dealership suddenly deciding to build cars instead. It doesn't really happen that often.

If all these big names were signing with Richard, they must have seen something in him. People tend to identify rising stars and always want to hitch their wagons to them. They must have seen that in him too. What a sight that must have been!

Just for the record, many of you were probably not born yet or were still too young to remember the songs that were on the radio or the eight-track back then or some of the artists that signed with Virgin. Such bands as The Rolling Stones, though, who had already established themselves as a permanent fixture on the charts from as far back as the early '60s, would not just jump to a new ship because they felt like it regardless of how well they knew Richard. It is still business.

A few things that Richard has said, though, provides insight as to why many bands signed with him. They were not wrong. Richard really did well and took many of them to global fame. Consider how Mike Oldfield and others, such as Genesis (Phil Collins), were also popular a decade before Richard came on the scene.

The answer lies in what he keeps telling us. The reason you do well in business is by giving your clients and customers more and real value. Such business ethics is rare these days and even less easy to find in the music industry. You can understand the level it was at by the speed that Richard's reputation spread across the industry, and some of the top names would rather hang their hat with him than anyone else.

To pose the question once again, was his meteoric rise in the record industry drive or luck? No, not so much about luck. Just consider the customer.

His dedication, his ability to connect with people, his innate nature to put the customer first, and his inability to follow standard practices made him rise through the ranks of the industry's elite. By the time it was all said and done, Richard had moved Virgin Records within the top six record companies in the world.

The '70s were good for Richard, and he focused on Virgin Records most of the time, making it a great company that would sell for a billion dollars in 1992! Consider this point. When you call someone a billionaire, the amount of cash they actually have is far less. Their value is tied to the stock price and their holdings. Two things would happen if they were to try and actually liquidate that stock: (1) the price would tank, and (2) they would not actually be able to get every single penny of that value. In reality, most billionaires are counted as such based on paper value. In Richard's case, just this single venture, Virgin Records, sold for $1 billion cash that went straight into his pocket, and that's not counting the profit over the previous twenty years.

In the hands of a genius with the right motivation, a billion dollars can go a long way. In this case, it took Richard across the Atlantic in a hot air balloon and got him a ticket to space among other things.

Richard had scaled his way from being a high school dropout to being the man behind some of the most famous names in the entertainment industry to being knighted.

This book is not actually a chronological account of everything he did and what happened to him. Some anecdotes are peppered throughout the book, but the value in this book is more about the underlying current that carried this man to the height of success and the reasons and circumstances for it. No man is common. All men are unique, yet we share certain traits and characteristics. If we just wait patiently, we will eventually find our own image in the composite of all that is available to us. When we do, we will benefit from all they have to teach us and all they have to advise us, which is why we long to hear about men who make their mark on this world, and that is also sometimes why we follow them wherever they lead.

Chapter 3 Transformational Leader

"One thing is certain in business. You and everyone around you will make mistakes."

What does a boy of sixteen do in the course of his adolescent life to earn the title of Transformational Leader by the time he gets close to retirement? For starters, he doesn't think of himself in these terms. He just thinks of himself as the critical cog in the wheel of transformation and revolution within his own orbit.

That is the kind of thinking that characterizes Richard Branson. He doesn't see what he doesn't have; he sees what he needs. It really is just another way of saying that there is no such thing as failure, and all you have to do to erase that form of failure is to get back up.

There are administrative leaders and those who are transformational. You don't need to invent something groundbreaking to be a transformational leader. Some leaders definitely do that, but that is not the essence of this sort of leadership.

Transformational leadership is about the ability to drive other human beings to achieve more than they originally thought possible. The world has seen a few transformational leaders, for example, Nelson Mandela and Mohandas Gandhi, otherwise known as Mahatma Gandhi.

Then you have such leaders as Steve Jobs, whom some would argue is not the same kind of transformational leader as Richard. The essence of such a leader is about the ability to move the world by moving people.

Regarding the incident when Richard was chairing one of his board meetings, he admitted that he didn't know the difference between gross and net income. One of his directors had to tell him.

This kind of transparency on Richard's part is exceedingly rare. Few people would ever admit that they do not know anything, much less something that basic. Their inability to admit would be based on two factors. The first would be that our enemies would have their knives out for us, and the second would be that I would lose positional authority over my subordinates.

What kind of confidence does it take to be able to stand there naked and do that? When you are a transformational leader, it doesn't matter if you know the nuts and bolts of the matter. That's not what your team is going to look to you for. They look to you to carry the endeavor to heights that only you can.

A transformational leader is someone who is not necessarily a nitty-gritty kind of person. That's not his contribution to the company or to its purpose. His contribution is the ability to harness the power that the people of many different skill sets possess and to unify their efforts. Without transformational leaders, the group of individuals, no matter how talented, are not going to be cohesive or coherent enough to tackle their common goal.

But people are not inherently going to just cede control of their direction to anyone. You cannot just walk up to a person or a group of people and suggest or demand that they now follow you. To be a leader, you need to have either positional or personal authority, but when you come from nowhere and are not awarded the job with a title, there is no positional authority to speak of. However, whatever positional authority one may have is eroded the moment others see that you consistently have no idea what you are talking about.

Then there is moral authority, which is the kind of authority that we need to cultivate before anyone even reaches out to shake our hand. It is the finder of truth that we use as the core of this authority. Truth does not need to be highly complex or a higher philosophical truth. It needs to be something simple that would be able to drive droves into your corner. Richard had this sort of moral authority from the get-go. His one guiding light and his true reason for existing was always about the ability to build people up.

He was all about achievement, yes. There is no question about that. He was not in it for charity, and he was not going to just move on after the good was done and leave the rewards on the table. He was in it for the returns as well. We all are, and if you don't think you are, you are kidding yourself. The basic nature of all relationships is based on a selfish intent. "What's in it for me?" It has to be there or you have a fundamental breakdown in the chain of existence.

If you find that hard to believe, consider the following. You are on board an aircraft and an emergency occurs because there is a rapid decompression event. You have your toddler with you who has no idea of the oxygen mask or how to use it.

Would you place the mask on him first or on yourself?

If you think when it comes to children that you have to be selfless and put the mask on him first or you will be a horrible parent, you are wrong. In this case, you have to be selfish and don your mask first because that child is in greater danger if you pass out from not having the mask. So in this case, you need to show selfishness, take the mask, get the oxygen, and then help the child get his on. It is the optimal result.

To help others, you have to first help yourself, which is a far cry from being greedy or cheating them. So, in Richard's case, the idea was not to give up his efforts for free but to make money in the process and then go on to be able to lead and help others.

This brand of selfishness is rooted in the desire to help people because you know that we are all connected. This sort of magnanimity is about contribution before the reward and the contribution to be able to help more and more people by pooling together the resources of the collective rather than directing them to do your bidding.

One key personality trait of transformational leaders is that they are able to keep their ego in check or not have one at all. Everyone would agree that Richard has his ego in check. For all his successes and the hurdles he has had to climb, he has no air of superiority and arrogance about him. He remains humble and centered in his approach to anything and everything. He has the ability to connect with people because there is no wall around him, and he does not believe that any authority he gains needs to come from the arrogance of positional leadership or the wielding of technical expertise.

Transformational leaders have another driving characteristic. They are able to easily connect with people. People like them, and they truly like people. Richard is actually one of the most personable people I know. He has the capacity to empathize, and that is one of his greatest assets for the brand of transformational leadership he possesses. Whenever he sees an employee or if he is on board one of his commercial aircraft, he is not egoistic enough to not greet and meet his staff and introduce himself. Of course, everyone knows him and don't need an introduction, but that's not the point. He still has the humility to try and touch their lives by being approachable. Automatically they fall in line with his cause just because he has such generosity and pleasantness about him.

One of the most prominent qualities of a transformational leader is the ability to take risks, which also distinguishes Richard. He has taken risks with everything he has done. He moves to the next level, taking on risk and vanquishing it, and then climbing higher. Risk is the key aspect of growth. You need to take risks as part of the definition of moving out of your comfort zone. The moment you decide not to take the risk and stay within your comfort zone, you not only end up not growing, but you also end up stagnating and possibly regressing.

When you take risks, you automatically end up facing many difficult decisions. When you combine the ability to take risks with the ability to be personable and genuinely care for your subordinates, you end up in a quandary when you need to make tough decisions.

When Richard sold Virgin Records, even though he was holding a check for a billion dollars in his hand, what he remembers most is how he wept for the sale of the company and seeing all those artists and staff that were his friends go. That broke him over the course of the years, in private, but the decision had to be made for the good of everyone and everything. By liquidating Virgin, he was able to save Virgin Atlantic and then continue on and start Virgin Galactic years later. Tough decisions always follow transformational leaders, but that is part of what makes them one.

To be a transformational leader, one needs to be able to expand from your comfort zone and cross into new areas. You don't just sit in your comfort zone and keep squeezing out the same old tired song. You have to move into areas that cross over to other skill sets and other demographics. Richard has done this all his life. From the days of the *Student* magazine to the days of the record shop and then on to the recording studio and then on to the other businesses, such as the airlines, money operators, and the two hundred to three hundred other companies that come under the Virgin wing, you will see that Richard displays the quality of a transformational leader across all his efforts.

Transformational leaders have vision, and in that vision they see the good that comes about by unshackling themselves from the old and embracing the new—to being inclusive rather than being exclusive, to being adaptive rather than afraid of change. All these are ways that the transformational leader sees the world around him, and he applies that to the things he does, and the result is that people follow him wherever he goes because in every society and every group we need a leader who is able to make us better than we can make ourselves—both as an individual and as a society.

Transformational leaders do not have any doubt about what they can achieve, and they will bring in whomever they need to crack the nuts and bolts of it to get it done. Just because they do not know how to fly a plane does not disqualify them from owning and operating an airline. Just because they do not know how cell phones work on the inside does not mean they cannot get someone who knows to help them. You don't have to do only what you know. He once said that when someone gives you an opportunity grab it and then figure out how to make it work.

What I have learned from knowing Richard can be categorized in two ways. First, you don't need to be an expert at anything to be able to become a billionaire (assuming you are looking for the reward). Second, to be successful, you need to understand what is really important and what are the distractions. Richard does that almost effortlessly. His focus on the experience of the customer has time and again made his endeavor more successful than the competitor because there is real desire to get the customer what he wants and keep the customer's needs first. He wasn't an expert at flying an airplane, yet he made the airline one of the best in the United Kingdom and then expanded that to a number of other countries.

Most of all, transformational leaders bring something to the table that no one else can—the vision to change the world around us that we all hope to do but have no idea how to do it. We all want to have our fingerprints on the changes that we leave behind for the next generation, but few of us have the ability to crystallize that desire into a vision and make it happen. When we lack that ability, we then subconsciously seek out the visionary who can make that happen for us. We follow them to the ends of the earth to be able to show us how to leave our mark, and we hope they can provide that road map for us.

Some schools will try to teach an entire class of people how to be transformational leaders, but the brand of leadership that Richard brings to the table for his fifty thousand employees worldwide is not something you can learn sitting in a chair in a classroom. You need the school of hard knocks to bang it into you while you go about your life.

If you look at the businesses that dominate the Virgin group, in fact even in its name—Virgin—you get the sense that they are always on the cusp of something new that no one else, including themselves, know much about. They are all virgins at whatever they are doing, without much experience in what they are providing to the world at large. The Virgin group is the perfect reflection of Richard. It is a company that mirrors all that Richard has become over the years. As he changed and grew, so did the company around him. As he advanced in new ways of looking at things and adapted to the new age, so did his companies. That is the mark of a truly transformational leader.

***

Chapter 4 Virgin Atlantic

"I've never gone into business to make money. Every Virgin product and service has been made into a reality to make a positive difference in people's lives. And by focusing on the happiness of our customers, we have been able to build a successful group of companies."

In most cases, the very mention of the name Virgin Atlantic or Virgin Airlines instantly evokes the thought of Richard's successful foray into the airline industry. Stories abound about how he laid it on the line and managed to pull it off—and how the sale of Virgin Records helped bolster the losses and the downward trajectory of the fledgling airline.

First, though, let's examine why Richard is the way he is and how that actually made a difference in his personality. As a child, he was extremely shy and would sometimes crawl into a shell. It is not uncommon for young children with his level of genius to have a sense of shyness about them, especially when these children have facility with both the left and right brain, as Richard so often has proven.

His shyness was a very inward way of going about life. Children can be shy and open to the world around them, but they aren't generally both. That's not something that you can do inherently; they occupy different halves of the brain. In Richard's case, at that age, it was the part of him that was shy that dominated his life. The one person who was able to pull him out of his shell was his mother. She was a flight attendant in her youth and a very pragmatic person. She was the person in his life who taught him that it is important to include others into one's thinking, and that was one of the best ways she could find to get Richard to come out of his shell.

As a mother, she realized that one of his greatest strengths was being able to empathize with others, and she was able to use that to gently bring him out of his shell. Richard, being shy the way that he was at that age, was not shy because of any form of disability. Richard's reluctance to look outside himself was more about his ability to think and his ability to live life within his mind. He still has that skill of being able to live within his mind except now it's much more advanced. He is able to brainstorm and generate ideas that are unconventional but typically get the job done. He even has a hammock in his office for this purpose.

From accounts that have been related to his youth, it seems that even though Richard appears to have eventually developed both halves of his brain, thereby working his EQ and IQ when he was young, it was his EQ that shone through more than his IQ. His mother was able to recognize Richard's stronger EQ and used that to appeal to his sense of empathy and kindness.

EQ is an acronym for Emotional Quotient; it is the counterpoint to IQ, which is Intelligence Quotient. EQ encompasses the artistic and softer side of the human condition, and it is not meant to be taken for granted, although it is in a world where logic and reasoning are designed to have a significant role. EQ is about what comes from the "heart."

With an EQ higher than most other people's, Richard was able to naturally assume the role as a change agent to the world around him, which made him a natural candidate to be a transformational leader. At the young age of being shy and inwardly turned, he had met only half the requirements necessary to become the transformational leader that he so eloquently became. With an increased EQ, such people are naturally empathetic to the plight and welfare of others, but they are not able to easily connect with them because connection would mean turning outward focus from a predominantly inward one.

That's where Richard's mother, Evette Huntley Flindt (later Eve Branson), comes into the picture. Understanding her son's innate abilities, she showed him how to look outward as much as he looked inward. In other words, she didn't get him to abandon the shell but taught him to use both when the time demanded it. She was able to draw him out and teach him how important it was never to become selfish, and that's what he would be if he just always kept looking inward.

The ability to be caring and empathize with people gave him the true desire to be able to become a change agent that gave others around him the ability to advance themselves and to be able to do better with their lives. He wanted to give them more value, and as it is always in this life, the more you give, the more you receive.

By doing this, she was able to get him to come out and shed his shyness because he now associated shyness with selfishness, and that was not what he was about. He was anything but selfish, and you could see that in later years when he has given so much to communities around the world.

In an interview about his mother, Richard spoke of five areas he could think of where she influenced his life and his thinking. He also talked about how his parents, both father and mother, who were always by his side, taught him to look at things the way he does now.

The first thing he mentions about her is that she taught him to live with no regrets. To many people, that would just be ghastly. They think that regrets are what prevent you from making mistakes. That's entirely not true. Living with regrets is the worst thing in your life, and Eve made sure that Richard knew that from the very beginning. By not regretting mistakes, he was able to then get up and try again instead of wallowing in the past and feeling sorry for himself. Richard admits that he is not that kind of person today, and whenever he makes a mistake, he has the sense to move on and make it right. Dwelling on a mistake does not make it better.

Richard's shyness was so prevalent in his youth that the only way to overcome it was with strict measures that his mother painfully instilled. There was a time, he recounts, when he was five and they were traveling on a country road about three miles from home. They had just gotten the groceries and were heading home while Richard was busy playing in the back and making a nuisance of himself. As a lesson to stop being such a distraction, Eve stopped the car, asked him to get out and told him to find his way home across three miles of country road. For a teenager, this may be daunting enough, but to a five-year-old, this must have been absolutely horrifying. For a boy of five, as shy as Richard was, the fear and pain must have been intolerable. There was a wiser purpose afoot here in Eve's mind. The punishment for the noise in the back was the least of it. She wanted him to talk to strangers and find his way home to help break his shyness and come out of his shell and find his way home, and he did.

Children with high EQ generally behave in ways that defy common understanding. We have a very unbalanced view of what it means to be smart. Those with a fantastic memory of their multiplication tables are considered smart, but those who are silent and observant are considered to be not as smart, especially in those days when EQ wasn't even a term, and no one knew what it was or how it manifested in later years.

The lesson that Eve taught Richard in this area extended to the ability to break out of his shell, and she taught him to put others first. It was a valuable lesson and one that was very brave of her to do. In many cases, parents are afraid to teach their children to put others first, but the ones who do, such as Eve, eventually hit the jackpot when their children start to see the value in teamwork and getting things done across the team with combined effort. This is a crucial part of being a transformational leader. By placing others first and combining that with his already high empathy from his high EQ, he was able to get into the world of customer-centric businesses and offer them value in whatever the product. By providing them with value, he inadvertently magnified the brand that people associated with it. Virgin, as a brand, is known the world over and has a brand equity that is difficult to value considering how the companies are all fragmented.

Until today, some think that Virgin is a budget company, budget airlines, budget insurance, budget cell phones . . . but it isn't. It is not a budget airline or a budget carrier. The reason it falls on people's minds is that there is such a drive in the company across the board that the perception customers have is that of value, and the perception of value translates to "budget" in their minds.

The most important lesson that she probably taught him, though, is that every day is a new day. Mistakes are just opportunities to learn, but they take on a whole new life when you spend your time in regret. There is a wonderful purpose to nightfall and daybreak; it gives you a new day fresh from the mistakes of the past so that you can metaphorically break the molds you created yesterday and start a new one today if the one you created yesterday is not one that will advance your core purpose. Indeed, every day is a new day, and you should be able to use it to advance yourself—not tie it around your neck and force it to drown you.

Finally, the lesson that Richard says he remembers from his mother is the constant need to stay grounded. As a child of sixteen making a living with a magazine and then breaking out into the record business and making it big from there can be a negative influence if you are not grounded. All that success will get to your head, and all that success will distract you if you allow it to. By being impervious to success and being able to keep your eye on the next prize, you are then able to extend your successes over time and make something great in the future.

Transformational leaders do not achieve their life's goals without bringing people together, and this is exactly what Richard does, and he does so because of the lessons his mother taught him.

Quintessential Richard

The high EQ that Richard displayed in his early years allowed Eve to balance the growth of her son to the point that he was able to develop both sides of his brain. Remember, too, that Richard was considered dyslexic, and because of that traditional teaching methods in school were not able to give him the benefit that he would have otherwise received. But that was just as well because the school environment would have diminished his career more than it would have enhanced it.

Nonetheless, he needed to balance his EQ with an equally high IQ potential, and since it was not possible for him to get it from traditional book learning, he went about it in another way. He paid attention and observed what people did around him and looked to the nature of things. Beethoven once said something that reminds me of Richard. He said that to do something well you always have to get to the nature of it. Of course, he said it more eloquently, but the point is that Richard was able to find the nature of all the things that he has gone out and transformed. If you look at it, the nature of the business is the nature of the person. Whether it is an airline or a record store, the nature of it is the person who is using it.

By having strong powers of empathy, he was able to understand the nature of a person, which allowed him to know what he needs to do to change that person's life. The ability to transform that person's world makes a big difference in Richard's ability to help people.

But his ability and desire to help people do not just stop at delivering great customer service in his companies. Being an airline owner, he had to contend with the environmental impact of his planes. In the beginning, not being a person of science, the effects were not as apparent to him as they should have been and as they soon became. The change happened when he met Al Gore, who broke it down for him one step at a time in a way that Richard could see the impact CO_2 had on the world around him. This suddenly appealed to his empathetic nature, and he seized it quickly.

As soon as Richard understood the catastrophe that was looming over all humanity, he initiated transformation. He committed ten years' worth of profits from Virgin Airlines to the research and development of biofuels that would allow aircraft to stop polluting the skies with the tonnage of CO_2 that each flight inevitably puts out. Within a few years, the research had started to pay off as researchers started to come up with solutions for formulations of organic biofuels that were able to change the CO_2 profile of aircraft without many mechanical modifications to the engine, its fuel system, or its operational characteristics.

Decarbonizing aviation has been a goal of Richard's aviation endeavors since then, and his team eventually used the Global Flyer, an aircraft designed by Burt Rutan and flown by Steve Fossett that circumnavigated the globe without refueling. Richard's Virgin Galactic sponsored the flight. The idea was to test the design needed to make flight more environmentally friendly and to advance further technologies. Indeed, it did advance the later technologies, as Richard joined forces with Burt to begin designs of a high-altitude vehicle that would be needed to send commercial passengers to space and bring them back in a reusable vehicle.

Setting up an airline and expanding it to become the UK's second-largest carrier was a great achievement by a man who had no previous experience whatsoever in the aviation industry. However, that was left to the professionals to do while he focused on what needed to be done and to understand the core nature of the business. He then took that and advanced it even further by launching a program that would launch customers into space. The first commercial flight is scheduled for some time in 2018.

Mistakes r'Us

Success is not about hard work. It is certainly not about luck, and according to Richard, it is also not solely about profit. Rather, it is about serving the customer, giving them what they want, and giving them what improves their world. He believes from the bottom of his heart that the whole point of a business's existence is to be able to provide and fulfill the needs of the customer whatever that may be whether they know it or not.

To be able to do that requires one of two things. You either have total insight into what everyone wants and you go out and build it, or you try and try, and try some more, until you get it right. Mistakes and failures are a part of every successful person's background. It is how we approach those mistakes and failures that makes the difference.

In Richard's case, he is one of those people who has no qualms about making mistakes and doing it over—thanks to his mother's teachings. He just gets back up and tries it again, but the one thing he never falters with, the one mistake he never makes, is always knowing that he needs to deliver for his customer and to do that he can never get his feet off the ground.

He also knows that the only way to serve the customer and to provide is to innovate constantly and be able to do better for his customer in ways they don't even realize. For instance, not many people know that the company was donating its profits from air travel into research and development of fuels and systems that would reduce the carbon footprint of his airline and airlines around the world. In total, that investment runs into the billions over the years. It involved trial and error, and when you are attempting to change the way fuel is made and used, it's par for the course.

The customer, sitting in one of Richard's aircraft, is not going to know that behind the scenes his ticket's dollar is going toward research that will make him and his children better off down the road. It's not always about the publicity either. Transformational leaders are the key agents of change that we need in society. It is because of them that things adapt and improve. It is because of them that we improve our lives, and it is because of them that we learn new ways of doing old things better.

That is why we need them. We do not need them to know what gross and net margins are, but we do need them to look beyond the horizon and see what is coming so that they can change our direction and allow us to adapt to the future.

Chapter 5 Brand Value

"I love creating hideaways. My idea is to go to the most beautiful, unspoilt places, buy the land, and make sure it is never damaged. I've always admired John D. Rockefeller, who bought up tracts of land to ensure they were left wild in perpetuity."

It is not easy to see the man by looking at him or reading about him. In fact, it's not even easy to understand a man by speaking to him for long intervals. If you really want to get to know him, you have to do so by observing his actions across a span of time, and you have to look at the reverberations that rippled from his epicenter. Using that same strategy to understand Richard has yielded the best results.

One of the things we learn about Richard is that even though he is one of the most visible CEOs and billionaires on the planet, he is also one of the most secretive. *Forbes* currently puts him in the top 5 of the list of UK billionaires and ranks him in the eighties globally, but that really is a best guess and not based on hard evidence. If you try to collate that data, you will run into a rather reclusive wall. It turns out that Richard is not an open book as he may first seem. For one thing, most of his companies are privately held, and many of his companies are also under layers of well-structured shell companies, proxies, and offshore holdings. None of this should come as a surprise, and none of this should reflect poorly on him. A lot of what he has done has been in the public good, and it has benefited him a great deal, so we should not in any way begrudge his rich compensation. The point, however, is that the analyst's valuation of his personal wealth is probably grossly miscalculated. It is probably much more than we imagine.

More than two hundred companies are in the Virgin group, each is owned through a different structure, and not all are uniform in their control or in their contribution. As you look deeper and find the purpose of this arrangement, it becomes apparent that this is not in any way a tax evasion scheme, as some have suggested; instead, it really does resemble the structure of a private equity holding that you would see in some private money enterprises. While Richard is not known for his banking (even though Virgin Money is considered a banking institution) expertise, he seems to be one of the wealthiest private equity holders. It's just not advertised that way. Genius!

In private equity firms, they usually take silent positions and then extract the lion's share of the profits. In the Virgin story, however, there is a little more to it than that. Richard brings two things to the table. First, he brings his transformational expertise to the game. The second is that he brings the Virgin brand to the table. Both of what he brings are extremely important and valuable to the company he is investing in.

Just to be clear, though, is not all the companies that are under the umbrella are ones that he bought into. Many of them were indeed started by him and then slowly liquidated. If you look at the list of companies he has liquidated over time, then this idea that he is mostly a private equity house takes on more credibility.

Yes, we are all caught up with the tears he shed at the sale of Virgin Records, and we don't seem to feel that he is in the habit of liquidating positions in companies, but that is in effect exactly what he is doing. He is not chopping them up and getting rid of them. He is turning a profit on them and then liquidating his position. There have even been investments where he has sold the company back to the management of the company in a management buyout.

Looking at his company structure, what you will find is that across the globe the almost three hundred companies that have his fingerprints and his brand are done under a specific pattern and held under a specific set of circumstances that all end up executing through a holding company structure in Switzerland—Virgin Investments SA. In fact, even Richard has said it as much. He claimed that Virgin indeed does look for investments to make, but he compared his organization to being a venture capital firm. Internally it is understood that they look for companies that have no less than 30 percent internal rates of return for them to be even considered acceptable.

To understand exactly how far this goes, remember that biofuel initiative that he made with the profits of Virgin Airlines. Well, that was invested in another Virgin-branded company called Virgin Biofuels. There is nothing wrong with any of this, but if you think that all of his efforts are just because he is a nice guy then you would be totally wrong.

Nice guys finish last, and there is no indication in history, or in the cards, that Sir Richard Charles Nicholas Branson is finishing last anytime soon.

***

Chapter 6 Brilliant Structure

"Those who know me know I'm passionate about lists, and top of my list of priorities is my family. My wife, Joan, and I do not consider our legacy to our children to be wealth or fame but the opportunity to pursue happiness by following their own path."

As we continue our quest to understand Richard, we need to look at the way he conducts his business. We can't find any fault in all that he has done. In fact, we find that he is one of the more compassionate businessmen in the world, but that doesn't mean he is not shrewd about what he does. He is just humble about it, and his mom's lesson still holds true—stay grounded. So his ability to stay grounded has left him looking like he is not such an accomplished billionaire unlike some who are not so much a billionaire in reality as they are in their dreams.

A detailed analysis of the structure of the company under Virgin Investments reveals that the companies across the board all pay their relevant taxes without any problems. There has never been a hint of tax evasion or anything sinister as that. Richard has always been a good corporate citizen.

That doesn't mean, however, that it does not benefit him to structure the entire group in a way that is designed to shield the lion's share of the profits in an astute tax-saving structure during the sale of the assets. This means that the structure is designed to be tax efficient at the point of sale.

This alone is enough to suggest that the companies and the holding organization as well as the methodology of acquisition, investment, and disposal are done through an existing formal structure. A board in Switzerland oversees and controls this structure.

The companies are made efficient for eventual sale, which is the purpose of his involvement or at least the point where he feels he deserves to extract the most profit. If you look at the list of the companies that indeed have been carved out systematically, what you find is that the lie that has been derived from the sale has always been significantly more than that they say Richard is worth, even taking into account that other costs and other expenditures are involved.

For someone who many people set aside as being unable to learn, the one thing that Richard has proven time and again is that the joke is on them. Not only is he a compassionate person and has the inherent ability to help others and see the path in doing so, but he is also able to instinctively navigate the legal waters of the financial world.

Much of his private holdings have been undergoing significant streamlining, and that has made the effort to understand the brand's efforts difficult. We can classify the company into at least four areas of business: transportation, communication, retail, and finance. But these are just the companies and the areas that contribute the greatest to the value that he holds. Other companies are in various diverse industries.

But that is not the end of it. The genius of the whole thing is that the Virgin brand has its own value. The moment Virgin provides its name, the group begins extracting a licensing fee that is above and beyond any of the holding profits that comes to it. So what you have is a company that gets paid annually from each of the hundreds of companies that are in the group, and then it takes a percentage of the profits, which can't be less than 30 percent IRR, and then they take on the sale of the company.

Remember that the sale of Virgin Records put $1 billion in cash in his pocket. That is where it started. He just keeps rolling the profits over and keeps making something more with it. There are at least three streams of revenue that flow from each company that bears his brand. So one of the things that profit the business is the taxes that are saved over the years by virtue of this structure, and that value is then monetized during the sale and all of that extracted from the equation and held tax free from that point on.

If you are going to look at a man and understand who or what he is, this structure should leave no room in your mind that this man is a genius, and he is one who knows from the bottom of his heart that he needs to add value to people's lives, and then he is free to extract value from his contribution.

In the end, the structure is moot. Why? Because those are just the metabolic steps that take you from one point in the process to the monetization of the whole thing. The rest is just processes that are in place. What's important is the business of a man who has made money from his smile and his ability to create a brand. The brand is not slapped onto just anything; remember that they consider at least a 30 percent return before they would even think about investing in it. So it has already proved to a certain point that it is going to do well. Then Virgin comes in, slaps its name on it, and there is a bump in the value of the company because the brand has value. Now the company is worth more, and they take that along for a while, and Richard brings his transformational value and then in a little while, down the road, they offload it and move on to the next one. One element, the intangible name, feeds into the tangible element of the company and its product. Richard just found the way to bring them together and pull the value out of it.

***

Chapter 7 Creative Instincts

"I believe in benevolent dictatorship provided I am the dictator."

A debunked theory says you can either be logical or you can be creative. For the longest time, it was hard for people to recognize that a person could be both, so it became part of the collective consciousness to be one or the other and never really did anyone try to do both.

If you look at Richard carefully and study his patterns and habits, his achievements and failures, what you find is a man who purportedly is more creative than logical, but that is not true at all. It may not be the perfect balance between logic and creativity, but who knows where that balance hangs. It's all just theoretical.

The point is that Richard has made it possible to be able to tap into both sides and eventually become a whole brain person rather than just creative or just logical. Such people as Richard Branson and even Jeff Bezos of Amazon and the likes of Elon Musk have healthy doses of both left and right brain characteristics.

Being able to structure companies to be tax efficient, structuring the maximum possible extraction of value, and being able to oversee all of them is really a creative process that has a little logic sprinkled over it.

By Richard's own admission, he thinks creativity is the root of all business success stories. He does believe that some businesses are better adapted to logical processes, but that's what it is limited to—processes. Richard is a firm believer in the fact that creativity is not about being artsy; rather, creativity is about seeing a bigger picture—things that science and logic can't really explain. That's the part of creativity

We get so caught up with the things that allow the logical mind to flourish, but we forget that the moment the creative mind is left out of the process things get stagnant. Einstein once wrote that you cannot solve a problem in the same plane that it was created. You need to be able to see it from a higher perspective. That higher perspective for such people as Richard Branson is the creativity that he was born with. This is not something he needed anyone to teach him. This is one thing that he had inside him. His mother and the experiences that came from there are all just things that focused his creativity and balanced it with the ability to channel it and logically call upon it.

When Richard looks at the purchase of a company or starting up something that he can positively contribute to, he takes a step back and looks at the narrative and the horizon of the story. He is not interested in the numbers and the projections simply because all that comes later, and all those things are what he has managers and technical people handle. He just wants to understand the crux of the thing.

For anyone starting a business, you should contact him. If he responds positively, you have the benefit of carrying his brand for the time he invests in your company and also the benefit that he will be able to channel much of his assets to helping you achieve your objective.

The key to being able to get him at "Hello" is to give him the elevator pitch that is void of the numbers. Forget the revenue, net income and profit, and forget all the balance sheet ratios that you learned in business school. Save that for the managers who will interview you later. Instead, focus on the story of the company. Talk about how your product or company is about to change the world and how customers are going to benefit from it at every turn. If you can do that, you have a good shot of having the Virgin brand on your letterhead.

If you can watch him and his companies, you will learn so much more than you could by watching any other business transformational leader. That is the greatest value-add that Richard brings to the table.

It turns out that the best way to kick-start a business is the way that Richard has always done it. From the time he created Virgin Records to the time he invested in the last company he got involved with, what stands at the center of the Branson name and the Virgin hallmark is that the customer's needs define the company's actions.

He even goes a step further in looking at what is good for the customer but not necessarily apparent in the beginning because he knows that whatever he does will find its way back to him in terms of profits and brand equity.

One of the reasons it seems that you can always trust the brands is that the entire value of the brand and by extension, his value, is based on how that brand is perceived. Each subsequent investment that he makes does well because, in part, it is the brand that imparts both perceived value, and when that perceived value sticks, it also advances the company's bottom line. It's a symbiotic relationship that has worked well for hundreds of companies that have been sprinkled with the Virgin stardust.

That has been his driving instinct, and the fact that he was able to monetize the brand as well as he does is something we can all learn from.

***

Conclusion

"Business opportunities are like buses. There's always another one coming."

The best way to understand a man is to see how he affects those around him. To take that one step further, to understand the man, you have to understand his habits.

What is almost a habit with Richard is that he never shies away from a problem. He believes in ramming it head-on. Whatever the problem, however complex, he either stands in front of it, owns it, and defuses it, or he gets someone else to do it if it needs some form of technical expertise. Even when someone else is in the thick of it, he doesn't leave their side; he remains in the midst of the problem. This is what happend when Virgin Atlantic first came about, and it was just a one aircraft operation.

One such problem that was the start of the airline was when he was in Puerto Rico waiting for a flight to get to the BVIs to meet his girlfriend (wife, now). The airline canceled the flight simply because it did not have enough passengers to make it profitable. So all the passengers were stuck on the ground.

Richard was furious because he had a date waiting, and so he charted a private plane to make the flight. As a joke, he took out a chalkboard and wrote on it an offering of one flight to BVI for anyone who wanted to go, charging just $39—one way. Within moments, the flight was full, and they all left for BVI. Virgin Atlantic started soon after that.

Most people I know, including me, would have just checked into the hotel and waited like good little sheep while the airline made us hang around. Richard has always had the habit, and it has been one of the driving forces behind his runaway success.

The second point is that this towering entrepreneur steps outside his comfort zone every time he can—from the time he set up the studio to the time he started the airline to the time he set up the Virgin Mobile. Many of the businesses that he has been a part of directly, excluding the ones that he invested in or lent his name to, were businesses that were opportunities that came his way, and he just jumped at it with both hands. The universe tends to reward those habits very well.

He is also always open to change. In fact, it can be said that he is the catalyst of change. In truth, he is open to change when he is not the cause of it, and he is the catalyst when he initiates it. Change drives profit. If all things stayed the same, there would be no room for profit. You have to live in that space. You have to live in the world of the transaction that is always evolving. When you are the master and catalyst of change, you will have moments that you fail, but that failure can never dissuade you to shift gears that go to something safe.

He also continuously challenges himself. The one aspect of every successful person is that they are never in competition with anyone else except themselves. When you look at the world, applaud the great successes you find, but don't compete with them; rather, you just make incremental changes to yourself. Just make yourself better than you were the day before, and soon you will be great. It did not take Richard a lifetime to make something of himself. By the time he was thirty, he was already far ahead of the game.

In all the successes he has had through the decades and with all the troubles he has faced head-on, the one saying that comes to mind each time is the following:

"The master fails more times than the beginner has even tried." —Stephen McCranie

What I seek from him each time my own challenges stare me in the face is that he instilled in me the simple truth that one need not be perfect to make a difference. Each time we go out into the world to make something, invent something, sell something—for anything, we are changing something. How big a change we make depends only on how many people our actions affect. We don't need to be perfect, and we must remember this point each time we make an attempt in good faith. We must know that we try, but if we fail, it doesn't make us worse off. It makes us better off.

This can be hard for many who want perfection before the launch and give up when it isn't perfect.

His wisdom is no doubt something we all hope to acquire, and we can. It just takes time, patience, and persistence.

Finally, remember that he believes deeply that nothing is impossible. He sincerely believes there is no such thing as undoable or impossible. He knows in his heart there is only what you can do and what you want to do. Your limit is only how far you are willing to go. If you are willing to get out of the safety of your mother's car and walk through a strange village and countryside to get home after three miles, then you will definitely grow up to believe you can indeed do anything.

Richard is not the playboy you see splashed across the tabloids. He is not the hippie kid who fell into good fortune. Nothing that happened to him was by accident. He has always been the master of his own destiny. The beauty of it all is that he has managed to do everything with such humor and poise, and he has been extremely good-natured about it. There isn't the slightest area of arrogance or the slightest hint of contempt. He is and always has been a man who knows that he is a part of all that is around him and has no delusions of his wealth and what it means.

He has conclusively proven that academics and structure are not as grand as they are made out to be. Structure comes at the cost of creativity and individuality. Structure robs you of your spirit to be more than you can be and forces you to become the same as everybody else. It is a soul-snatching endeavor to be part of the established order and just another brick in the wall in the words of Pink Floyd, a fellow Briton.

***

If you enjoyed learning about these great men, I would be forever grateful if you could leave a review on Amazon. Reviews are the best way to help your fellow readers find books worth reading, so be sure to help them out!

Made in United States
North Haven, CT
13 December 2024